THE
DUNKIRK
EVACUATION
IN 100 OBJECTS
THE STORY BEHIND
OPERATION DYNAMO IN 1940

Martin Mace

Frontline Books

THE DUNKIRK EVACUATION IN 100 OBJECTS
The Story Behind Operation Dynamo in 1940

This edition published in 2017 by Frontline Books,
an imprint of Pen & Sword Books Ltd,
47 Church Street, Barnsley, S. Yorkshire, S70 2AS,

ISBN: 978-1-52670-990-5

Pen & Sword Books Limited incorporates the imprints of Atlas, Archaeology, Aviation, Discovery, Family History, Fiction, History, Maritime, Military, Military Classics, Politics, Select, Transport, True Crime, Air World, Frontline Publishing, Leo Cooper, Remember When, Seaforth Publishing, The Praetorian Press, Wharncliffe Local History, Wharncliffe Transport, Wharncliffe True Crime and White Owl.

For more information on our books, please visit
www.frontline-books.com
email info@frontline-books.com
or write to us at the above address.

Printed and bound by Replika Press Pvt. Ltd., India

Typeset in 10/12 Avenir

Contents

CONTENTS

Introduction

The news from the Continent had been full of alarm and despondency. The French armies had been pushed back in the north and broken in the east. But the Battle of France was scarcely more than a week old and the British Expeditionary Force was still intact and unbowed. Hope, if not expectation, that such setbacks could soon be reversed remained high. It was therefore with a mixture of disappointment as much as disquiet, that Winston Churchill's War Cabinet received the latest depressing message from the British field commander, Lord Gort, on 19 May.

The previous night Gort had a meeting with General Billotte, Commander-in-Chief of the French 1st Army Group, and the man who was responsible for co-ordinating the movements of the British, French and Belgian Forces. Billotte told the British commander that he had little hope of stopping the German advance from the east which had crossed the River Meuse, pushed past the French 9th Army and was heading rapidly across northern France towards the Channel coast. This meant that there was an imminent danger of the Allied armies in the north-west being irretrievably cut off from the other French forces in the south.

The two generals considered the options available to them. The first, and most desirable, was for the British and French to counter-attack and cut the German lines of communication, which would halt the panzer divisions of Army Group B and buy time for the Allies to regroup.

The second possible course of action was for the northern armies to immediately withdraw south beyond the River Somme to link up with the other French armies.

If neither of these operations were practical, which seemed likely, there was only one option available to Gort – to evacuate the entire BEF back to the UK. 'I felt,' Gort said, 'that in the circumstances there might be no other course open to me'.

After the meeting, Gort relayed this information to London, to the dismay of the British Prime Minister and his Cabinet. Though the Chief of the Imperial General Staff, General Ironside, was sent to France to urge the French to mount a counter-attack, measures were also put in hand to evacuate the BEF in case Gort's prediction proved correct.

The Allies did indeed counter-attack at the key communications centre of Arras. Whilst the attack was beaten off by the Germans, it did succeed in delaying the encirclement of the BEF. But its failure left Gort with no choice other than to try and save his army. The retreat to Dunkirk began.

The story of the evacuation of the BEF and other Allied troops has been told many times in both print and film, and has become one of the defining moments in the history of the British nation. Yet there are artefacts from that operation which can still be seen today, and many places to visit, which bring that fateful history back to life.

Dunkirk and its environs can easily be explored, with its long stretches of open beaches remaining largely untouched, where wrecks of sunken ships reveal themselves at low tide. Many of the surviving sand dunes into which the British soldiers tried to hide from the bombs and bullets of the Luftwaffe and the shells of the German artillery are today protected from development and are accessible to all. At the farthest extremity of the evacuation beaches, at the town of La Panne (De Panne to the Belgians), the former sanitorium where the British casualties were treated still bears the scars of the fighting, and the building where the Casualty Clearing Station No.12 was located, the Château Coquelle, stands unperturbed though battle-scarred in its quiet side street.

Dunkirk itself was almost bombed into oblivion, and signs of that destruction mark the stones of the church of St Eloi, and towards the east of the town is the Dunkirk Memorial which stands at the entrance to the British War Graves Section of Dunkirk Town Cemetery, where so many of those who died now rest in peace or are commemorated.

In the heart of the port of Dunkirk stands Bastion 32, the headquarters of *Amiral du Nord, le contre-amiral* Jean-Marie Charles Abrial, the senior French naval officer during the Dunkirk evacuation. It was from there that Captain William Tennant controlled operations as Senior Naval Officer, Dunkirk; it is now a museum and memorial to the Battle of Dunkirk, in which the French fully played their part.

The most famous of all the locations associated with the Dunkirk evacuation must surely be the East Mole, often referred to simply as the Mole. Though mostly gone, the spot where it stretched out into the sea on the eastern edge of the harbour can still be reached.

The defensive perimeter, which so successfully held the Germans at bay, was largely defined by the series of canals which run from the sea at Nieuport north to Furnes and then in a westerly direction towards Bergues. Alongside the canals are roads that can be driven or strolled along, where for days the most bitter fighting ensued and was the scene of the action in which Captain Marcus Ervine-Andrews was awarded the Victoria Cross.

The once-fortified town of Bergues marked the most westerly part of the perimeter held by the regiments of the BEF, the line beyond to the west being manned by the French forces under General Fagalde. Bergues came under persistent attack, evidence of which marks its ancient walls.

Operation *Dynamo* gained its name from the room in the complex of tunnels below Dover Castle. There the vast collection of vessels of all shapes and sizes that rescued the BEF was organised and controlled.

As well as these rooms, preserved as they were during the Dunkirk evacuation, there are memorials relating to Operation *Dynamo* around Dover, such as the statue to Admiral Ramsay, erected in the castle grounds. Beyond Dunkirk, at Teddington Lock on the River Thames, there stands a memorial to the collection of 'Little Ships' assembled there before sailing down to the coast for the journey across the Channel. Another memorial sits in St Clements churchyard at Leigh-on-Sea, dedicated to local fishermen who sailed into the horrors of Dunkirk in their little cockle boats, never to return.

Many other vessels that were lost in Operation *Dynamo* are remembered around the UK. Among these is the former Isle of Man Steam Packet *Mona's Queen*, which struck a mine and sank on the morning of 29 May. Seventy years after her loss, *Mona's Queen's* anchor was raised from the sea bed and placed on display at Port St Mary in the south of the Isle of Man.

A number of the vessels taking part in the great evacuation have survived the ravages of time. The Thames barge *Pudge* is now at Maldon and is maintained in all her glory and in full working order; and the beautifully preserved steam tug *Challenge* is proudly berthed at Southampton. Appropriately, sitting in Dunkirk harbour, is the paddle-steamer *Princess Elizabeth*, which made her final trip to the port in 1999, where she now serves as a venue for city events and festivities.

Artefacts from those dramatic days in May and June 1940 abound. Reports from friend and foe can still be handled and read, as can personal letters and official despatches. Rifles, vehicle parts and propaganda leaflets dropped to the men on the evacuation beaches, flags and medals can still be found.

All of these items, objects, buildings and places, together graphically portray the great evacuation which the British Army's Quartermaster-General described at the end of May 1940 as being, 'on a scale unprecedented in the history of war'.

Acknowledgements

This project would not have been possible but for the help and assistance of my wife, Leanne, Sara Mitchell, Robert Mitchell, and John Grehan, for his knowledge and advice on the people and events of Operation *Dynamo*.

I would also like to acknowledge the invaluable contribution of Dave Cassan, Terry Heard (www.ww2cemeteries.com), Arie-Jan van Hees, Ben Luto, James Luto, Andy Saunders, and Geoff Simpson.

All images used in this publication are from the Historic Military Press archive unless stated otherwise.

For their support and assistance with images, I am grateful to Frans Ammerlaan, Martin Baxter (www.hampshirechurchwindows.co.uk), Geoff Davies, Chris Goss, Jean-Claude Graux, Richard Hoare, Simon Moores (www.airads.co.uk), Hans de Regt, Bill Scott, Martin J. Smithson, and Mick Wenban.

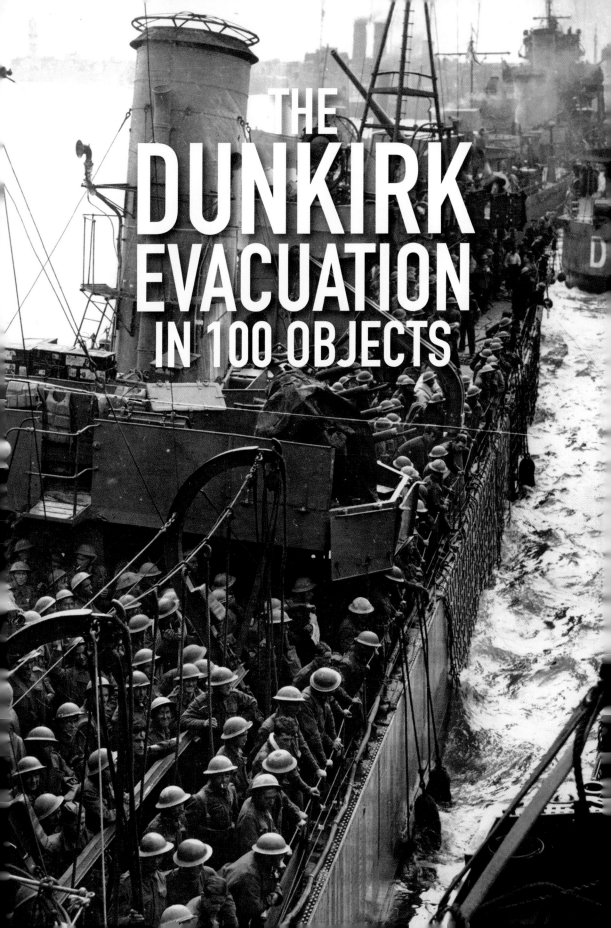

THE
DUNKIRK
EVACUATION
IN 100 OBJECTS

Wartime Postcard of General Lord Gort

Facing the Reality of The German Blitzkrieg

Following the start of Germany's Blitzkrieg, at around midnight on 18/19 May 1940, the Commander-in-Chief of the French 1st Army Group, General Gaston-Henri Billotte, travelled to Lord Gort's headquarters to discuss the deteriorating strategic situation on the Western Front. Billotte brought with him little good news. Though the French commander stated that efforts were being made by the 9th Army to halt the German advance, he admitted that the outlook was 'not encouraging'. Gort, who is depicted here in a postcard published in the winter of 1939-1940, saw that there was a real prospect of the British, French and Belgian armies in the north being irretrievably cut off from the main French forces in the south.

This meant, as Gort and Billotte saw it, that there were just three courses of action available to them. The first was to close the gap in the French line through which the Germans had poured by counter-attacks against the enemy's lines of communications. Whether such attack would succeed was highly problematical, considering the French failures so far.

The second was to withdraw immediately to the Somme to join up with the rest of the French armies. This had the attraction that the British Expeditionary Force (BEF) would be falling back own its lines of communication and if it was successful would not entail the abandonment of large quantities of equipment. But it would obviously mean that the Belgian Army would be faced with the choice of abandoning Belgium or of fighting on its own; or of surrendering to the enemy. Clearly, such a move would be politically unacceptable. It was also probably too late to attempt this move, so rapid had been the advance of General Guderian's panzers across the rear of the northern armies.

This left just the third option – a withdrawal to the Channel ports with a view to abandoning France and evacuating the BEF back to the UK. 'I realised that this course was in theory a last alternative, as it would involve the departure of the B.E.F. from the theatre of war at a time when the French might need all the support which Britain could give them,' Gort wrote. 'It involved the virtual certainty that even if the excellent port facilities at Dunkirk continued to be available, it would be necessary to abandon all the heavier guns and much of the vehicles and equipment.'[1]

Terrible as it would be to leave his allies to fight on alone, Gort came to the conclusion that this was likely to prove to be the only course of action open to him.

So it was, that around 01.30 hours on 19 May, Gort had to explain this to the Chief of the General Staff, who in turn telephoned the Director of Military Operations and Plans at the War Office. Later that same day, the first discussions were held in London to consider the evacuation of the BEF.

Opposite: Field Marshal John Standish Surtees Prendergast Vereker, 6th Viscount Gort, was given command of the BEF in September 1939. John Gort had fought in the First World War, during which he was Mentioned in Despatches eight times, was awarded the DSO with two Bars and received the Victoria Cross for his actions at the Battle of the Canal du Nord in September 1918.

The War Office, Whitehall

The Decision Is Made To Evacuate The BEF

The disquieting assessment of the situation facing the Allied armies in northern France, relayed by Lord Gort to the War Office, was passed onto the War Cabinet. There, Winston Churchill presided as both Minister of Defence and Prime Minister, bearing the burden of ultimate responsibility. He conceded that the apparent paralysis of the French First Army and the uncertainty about what was happening in France was causing the members of the War Cabinet 'extreme anxiety'. Things, though, were about to get even worse.

At 16.30 hours on 19 May the War Cabinet was informed that Lord Gort was 'examining a possible withdrawal towards Dunkirk if that were forced upon him'. Quite why this information had taken so long to pass through the hands of the staff at the War Office is unclear. This must have been met by the War Cabinet with profound dismay. Churchill, however, recorded, with his usual rhetoric, that 'all our proceedings were quiet and composed', and that, 'we had a united and decided opinion, behind which there was silent passion'. Nevertheless, the War Cabinet could not bring its collective self to agree with Gort's pessimistic appraisal.

The Chief of the Imperial General Staff, Field Marshal Sir Edmund Ironside, refused to acknowledge Gort's belief that an evacuation of the BEF was an option. Instead, he favoured a march south to link up with the other French armies behind the Somme. The War Cabinet agreed and decided that Ironside should go over to France and see what was happening for himself. 'We therefore sent him to Lord Gort with instructions to move the British Army in a south-westerly direction and to force his way through all opposition in order to join up with the French in the south,' the Prime Minister recalled, 'and that the Belgians should be urged to conform to this movement, or, alternatively, that we would evacuate as many of their troops [the Belgians] as possible from the Channel ports. He was to be told that we would ourselves inform the French Government of what had been resolved.'

This was all well and good, but the War Cabinet was then made aware by further communications from France that the BEF possessed only enough food for four days and sufficient ammunition to fight one more battle.

Ironside duly arrived at Gort's headquarters at Wahagnies on 20 May, and relayed the War Cabinet's instructions. By then, in the rapidly changing circumstances the Allies found themselves in a march south which had already become impracticable. After travelling over to the French First Army headquarters for a meeting with Generals Billotte and Blanchard, Ironside was forced to agree with Lord Gort.

Ironside returned to London to tell his political masters that the unacceptable choice is the one that would most likely have to be made – the BEF would have to abandon France.

Opposite: The Old War Office buildings in Whitehall, London, where a number of key decisions were made in the days before Operation *Dynamo*. Originally built in 1902 for the Imperial General Staff, the building was a focal point for military planning throughout the major conflicts of the 20th Century. The buildings were placed on the open market by the Ministry of Defence in 2013, and are set to become the location of a hotel and residential apartments. (MoD/Crown Copyright, 2013)

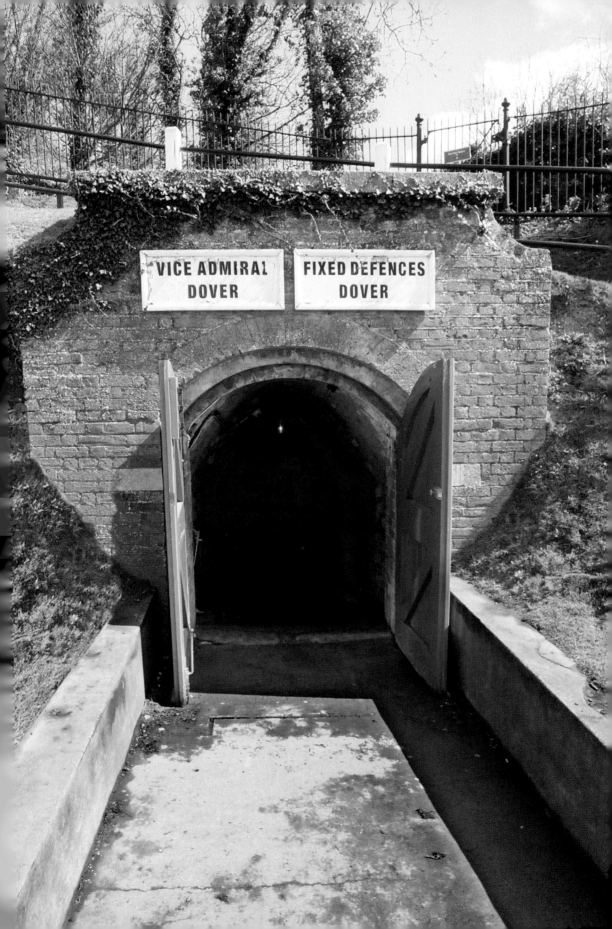

Vice-Admiral Ramsay's Headquarters

Planning an Evacuation 'Unprecedented in The History of War'

Following Gort's disturbing disclosure that the situation in France had deteriorated so rapidly that the BEF might have to be evacuated back to the UK, later on 19 May Vice-Admiral Bertram Ramsay, Flag Officer Commanding Dover, was summoned to the War Office in London for a meeting chaired by General Riddell-Webster, Quartermaster-General to the Forces. The subject they were to discuss, was 'the hazardous evacuation of very large forces' through Dunkirk, Calais and Boulogne. Ramsay was present because it was he who would be responsible for the evacuation and all available shipping would be placed at his disposal.

It was envisaged that, starting on the 20th, the 'useless mouths', in other words the non-combatants, would be shipped back to the UK at the rate of 2,000 per day. Then, starting on the 22nd, the base personnel would be evacuated – some 15,000 in total. This would free the roads and the shipping for the vital third stage of the operation, to rescue the fighting divisions of the BEF.

Just how many men would eventually be saved remained unknown, but even at this stage, the evacuation of tens of thousands of troops was seen as 'formidable' and was likely to be, as described by the Quartermaster-General's Department, 'on a scale unprecedented in the history of war'.[2]

Even at this preliminary stage, the difficulties that were likely to be experienced were understood, and proved all-too accurate: a) It would only be possible to evacuate the personnel, and all the equipment not carried by hand would have to be abandoned; b) That the organisation of units and formations could not be preserved, but that bodies of men would arrive haphazard, separated from their own officers and non-commissioned officers and without any knowledge of the whereabouts of others of the same unit; c) That the normal machinery for providing the men with quarters, pay, clothing, blankets, and above all, food, would have ceased to exist; and that d) suitable transport would often be difficult to obtain.

Ramsay had much to consider. He had to discover the number of personnel vessels and small craft that might be made available, the safest route the ships should take across the Channel, and for the reception of the troops at the points of disembarkation. It was also understood, even at this preliminary stage, that it might not be possible to embark all the troops from Dunkirk harbour and what other ports might still be in Allied hands, and that many of the soldiers might have to be lifted directly from the beaches. But all that the Royal Navy had at its disposal were its ships' own cutters and whalers. This was, Ramsay pondered as he headed back to his headquarters at Dover, seen here, just another of the many problems that he would have to solve.

Opposite: The entrance to Vice-Admiral Bertram Ramsay's subterranean headquarters at Dover Castle, below. (Courtesy of Robert Mitchell)

The Tunnels at Dover Castle

Codename Operation *Dynamo*

Deep inside the famous White Cliffs of Dover is an extensive network of tunnels that became the headquarters of Bertram Ramsay who, since 24 August 1939, was Vice-Admiral Dover. The tunnels were first constructed under the Castle in the Middle Ages to provide a protected line of communication for the soldiers manning the northern outworks of the castle and to allow the garrison to gather unseen before launching sorties against besiegers.

The fear of invasion by the French in the Napoleonic Wars led to Dover being powerfully garrisoned. Soon the castle was overflowing with troops and so to create further accommodation and storage space the tunnels were considerably expanded, the work being undertaken by French prisoners of war. When complete, the tunnels, seven in number, could accommodate up to 2,000 men.

After the threat from Napoleon had finally ended at Waterloo, the tunnels were used by the Coast Blockade Service but, in 1827, they were abandoned and remained largely so until the outbreak of war in 1939. In the early months of the Second World War the tunnels were re-opened as an air-raid shelter and then converted into an underground hospital.

The tunnels also became the naval headquarters at Dover. The nerve centre of the headquarters was a single gallery which ended in an embrasure at the cliff face. This was used as an office by Ramsay. When he first arrived at Dover, he had not been impressed with the resources. As he wrote to his wife: 'We have no stationery, books, typists or machines, no chairs and few tables, maddening communications. I pray that war, if it has to come, will be averted for yet a few days.'

A succession of small rooms leading deep into the chalk away from Ramsay's office housed the Secretary, the Flag Lieutenant, the Chief of Staff (Captain L.V. Morgan) and the Staff office itself. Beyond these was a large room used normally for meetings/conferences in connection with the operation of the base. In the First World War it had held an auxiliary electrical plant and was known as the 'Dynamo Room'.

It was in this room on 20 May 1940, following his meeting in London the previous day, that Ramsay called a conference with his staff to discuss the evacuation of the BEF. At this stage it was hoped that 10,000 men would be rescued every twenty-four hours from each of the three Continental ports – Dunkirk, Calais and Boulogne – with the thirty or so cross-Channel ferries, twelve steam-powered drifters and six coastal cargo ships that had been allocated to the task by the Admiralty. The ships would work the ports in pairs, with no more than two ships at any one time in the three harbours.

During the meeting it also became obvious that a reorganisation of the base staff at Dover would be necessary to cope with the sudden rush of additional work. It was decided to set up this new body in the conference room itself. Thus, it was in this former Dynamo Room that the preparation, planning, and organisation of the evacuation of the BEF from France took place. Two days, at 19.44 hours on 22 May, the Admiralty issued a blunt message to its various commands: 'The operation for which these ships are being prepared will be known as *Dynamo*.'[3]

Opposite: One of the tunnels beneath Dover Castle which formed part of Vice-Admiral Bertram Ramsay's headquarters at the time of the Dunkirk evacuation. The Dynamo Room itself can today be seen by visitors to the Castle, as can the Operation Dynamo Experience. For more information, please see: www.english-heritage.org.uk. (© English Heritage)

Official Evacuation Chart

The Only Option was Dunkirk

Following Ramsay's return to Dover on 20 May, the task of deciding exactly where the evacuation of the British troops would take place from was handed to the BEF's acting Operations Officer, Lieutenant Colonel the Viscount Robert Bridgeman. Aware of the need for speed, Bridgeman set about his task immediately, and worked throughout the night. He started on the premise that an evacuation could take place anywhere between Calais and Ostend, he had to find a stretch of coast that could be easily reached by the retreating troops, and easily defended by the three corps of the BEF.

Bridgeman had, therefore, to consider which port had the best approach roads and which might offer some degree of protection from the air, and which ports had the best facilities. He had to answer such questions as, were there canals or other features which could be held against the enemy, particularly on the flanks, were there towns that could be held as strong-points and were there dykes that could be opened to flood the ground and stop the German panzers?

After pouring over maps of the French and Belgian coasts, Bridgeman decided that the twenty-seven-mile stretch between Ostend and Dunkirk was the most suitable. By the morning of Tuesday, 22 May, Bridgeman had covered every detail he could think of. Each corps was allocated the routes it would use to reach the coast, and which stretch of coast each would hold. If the decision to evacuate was taken, there was now a plan in place.[1]

Ramsay attended a further meeting in London on that same day, Tuesday 22nd, to determine the number of vessels and small craft that could be employed in the rescue mission. Over the course of the following two days the evacuation of troops from Boulogne was started, and completed on 24 May. The evacuation at Calais was limited to lines of communications personnel, the fighting troops having to remain at the port to prevent German forces moving up from the south to cut off the BEF from the coast. This meant that if the BEF was to be evacuated, it could only be from Dunkirk and its adjacent coast.

In the few days following the first meeting in the War Office, the military situation had deteriorated so sharply that Ramsay was advised by the Admiralty on 26 May that Operation *Dynamo* was to be implemented immediately 'with the greatest vigour'. Ramsay was told that it was expected that the evacuation was likely to last for just two days before it would most likely be terminated by enemy action. He was advised that he would probably only be able to rescue 45,000 men.

Left: A street sign on the old D16 running into Dunkirk during or just after Operation *Dynamo*. Main image opposite: An official plan, based on Admiralty Chart No.1406, showing the routes used during Operation *Dynamo*, together with their distances, which were used during the evacuation. Opposite bottom: A French Char B1 bis tank knocked out during the German advance into France. Nicknamed *Ouragan*, this tank, No.260, was put out of action in the town of Guise which is in the Aisne department to the east of Saint-Quentin. *Ouragan* was operated by the 8e Bataillon de Char de Combat. (Conseil Régional de Basse-Normandie /US National Archives)

HMS Wolsey Underway

The First Warship to Sail During Operation *Dynamo*

It was on 22 May that the W-class destroyer HMS *Wolsey* set off for Dunkirk to take on board around 200 wounded soldiers, all of who were walking wounded. After landing the soldiers at Dover, the following day *Wolsey* acted as a guide for the Hospital Ships *Isle of Thanet* and *Worthing* on their first voyage to Dunkirk. The destroyer's next task was to assist her sister ship *Windsor* in taking demolition parties to Le Havre. *Wolsey* then joined HMS *Wolfhound* on the afternoon of 26 May in bombarding the approaches to Calais to help the British troops in defending the port.

Wolsey returned to Dover at 18.50 hours, and then at 19.30 hours received orders to proceed to Dunkirk to act as a wireless link ship between the French port and Dover. In so doing she became the first warship to make the crossing after the announcement of the start of Operation *Dynamo*.

Despite encountering fog on the passage, *Wolsey* secured to the Quai Félix Fauré at 23.50 hours. She had to shift berth on the morning of the 27th to allow troop transports to go alongside the jetty, with *Wolsey*

moving into the anchorage just outside the harbour. This move placed *Wolsey* at the edge of the range of the shore signal station, making communications difficult. So, the destroyer berthed against the East Mole at 07.00 hours.

Lieutenant Commander Colin Henry Campbell RN, *Wolsey*'s captain, estimated that he could remain at the East Mole until one hour before low water, but by 09.15 hours the tide had retreated a little faster than he had calculated, and when an air raid on the port began a few minutes later, he decided to return to the anchorage. As *Wolsey* tried to pull away, its propellers grounded and the destroyer was stuck by the Mole until hauled off by a French tug at 10.30 hours.

Back in the anchorage, *Wolsey* again struggled to communicate with the shore due to dense clouds of smoke and almost continuous air raids. The warship had to remain at Action Stations the entire day, with more than seventy rounds being fired by all its guns. Six times the anchorage was bombed but no bombs fell dangerously close to *Wolsey*.

With its role as a communications link proving unsatisfactory, at 18.00 hours *Wolsey* moved inshore as close as she could, and took off 150 troops. Lieutenant Commander Campbell then headed back to England, reaching Dover at 01.00 hours. After refuelling and taking on more ammunition, *Wolsey* set off for France at 18.50 on the 28th, arriving off Braye at 23.00. This time Campbell took on board 500 troops before returning to Dover. A third trip on the 29th, saw *Wolsey* rescue a further 800 men and in her final trip another 600 troops were taken on board.

Main image: HMS *Wolsey* underway whilst generating a smoke screen. Left: A party of Royal Engineers disembarking from a destroyer at Dover, 31 May 1940. One soldier is carrying a ceremonial sword, presumably a 'souvenir' of the campaign. Above: The future Duke of Edinburgh, Prince Philip, makes a royal visit to HMS *Wolsey* after Operation *Dynamo*.

The Steamer Mona's Isle

First Ship of Operation *Dynamo* to Make a Return Trip

At about the same time that HMS *Wolsey* had departed from Dover for Dunkirk, the steamer *Mona's Isle* also headed out across the Channel. Originally built for the South Eastern and Chatham Railway in 1905, this steamer was first named *Onward*. After being purchased by the Isle of Man Steam Packet Company, *Onward* was renamed *Mona's Isle* in 1920. Requisitioned for service as an Armed Boarding Vessel, HMS *Mona's Isle* spent the first winter of the war patrolling the North Sea.

As her captain, Commander J.C.K. Dowding noted, *Mona's Isle* was off the entrance to Dunkirk Harbour by 01.15 hours the following morning. Having received no response to his signals, Dowding decided to enter the port: 'Being ignorant of conditions and harbour, attempted to enter slowly. Star[board] engine failed owing to wire round propeller. Considered entrance might be fouled so backed out. Propeller cleared itself.'[4]

Main image: Pictured here in her civilian role with the Isle of Man Steam Packet Company, the steamer *Mona's Isle* was the first ship to complete a round trip during Operation *Dynamo*.

Above: British troops making
their way into Dunkirk as the evacuation gathers pace. According
to the original caption, as 'the stream of soldiers and trucks must not be held up', a 'French marine
fills in a crater caused by a German aerial bomb'.

Having moved back out in to open water, Dowding was instructed to wait until daylight before attempting to enter the harbour again. This he did at 04.16 hours, berthing, like *Wolsey*, at the Quai Félix Fauré, though 'with all guns firing at enemy aircraft'. Embarkation began at 05.30 hours, a process that was completed just over an hour and half later, by which time 1,420 men had boarded *Mona's Isle*.

If the steamer's journey to Dunkirk had been relatively trouble free, the same could not be said for the return. Whilst off Gravelines at 07.30 hours, the crew observed several small British vessels and a hospital ship (possibly *Dinard*) being shelled some distance ahead. *Mona's Isle's* turn came twenty minutes later when she was heavily shelled and straddled by several German guns, Dowding noting that there were 'several hits of sorts and casualties'·

Then, at 08.25 hours, it was the turn of the Luftwaffe. 'Six Messerschmitt appeared,' continued Dowding. 'Opened fire with 4" and 2 Lewis guns and 12 pdr. Aircraft carried out about four attacks, from the sun, invisible to us. From astern. Terrific machine gun fire, a great deal of which missed ahead, but many direct hits with cannon, especially round 12 pdr. whose crew under Sub Lt A.E. Neave R.N.R. stood up to it extremely well, but sustained casualties, including the sub lieutenant. The packed troops on the open deck suffered badly; had the shooting been accurate the losses would have been very much greater.'

After ten minutes, perhaps having run out of ammunition, the Messerschmitt Bf 109s abandoned their attacks. One of the shells had hit *Mona's Isle's* tele-motor pipes, rendering the rudder inoperable. At the same time, steam pipes and wiring, including the W/T set wireless aerial, had been damaged, as had all of the lifeboats, which were rendered unusable. Nevertheless, with steering achieved by using the port and starboard engines to adjust the speed of the screws, *Mona's Isle*, assisted by the destroyer HMS *Windsor* and a number of tugs, was able to reach Dover at 10.00 hours.

Because of congestion *Mona's Isle* was not able to berth alongside Admiralty Pier until 13.53 hours, at which point the disembarkation of this first batch of *Dynamo* evacuees safely brought home began – a moment that was tempered, however, by the fact that sixty wounded and twenty-three bodies, all the result of the air attacks, were unloaded on to the quayside.

Battle-Scarred Château Coquelle

The Location of Casualty Clearing Station No.12

In both world wars, medical facilities were established behind the front line. A casualty would first receive treatment at his regimental aid post and then, if the wound was serious enough, he would be transported to a Casualty Clearing Station. There, casualties would be assessed and, if required, emergency operations undertaken.

One such unit within the structure of the BEF was No.12 Casualty Clearing Station. When the army advanced into Belgium, it was set up in the sports ground at Annezin near Béthune in Northern France. On 26 May, with the BEF falling back to the coast, No.12 CCS was ordered to pull back to Dunkirk. It was re-established in Château Coquelle in the Le Chapeau Rouge area of the town. One of the surgeons, Major Philip Newman, kept a diary, which is taken up here on 28 May: 'In the morning, there was a hectic drive to Chapeau Rouge just after another air raid. Picked up two soldiers burnt to a cinder and arrived at the Château in Rosendael on the outskirts of Dunkirk. We now knew that we were left holding the baby and that the BEF were pouring as hard as they could out of Dunkirk. Straightaway I organised a theatre in the drawing room of the Château and within two hours had two operating teams going.'[5]

Having being told, on arrival, to expect as many as 700 casualties, there was little doubt that the staff of No.12 CCS were going to be busy. 'Bombing around us was frequent. This first day we plodded on steadily with the operating with the promise of relief in the evening by some field ambulance people. They never turned up — they had bunked off home.'[6]

For two days Newman's team worked almost non-stop. Each day would begin at 05.00 hours as the casualties started pouring in. 'Shelling and bombing became worse, a 500lb bomb fell within 50yds of the house and a smaller one within 20yds,' Newman continued. 'Wounded increased until the house was packed full and the driveway was full of ambulances loaded up. I shifted my operating theatre to the cellar with one electric lamp.'

Eventually, with the staff in a state of exhaustion, news came through that No.12 CCS would be evacuated at 23.00 hours on 30 May. A second order was then received, which read: '12th C.C.S to remain open, only patients to go.'

So Newman and his team stayed on, treating more casualties. By 1 June, Newman noted that, 'Things were in an awful mess. Shells were bursting very close to the house and the wounded were in a terrible state.' The twenty-eight-year-old surgeon stayed at his post to the very end, having lost the ballot held to see who would remain as part of the skeleton staff, when the time came for the majority of the medical personnel to depart. He was taken prisoner by the Germans on 4 June.

Opposite: The imposing Château Coquelle is located in a small park, which is open to the public, off Rue de Belfort in Dunkirk, about a kilometre from the port and a little less from the beach at Malo-les-Bains. Inset: Wartime scars can still be seen on the walls of Château Coquelle, particularly on the west-facing façade. This damage may well have been caused by the bombs described by Major Philip Newman in his diary.

A Spitfire Survivor

Lost In Combat Over Northern France

During the Battle of France and in the period leading up to and during the evacuation from Dunkirk nearly 2,000 RAF aircraft of all types were lost. Although a number were left behind during the retreat, many of these were Fighter Command aircraft that had been shot down or crashed whilst operating over France and Belgium in support of the BEF. One example was Supermarine Spitfire Mk.Ia N3200, an aircraft flown by Squadron Leader Stephenson of 19 Squadron.

It was at 07.40 hours on the morning of Sunday, 26 May 1940, that Stephenson took off in N3200 from RAF Northolt at the head of his squadron, which had moved there from Duxford the previous evening. The pilots' instructions were to patrol the Calais-Dunkirk area. 'They met 21 Ju.87s escorted by 30 Me.109s. Approximately 10 E/A [enemy aircraft] were shot down. S/Ldr Stephenson and P/O Watson failed to return. F/O Ball was wounded in the head and arm.'[7]

Below: Spitfire N3200 on display at IWM Duxford – where it is based and can be seen by visitors. It carries the markings it wore on the day it was shot down during its first, and only, operational sortie. Sadly, Stephenson never lived to see his aircraft recovered. Having continued his RAF career after the war he was killed in 1954 while test-flying in the United States.

Above: The wreckage seen here is thought to be the burnt-out remains of Spitfire P9377 of 222 Squadron. It was force-landed on the beach near Bray-Dunes on 1 June 1940 following combat with Messerschmitt Bf 109s of I./JG 26 and Messerschmitt Bf 110s of 1./ZG 1, during which the Spitfire's engine was hit and damaged. Pilot Officer R.A.L. Morant belly-landed and then set fire to his aircraft before making good his escape and getting on board a boat bound for Britain. Interestingly, the wreck of a Hurricane can be seen in the distance. This is almost certainly P2902 – which we will encounter later in this book. A 245 Squadron aircraft, P2902 had been shot down the day before P9377. (Courtesy of Chris Goss)

It was after he had shot down one of the Stukas that Stephenson's N3200 was hit. He managed to crash-land his stricken aircraft on a beach at Sangatte, near Calais. One account describes what Stephenson did next: 'Fleeing from the wreckage, he was helped by Frenchmen who disguised him in their clothes before he began his journey to the Belgian capital, which was occupied by the German forces. In his diary … Stephenson reached the American embassy where "an extremely considerate and friendly" diplomat explained that there was no chance of escape from the city. Embassy staff could not help him "as this would compromise their chances of aiding the British interests for which they had been made responsible" …

'Abandoning hope of escape, Stephenson walked to Evere aerodrome outside Brussels where he surrendered to the "very charming young men" of a German fighter squadron … "I might have been a member of a visiting squadron. I was introduced and shook hands all round amid much friendly laughter … I felt almost sinful so at ease and merry."'[8]

Whilst Stephenson spent the rest of the war in captivity, his Spitfire gradually sank into the sand. Spitfire N3200 had been built under contract number B527113/36 at the Vickers Armstrong (Supermarine) Ltd factory in Southampton. Fitted with a Rolls-Royce Merlin III, it rolled off the production line as part of a batch of 200 Mk.Ias. Having undertaken a successful factory test flight, N3200 was delivered to No.8 Maintenance Unit at Little Rissington on 2 December 1939. It was not until 19 April the following year that N3200 was finally issued to 19 Squadron.

The wreckage of N3200 was re-discovered in 1986 after being exposed by bad weather and strong currents. The remains were excavated during the spring of that year and, being reasonably intact, were put on display in a French museum. In December 2000, N3200 was purchased and returned to the United Kingdom for restoration by Historic Flying Ltd.

After a painstaking and meticulous rebuild, an engine test was carried out on 21 February 2014. Then, after final checks, N3200 took to the air again on 26 March 2014 – seventy-four years to the day after she had been shot down at the start of Operation Dynamo.

"ISLE OF GUERNSEY"
WAR SERVICE
1939 - 1945
HOSPITAL CARRIER
DUNKIRK EVACUATION
ROYAL NAVAL AUXILIARY
NORMANDY INVASION

S. R

Steamer's War Service Plaque

Honouring the Hospital Carrier *Isle of Guernsey*

On a wall in the National Railway Museum, York, are a series of wooden ship's war service plaques from vessels that had been owned by the Southern Railway and which had 'done their bit' during the Second World War. One of these plaques was for the steamer *Isle of Guernsey*. Requisitioned from civilian service on 23 September 1939, *Isle of Guernsey* was converted to fulfil the role of a hospital carrier.

Under the command of Captain E.L. Hill, *Isle of Guernsey* first sailed to Dunkirk, in company with fellow hospital carrier *Worthing*, at midday on 26 May, returning with 346 wounded men. It was during her third crossing, on 29 May, that disaster struck, as Hill himself later recounted:

'At 5-16 p.m., having received orders, we proceeded towards Dunkirk … At 7-30 p.m. an airman was observed descending by parachute close ahead of us and the vessel was stopped to save him. One of the seamen [Able Seaman J. Fowles] went down a rope ladder to assist the airman, but before he reached the bottom, 10 enemy 'planes attacked the ship with bombs, cannon and machine guns. By a miracle none of the bombs struck the ship, although considerable damage was done by the concussion, shrapnel, cannon shells and machine gun bullets. British fighter planes drove off the enemy and we proceeded towards Dunkirk with a terrific air battle taking place overhead.

'Arrived off the port at 8-20 p.m. we found it was being bombed and shelled, and we had orders from the shore to keep clear. Returning along the channel in company with two destroyers, we later received orders to wait until darkness had fallen and then return to Dunkirk.

'At 11-30 p.m. we entered between the breakwaters, the whole place being brilliantly lit up by the glare of fires, burning oil tanks, etc., and managed to moor up alongside what was left of the quay at 12-30 a.m. Loading commenced at once and by 2-15 a.m. we had taken on board as many as we could, numbering 490. All the crew and R.A.M.C. personnel behaved splendidly throughout, carrying on with their duties and doing their utmost to load the ship as quickly and as fully as possible, although the ship was shaken every few minutes by the explosion of bombs falling on the quay and in the water.

'Leaving the quay at 2-15 a.m. we proceeded out of the harbour and just outside we found the sea full of men swimming and shouting for help, presumably a transport had just been sunk. As two destroyers were standing by picking these men up, we threaded our way carefully through them and proceeded towards Dover. It would have been fatal for us to attempt to stop and try to save any of these men, as we made such a wonderful target for the aircraft hovering overhead, with the flames of the burning port showing all our white paintwork up. Everything was comparatively quiet on the way across.'[9]

Travelling via Dover, *Isle of Guernsey* reached Newhaven at 11.15 hours, the latter having previously been designated as the main ambulance port for the BEF. 'No further trips were made to Dunkirk,' concluded Hill, 'because by the time our damage had been repaired, the evacuation was completed'.

Opposite page top: *Isle of Guernsey*'s war service plaque at the National Railway Museum in York. Background image: A pre-war image of the ferry *Isle of Guernsey*.

Admiral Tennant Memorial

A Bust Commemorating Operation *Dynamo*'s Man on the Ground

Despite the fact that the Admiralty had issued the directive ordering the start of Operation *Dynamo*, the situation at Dunkirk was far from clear. In an effort to resolve the matter, at 18.00 hours on the evening of 26 May, Captain William Tennant, chief staff officer to the First Sea Lord, was ordered to make his way to Dunkirk. Tennant himself later described his journey, having left London at 20.35 hours on the 26th and travelled via the Nore to arrive at Dover early the following morning:

'I left Dover in HMS *Wolfhound* at 1345 [on the 27th] with a naval party consisting of 12 officers and 160 ratings, plus signal staff. The weather was fine and clear.

'We proceeded North of the minefield – a voyage of some 90 miles – and about half way over the first dive bombing attack took place. These attacks continued at about half hour or 40-minute intervals until we reached Dunkirk at about 1800. There were several very near misses but only minor damage was done to the ship. This was an unpleasant introduction to the war zone, and dive bombing was certainly more alarming afloat than ashore, as we were soon to discover.'[10]

One of these attacks was carried out by a group of four Junkers Ju 87s, two bombs hitting the water close to *Wolfhound*'s starboard bow. 'Splinters came on board,' reported her Captain, Lieutenant Commander J.W. McCoy, though 'the remaining salvoes were not close. *Wolfhound* opened fire and it is considered that two aircraft were hit. One aircraft emitting heavy smoke and another jettisoning its bombs about two miles away.'[11]

It was at 18.00 hours that *Wolfhound* finally pulled into Dunkirk, just as the port was under attack from an even larger force of Stukas. The author Robert Jackson described the scene faced by Tennant and his team: 'As *Wolfhound* approached Dunkirk … the pall of smoke assumed frightening proportions as it coiled and billowed in the summer air, and at its foot the whole waterfront seemed to be ablaze. Rivers of flame seethe along the quay from lines of burning warehouses, and as the destroyer approached the harbour a carpet of soot descended on her like black rain. The *Wolfhound* berthed to the screech and crump of bombs.'[12]

As Private William Ridley, 9th Battalion, Durham Light Infantry, recalled, Dunkirk 'had the stink of death. It was the stink of blood and cordite.'

Having disembarked his party and divided them up into sections, Tennant 'told the officers in charge of each section to scatter them round the port' to make them less vulnerable to bombing attacks. For his part, he 'proceeded to the Bastion Naval Headquarters to investigate the local situation'[13]. Despite the devastation around him, Tennant began to complete his initial assessment, setting in motion the extraordinary rescue effort by vessels of all shapes and sizes that came to characterise Operation *Dynamo*.

Opposite: The memorial bust to Admiral Sir William Tennant which is located in the grounds of the Bell Tower (often referred to as the 'Pepperpot' by virtue of its distinctive appearance), which dominates Church Street in Upton-upon-Severn, Worcestershire.

Teddington Lock Memorial

Remembering the Gathering of the Little Ships

As Captain Tennant's message from Dunkirk had indicated, and Ramsey was quickly realising, the need to find enough vessels with a shallow draught was intensifying, such craft being suitable for taking troops off the beaches where the larger ships could not penetrate. However, some preparation in this respect had already been made when, during the nine o'clock news on 14 May 1940, the following announcement was broadcast by the BBC: 'The Admiralty have made an order requesting all owners of self-propelled pleasure craft between 30' and 100' in length to send particulars to the Admiralty within fourteen days from today if they have not already been offered or requisitioned.'

How Teddington's "*Little Ships*" helped win the Second World War

In the Spring of 1940, allied troops were trapped between the German advance and the sea at Dunkirk in northern France. The evacuation of those troops, "*Operation Dynamo*", was helped by private boats which crossed the Channel and, whilst under constant attack from the Luftwaffe, ferried men from the shallow beaches to larger ships offshore. Douglas Tough assembled 100 of these "*Little Ships*" at Tough Brothers' boatyard which once stood opposite this plaque. During the 10-day operation they helped in the rescue of 338,226 British and French troops who were saved to fight another day. Wartime leader Winston Churchill called this "*A miracle of deliverance*".

This instruction's timing was quite coincidental, being a step taken by the Admiralty because of the increasing demand for vessels due to the general war situation, and was not a direct consequence of the Dunkirk evacuation. Soon all the owners or operators of tugs, ferries, barges, motor-launches, lighters, fishing boats and schooners, as well as boat-yards, boat-builders and yacht clubs up and down the Thames and along the south and south-eastern coasts, were being contacted by the Ministry of Shipping.

Early on the morning of the 27th, the Admiralty had already asked the Ministry of Sea Transport to find between forty and fifty such small craft to assemble at Sheerness for 'a special requirement'. The Director of the Small Vessels Pool, Vice Admiral Sir Lionel Preston, provided a list of those vessels from the Small Craft Register that he thought would be able to assist with the evacuation, but it was soon found that many were not suitable.

A meeting was hurriedly arranged with the Director of Sea Transport, H.C. Riggs, in which it was agreed that Vice Admiral Preston would despatch some of his officers to examine the boat-yards from Teddington to Burnham and Brightlingsea, and to send all vessels that they thought fit for service round to Sheerness.

As the Association of Dunkirk Little Ships (ADLS) points out, 'very few owners took their own vessels, apart from fishermen and one or two others', as 'in many cases the owners could not be contacted and [so] boats were taken without their knowledge – such was the speed and urgency of the Operation'.[14] At William Osborne's yard in Littlehampton, West Sussex, for example, the cabin cruisers Green Eagle and Bengeo seemed to fit the bill. Local volunteers were quickly rounded up by the harbour master and both vessels headed east up the Channel. Green Eagle certainly crossed to Dunkirk but is recorded to have been lost during the operation.

At the Tough Bros. boatyard at Teddington, the proprietor, Douglas Tough, received an early-morning telephone call from Admiral Sir Lionel Preston. Taking Tough into his confidence, Preston briefly outlined Operation Dynamo, the kind of boats needed and, most importantly, the pressing nature of the situation. The results were dramatic.

Assisted by individuals such as Ron Lenthall and Chief Foreman Harry Day, Douglas Tough set about gathering the small craft asked for, starting with fourteen in his yard opposite Teddington Lock. 'More than l00 craft from the Upper Thames were [duly] assembled at the Ferry Road Yard of Tough Bros.,' continues the ADLS account. 'Here everything unnecessary was taken off and stored … The boats were then checked over and towed by Toughs and other tugs down river to Sheerness. Here they were fuelled and taken to Ramsgate where Naval Officers, Ratings and experienced volunteers were put aboard and directed to Dunkirk … The whole Operation was very carefully coordinated and records exist of most of the Little Ships and other larger vessels that went to Dunkirk.'

Opposite: The black granite plaque at Teddington Lock, which is a complex of three locks and a weir on the River Thames. The lock is situated in Ham, about a mile below Kingston-upon-Thames. It can normally only be reached on foot. The nearest road is Riverside Drive in Ham. Alternatively the lock can be reached from Ferry Road, Teddington, over the footbridges which cross the river there. Some scenes from the 1958 feature film Dunkirk were filmed around Teddington Lock. (Courtesy of Robert Mitchell) Right: One of the 'Little Ships' pictured in its peacetime role. This is the Southend pleasure boat Princess Maud providing a good illustration of how just many people could be carried. Accompanied by other Southend pleasure boats, Princess Maud crossed to Dunkirk on 29 May 1940, but ran aground and was lost after getting too close inshore.

Hôtel du Sauvage, Cassel

The Dunkirk Perimeter is Agreed

It is unsurprising to learn that the old fortified town of Cassel, sitting high above the flat Flanders fields, has been fought over many times in its past and, in May 1940, would once again be the scene of much bloodshed. It was to this historic town that, on 27 May, Lord Gort travelled to meet with Général de corps d'armée Bertrand Fagalde, commander of the French XVI Corps whose forces were stationed in the area around Dunkirk, and Admiral Abrial, Commander-in-Chief of the French northern naval forces, to discuss the arrangements for the evacuation of the BEF.

Gort took with him Lieutenant General Sir Ronald Adam, who had been relieved of his command of III Corps to take responsibility for the evacuation and the defence of Dunkirk, and Lieutenant Colonel Robert Bridgeman, who had earlier been tasked with deciding where the embarkation of the troops would take place. The meeting took place in the Hôtel du Sauvage in the town's main square. Cassel had already been shelled by the Germans and the hotel had been abandoned by its staff, leaving cloths and empty bottles on the tables.

The main subject under discussion was the establishment and extent of the defensive perimeter around the embarkation areas. It was eventually agreed that the perimeter would run from the coast at Nieuport in the east to Furnes, then westwards to Bergues along the line of the Furnes-Bergues Canal, before cutting back towards the coast at Mardyck. This meant that the perimeter, into which the BEF would withdraw, was twenty-three miles east to west and seven miles wide at its deepest point (between Dunkirk and Bergues). The British troops were to hold the perimeter from Nieuport round to Bergues, with the French occupying the western sector down to Mardyck.

The meeting was a somewhat strained affair, as it had not been until Fagalde was driving up from Dunkirk to this meeting that he became aware that the British had already decided to abandon France to its fate. He had learnt this not from his own government, which did know, but from the British troops he had encountered on his way to Cassel. The road from Dunkirk had been choked with abandoned British Army vehicles. When Fagalde stopped to ask a British officer why so many large lorries had seemingly been left by the roadside by their drivers, he was told that they had been ordered to leave their vehicles and to evacuate to Dunkirk. It was also at the meeting that Admiral Abrial was first informed of the decision to evacuate. It is, therefore, to the great credit of Fagalde and Abrial that agreement was reached in such strained circumstances.

Opposite page: The Hôtel du Sauvage in Cassel's main square. (Courtesy of Hans de Regt) Right: Bomb or shell damage on a building in the main square at Cassel – a photograph taken just a few doors down from the Hôtel du Sauvage.

Bastion No.32

The French Naval Headquarters at Dunkirk

In 1940, Dunkirk still possessed a series of old fortifications that provided both seaward and landward defence. The most powerful of all these fortifications, known as Bastion 32, was used as a naval headquarters for the northern region of France. Situated on what was towards the head of the western side of the main channel of the harbour, it sits today by the Rue des Chantiers de France.

Built in 1874, its thick walls housed the command post of the naval officer in charge of Dunkirk, *Amiral du Nord, le contre-amiral* Jean-Marie Charles Abrial. When Captain William Tennant arrived in Dunkirk on 27 May, the same day that Abrial was informed that the British were evacuating during the meeting the Hôtel du Sauvage in Cassel, he duly made his way to Bastion 32. Tennant would provide his own graphic account of the sights that greeted him:
   'The town was heavily on fire, the streets being littered with wreckage of all kinds, and every window was smashed. Great palls of smoke from the oil depots and refineries enveloped the docks and town itself.
   'On our way up to the Bastion we had to take shelter from two more raids by enemy bombers, the bombs from the last of which fell unpleasantly close. There were a number of British troops in the town and we passed a good few dead and wounded in the streets – evidently the victims of these air raids.'
   Following his arrival at Bastion 32, Tennant met Allied army and navy officers to discuss the evacuation: 'I held a meeting with Brigadier Parminter, Colonel Whitfield, Area Commandant, and Commander Henderson, B.N.L.O. After this meeting the pier and beach parties were at once organised, told off and dispersed. At 1900 I took over as S.N.O. Dunkirk.'[15]
   Within two hours Tennant had made an assessment of the situation; he duly sent the following signal to Dover: 'Please send every available craft to beaches East of Dunkirk immediately. Evacuation tomorrow night is problematical.' This message was timed at 19.58 hours.
   At 20.25 hours, Tennant sent a further signal to Ramsay: 'Port consistently bombed all day, and on fire. Embarkation possible only from beaches east of harbour … Send all ships and passenger ships there to anchor.'
   Tennant continued to control the embarkation from Bastion 32 along with Admiral Abrial, who had not been informed by the French Government of its decision to support the evacuation of the BEF or that French soldiers could also be rescued. Tennant also continued to press Dover for more vessels, requesting that, 'all possible shipping whatever their breed be sent for troops during dark hours'.

Opposite main image: Today Bastion 32 houses the excellent Dunkirk 1940 Museum, which, formerly known as the Mémorial du Souvenir, helps tell the story of Operation *Dynamo*. For more information, please visit: www.dynamo-dunkerque.com. Inset left: British troops entering Dunkirk pass the smouldering wreckage of a lorry, a small part of the debris of war that came to increasingly litter the streets of the port. Inset right: A French soldier passes the same burning lorry.

The East Mole Information Panel

A 'Magnificent Disregard for the Consequences'

Dunkirk was a fine port and had the harbour not been largely destroyed by the *Luftwaffe* it would have proven an ideal point of embarkation for the BEF. Though much of the port was denied to the ships of the Royal Navy, the outer breakwaters, or moles, could still be approached.

The East Mole, or East Pier as it is also referred to, was not a stout stone wall with berthing places along its length, as might be imagined around a harbour. It was a narrow plank-way barely wide enough for three men to walk abreast. On either side was a protective railing made of strong timbers with, at intervals, taller posts which could be used by ships to secure themselves against the Mole in emergencies. At the far end of the Mole was a concrete 'nose' upon which stood a short lighthouse. The Mole was built in this fashion to allow the tides to roll in and out and to put less strain upon its structure. This, though, meant that ships which did try to berth alongside had to ride the waves, making every approach difficult. Embarking troops in such circumstances was going to be no easy matter.

It is Captain Tennant himself who is credited with the decision to stop trying to recover troops from Dunkirk harbour and use the East Mole. The harbour had been so frequently attacked, and was such a large and easy target, that it was obvious by the second day of the evacuation that it could not be safely used. Seeing this, when he arrived at Dunkirk on 27 May, Tennant initially ordered all the ships to be diverted to the flat beaches beyond the East Mole. However, at this early stage in the operation, the only small boats available to go inshore to pick up the troops were the ships' boats. These few vessels alone would never be able to recover more than a tiny fraction of the tens of thousands of men on, or making their way to, the beaches.

Though the call had gone out for more small boats, it would be days before they could be gathered together and taken over to France in sufficient numbers. Faced with this dilemma, Tennant looked for an alternative and decided to try and see if ships could berth alongside the East Mole.

With, as one historian described it, a 'magnificent disregard for the consequences', Tennant ordered one of the destroyers to go alongside the Mole and see if she could tie up. The ship sailed up to the Mole and berthed without incident. The pattern had been set.[16]

As Captain Tennant himself realised on the night of 27-28 May, 'it was originally decided to embark a small proportion from the East Pier and the rest from the beaches by lighters or barges. The pier method, however, proved so effective as regards speed and order that it was used exclusively, parties of 50 men coming along the beaches to the pier and embarking.'[17]

Whilst the use of the East Mole appears obvious in hindsight, the decision to attempt the evacuation of thousands of troops from this narrow breakwater was at the time quite extraordinary. That so many men were rescued is, in large measure, due to that fateful decision made by Captain Tennant.

Opposite page main image: Though the East Mole at Dunkirk no longer exists, this information panel on the quayside at Dunkirk stands on what had been the approach to it – a spot which many of the evacuating Allied soldiers must have passed. Background: The scene on the quayside in Dunkirk after a Luftwaffe air raid.

11 L'esprit de Dunkerque 1840-1945 2015

Les Anglais embarquent depuis la jetée est

Sur la jetée est du port, de nombreux britanniques s'apprêtent à monter à bord des navires afin de rejoindre leur patrie et échapper à la captivité.

The English boarding from the east jetty

On the jetty on the eastern side of the port, the many british preparing to board the ships, to return to their « home » land and to escape captivity.

De Engelsen schepen in vanaf de Oostelijke Pier

Op de Oostelijke Pier van de haven maken talrijke Britse soldaten zich klaar om aan boord te gaan van de schepen die ze terug zullen brengen naar hun moeder land. Zo ontsnappen zij aan de

The Droit Office

Margate's Operation *Dynamo* Command Centre

Whilst hurried steps were being taken to evacuate as many men as possible from Dunkirk, frantic preparations were also being made at several South Coast ports to receive them. One of these ports was the Kent resort of Margate. The following account was published in 1950 to mark the tenth anniversary of Operation *Dynamo*:

'Margate was but a skeleton of its peace-time self when, on the afternoon of May 28, the first ship loaded with troops from Dunkirk steamed round North Foreland, but to the 200 men on board, the town's Jetty, set in a becalmed sea and silhouetted by a brilliant sun, appeared like a haven of peace and safety.

'A few days before the Mayor (Alderman G.B. Farrar), the Town Clerk (Mr. P.T. Grove) and the Chief Constable (Mr. W. Palmer) had been secretly advised to be ready for an emergency – the possibility of an enemy invasion was hinted – and the Civil Defence services were ordered to stand by.

'It was in the early hours of Monday, May 27, that the seriousness of the situation became known. Local military commanders received a message that "something had gone wrong over the other side", and were ordered to withdraw their troops from the town. Three thousand left that day. Two men of the Royal Engineers remained to blow up the jetty, should invasion become imminent. Mines for this purpose were actually laid the day before, and the place was closed to the public.

'It was intimated that some boats might arrive with men evacuated from Dunkirk … The first indication that the evacuation had started was the appearance of a hospital ship round the Foreland at daybreak on May 27. There were casualties on board, but they were not landed at Margate.

'That day the Royal Navy took over the jetty, and Commander Stanistrett and Lieutenant Newman, who were in charge, established themselves in the Droit Office. No one knew what to expect. There was no military transport available, no stores or equipment, no blankets, and no Service personnel to handle a major situation …

'Not until May 29 did troops begin to arrive in large numbers … At one time there were as many as 52 ships lying off the town, some so overcrowded that they presented a mass of khaki on the waterline; others, having completed one, two or even three journeys from the beaches, were waiting for orders or supplies before returning. There was not a ripple on the sea; not a cloud in the sky throughout those eight days. The sun shone continuously. The atmosphere was one of tranquillity, disturbed only by the realisation that but a few miles across the water one of the greatest epics in our history was being enacted.'[18]

Opposite: The Droit Office on Margate's seafront as it appears today. Badly damaged in an air raid in 1941, the Droit Office stood at the entrance to Margate's jetty. (Ron Ellis/Shutterstcok) Inset:The commemorative plaque on the wall of the Droit Office which points out that 46,772 men were landed at Margate during Operation *Dynamo*. (Courtesy of Robert Mitchell)

THIS TABLET COMMEMORATES THE LANDING ON MARGATE JETTY OF 46,772 TROOPS OF THE ALLIED FORCES ON THE EVACUATION OF DUNKIRK IN MAY, 1940.

The Barn at La Plaine Au Bois

Remembering the Wormhoudt Massacre

Of vital importance to the troops assembling in the evacuation areas was that the 'pocket' into which the BEF had withdrawn was held for as long as possible. This included the main road from the east to Bergues, which passed through the towns of Wormhoudt, Cassel and Hazebrouck, which were garrisoned by troops of the 144th Brigade of the 48th (South Midland) Division.

At the key road junction at Wormhoudt were the men of the 2nd Battalion, Royal Warwickshire Regiment, the 8th Battalion, Worcestershire Regiment and the 4th Battalion, Cheshire Regiment, along with supporting artillery. A little after midday on 27 May, Wormhoudt came under attack for the first time, with German aircraft dropping around ten bombs on the town, but it was not until the following day that the battle for Wormhoudt began in earnest.

At 09.40 hours on the 28th, convoys of German trucks arrived, out of which poured large

numbers of infantry. They took up battle positions and opened fire on the Warwicks holding the west and south-west perimeter. German artillery then began shelling the town. The defenders held their ground staunchly until tanks of the 3rd Panzer Regiment rumbled up, and though the British Boys anti-tank guns crippled four of the panzers, it was an uneven fight. Even so, the defenders held out until all their ammunition had been exhausted, at which point the Germans overran their positions. They dropped their weapons and surrendered to the 1st SS Panzer Division Leibstandarte SS Adolf Hitler (often abbreviated as LSSAH).

A number of the survivors from the Warwickshire and Cheshire regiments, a few from the Royal Artillery, and some French PoWs, amounting to around eighty to ninety men, were rounded up by elements of the LSSAH commanded by Hauptsturmführer Wilhelm Mohnke and marched into a barn at the small hamlet of La Plaine au Bois. Amongst those men was Gunner Brian Fahey:

'There must have been about 100 men in the barn, and then the Germans surrounded it, and threw in hand grenades. It was apparent that they were going to murder us all. I suppose the men in front took the full force of the blast, but we all went down like a pack of cards. I heard the noise of the explosion, and it hadn't damaged me'.

When the officer commanding the SS troops saw that not all the men had been killed by the grenades, he ordered the survivors outside, where they were shot. Brian Fahey had only been wounded by the grenades but was taken outside and shot in the back.

'When I finally came to, it had all gone quiet in the barn, and I could feel this bubbling in my lung but I realised that I wasn't dead … I crawled back into the barn and there were men in there. Most were dead and some were dying.' Fahey was one of only a handful who lived to tell of this terrible ordeal.

Main image: The barn at La Plaine au Bois, near Wormhoudt, which marks the site of the massacre on 28 May 1940. This is a reconstruction of the original structure that stood on the site at the time of the killings, the latter having been demolished around 1960. Below: The interior of the barn at La Plaine au Bois. The reconstruction was unveiled in 2001 by two survivors of the massacre, Alf Tombs and Bert Evans.

18

Wormhoudt Lake

Surviving the Wormhoudt Massacre

As well as Brian Fahey, another amongst the few who survived the Wormhoudt atrocity was Gunner Bert Evans, who later recounted the horrors of that day: 'The fighting was non-stop. Mortar attack after mortar attack. The noise, the fire, it was endless,' Evans recalled. 'I was captured with a group of "D" Company soldiers. We knew we were up against Hitler's elite. But we could never have expected the treatment they would mete out.

'First they [the men of the LSSAH] took all our personal effects – my letter, my photographs of my mum and dad and my two sisters, even the photograph of Elizabeth, my wife, who was serving with the ATS. They were torn up and burned. They didn't want any of us identified.

'Then some [of us] were rounded up and driven into the town square, where Germans with our Tommy guns opened fire. Then 15 or 20 of our boys were stripped to the waist and lined up. Opposite them were four machine guns mounted on stands. Then the guns fired and the men fell down like rag dolls. We were marched about a mile out of the village to the barn.

'It was bedlam. They were shouting, pushing us with the butts of their guns. We were jammed inside the barn. They pushed more and more in. No one could breath. Our wounded were falling and we were falling over them. When the captain called out that there was no more room we knew from that German's answer that this was where we would die.'[19]

The Germans then threw the grenades into the barn hoping to kill all the men. Two of the soldiers, Corporal Moor and Company Sergeant Major Jenkins, heroically threw themselves on top of the grenades to minimise the carnage. But scores died. When the smoke and machine-gun fire stopped, Bert looked down and saw that his right arm was hanging from his shoulder by little other than mangled muscle.

Captain James Lynn-Allen also survived the explosions and realised that the Germans would make sure none of the British soldiers lived to tell of the atrocity. He knew that if he remained where he was, he would certainly be killed, so he made a bid to escape. Seeing that Evans was also still alive, Lynn-Allen pulled him out of the barn with him, as the former recalled:

'While I was still feeling dazed, and as another grenade came in through the door, Captain Lynn-Allen, who was at this time unwounded, seized me, and dragged me out through the door, and round the corner while the Germans who had thrown the grenades were taking cover against the explosions. Captain Lynn-Allen practically dragged, or supported me, the whole way to a clump of trees which was about 200 yards away. When we got inside the trees, we found there was a small stagnant and deep pond in the centre. We got down into the pond with the water up to our chests. Captain Lynn-Allen was standing some little distance from the edge. I, because of my condition, stood closer to the bank, and presumably lower in the water.'[20]

The pair's escape attempt, however, had not gone unnoticed. 'Suddenly, without warning, a German appeared on the bank of the pond, just above us' recalled Evans. The German raised his pistol and opened fire, shooting Lynn-Allen in the forehead and Evans in the neck.

The captain was killed, but Evans was alive – just. Having staggered around in the pond trying to find Lynn-Allen, Evans then crawled to the bank and struggled out of the water, making his way across open fields to the nearby Bollengier Farm. He was eventually found by a German ambulance unit. Evans became a prisoner of war, his arm being amputated. He was repatriated in late 1944, surviving to provide testimony of the events that unfolded at La Plaine au Bois.

Opposite: Looking down from the memorial mound at the La Plaine au Bois site towards the pond in which Lynn-Allen and Evans sought cover. Note the white marker to the left of the lake which looks out towards Bollengier Farm. Top of page: Looking across the fields from the 'Wormhoudt Lake' towards Bollengier Farm. It was across this ground that Evans made his way after pulling himself out of the lake. Right: Captain James Lynn-Allen. Lynn-Allen's body was never found. He is commemorated on the Dunkirk Memorial.

19

The Beach At Malo-Les-Bains

Rescue from the Sand

Shortly after arriving at Dunkirk, Captain Tennant saw that the port of Dunkirk was being bombed to destruction by the Luftwaffe and that embarkation from there would become increasingly problematical. It had already been accepted by Ramsay that the beaches to the east of Dunkirk would have to be used for embarking the troops and, at 20.25 hours on the 27th, he received the following 'Most Immediate' message from Tennant: 'Port consistently bombed all day, and on fire. Embarkation possible only from beaches East of harbour A.B.C.D. Send all ships and passenger ships there to anchor.'

What Tennant was referring to was the stretch of the shoreline east from Malo-les-Bains through Bray Dunes to La Panne had been divided to four zones – A, B, C, and D. So Tennant then sent parties along the shore all the way to La Panne to organise the beaches to allow for the orderly passage of the troops through the beaches onto the boats. All the ships that subsequently reached Dunkirk that night were ordered to the beaches.

These beaches stretch to the Belgium border, eight miles away, and from there to Nieuport, nine-and-a-half miles farther still. For the whole seventeen-and-a-half miles the shore is a wide belt of shelving sand behind which, in many areas, are mile after mile of sand dunes, partially clothed in long, sharp spouts of grass and patches of sea thistle. It is amongst these dunes that the resorts of Malo-les-Bains, Bray Dunes and La Panne, mentioned above, can be found. Away from the coast beyond the dunes was, in 1940, a wide strip of open land – common and meadow – leading to the Dunkirk-Furnes canal.

The naval party that had arrived at Dunkirk with Tennant was spread out along the beaches to act as police, and as the troops walked off the road onto the sand, the troops were met by seamen who marshalled them into parties of fifty and then led them on to the beaches. The soldiers were then ordered to disperse along the sands so as to afford smallest possible targets for enemy planes.

Captain Howson was one of the Royal Navy officers at Malo beach, and he noted early on that, 'Very large numbers of British troops were gathered at Malo and we continuously met many large bodies making their way towards Dunkerque: these included some French troops who were told that some French ships might be expected for them, a pious hope.' What Howson also found was that it was immensely difficult to communicate with the boats from the beach by loudhailer. Communication between ship and shore proved to be one of the handicaps which bedevilled the evacuation throughout its nine days.

Main image: Looking down the open expanse of the beach at Malo-les-Bains towards Dunkirk – the harbour can be seen in the distance. (Shutterstock) Left and below: Two views of the wreck of *L'Adroit* at Malo-les-Bains. Despite frequently appearing in pictures relating to Operation *Dynamo*, her loss predates the official start of the evacuation.

The Dunes at Bray

The Queues of Waiting Soldiers Formed on the Beaches

To the east of Malo-les-Bains is the tiny resort of Bray-Dunes. There, as elsewhere, the troops waited with astonishing order and discipline to be taken from the beach to the ships anchored further out at sea, as Captain Anthony Rhodes of 253 Field Company, Royal Engineers described:

'Towards early morning great queues formed to go to the water's edge where at about four o'clock, out of the darkness, we saw boats coming in. Where they came in, there was a little nucleus of men at the head of the water, and a great queue running from the dunes behind, perhaps a quarter of a mile long. Nobody told us what to do, but it seemed the decent thing to get into the queue and not to try and jump it.

'At the head of each little nucleus there was a naval officer. There must have been ten or twelve of these queues, and when we were halfway up our queue, the bombing started again. One man ran out of place to the head of the queue when he saw a boat coming. The naval officer turned on him, and I heard him say, 'Go back to the place you've come from, or I'll shoot you!' He said it very loudly for everybody to hear, and the man went back with his tail between his legs.'

The orderly queues from the beach stretching into the water as the boats came in, was one of the hallmarks of the Dunkirk evacuation. Signaller Alfred Baldwin of the 65th Field Regiment, Royal Artillery said that the impression he had was of people standing waiting for a bus. He recalled that even when the German aircraft attacked, the same discipline was maintained: 'Every time a 'plane strafed the beach, all the queues vanished miraculously, then as soon as the staffing finished, they all came up and formed up again where they were before.'

It was also at Bray that men of the Royal Engineers, assisted by soldiers of the 1st Division constructed a long pier of lorries which were lashed together and fitted with planks. The pier stretched out into the deeper water off the shallow beach. This created a walkway some ten feet high and whilst insufficiently stable for large ships to berth against, it proved to be ideal for smaller craft. Instead of the troops having to try and climb onto small boats bobbing and swaying in the surf, the troops could walk out to the boats secured against the narrow pier. This stratagem was so successful that further lorry-piers were constructed at La Panne.

Main image: Looking down on the gently shelving beach from a section of the dunes at Bray. The beaches east of Dunkirk can be reached at a variety of locations. One site is the Reserve Naturelle Dune Marchand, a nature reserve to the west of Bray-Dunes. The reserve covers a total of eighty-three acres, and is signposted off the D-60 coast road. (Shutterstock) Below: Allied troops pictured on one of the beaches near Dunkirk forming into long winding queues ready to take their turn to board small boats which took them to larger vessels.

Bombed at Dunkirk

Australian Newspaper Cutting Recalls Minesweeper's Role

The Hunt-class minesweeper HMS *Pangbourne* made its first trip to Dunkirk on 28 May.[21] The vessel's approach to Dunkirk was recorded by an unnamed sub-lieutenant, who was *Pangbourne*'s Duty Officer. The first part was published in *The West Australian* on 9 June 1945. The introduction states that 'this vivid personal narrative of the epic evacuation from Dunkirk was written by an officer of a British naval vessel which took part in the operation. It was written – not with a view to publication – when the officer was lying in hospital at Leeds in June, 1940 and was received recently by a friend of the officer in Western Australia.'

'A peculiar smell is in the air,' wrote the sub-lieutenant. 'I know it from my days in the Merchant Service. It's burning oil fuel and there on the horizon ahead is a black cloud – smoke from the burning tanks of Dunkirk. It is flat calm now, and the wind has dropped, and as we draw nearer the eastern sky glows from a million fires.[22]

'We round Nieuport buoy and turn to the southward; I turn my glasses on the beaches. The silver sands are stained with black. I look again. The stain is a packed mass of people. Thousands upon thousands of them, looking to seaward to watch the flotilla arrive. And now I can see

something more – something which my bewildered mind is unwilling to believe. The people are soldiers in British khaki! Can things be going so badly for us that we are evacuating our army?

'We tie up [alongside the Mole] and they swarm aboard us. Dirty, ragged, weary soldiers, with a forced smile on their white faces and a cheery word for the sailors although they are dead on their feet. They come without coats, some without shoes or socks – but few without some sign of an unbeatable spirit. We stow them wherever there is an inch of space, and they flop down as they are and relax. They seem to think because they are aboard a ship danger is past. And now we have received a message that we must shift berth into the inner harbour, where an ambulance convoy is waiting with stretcher cases.'

Having found its way to Dunkirk's inner harbour with great difficulty, *Pangbourne* was secured to the dock wall, at which point the stretcher cases were brought aboard, being deposited wherever space could be found. Fully loaded, the minesweeper headed back out to sea, bound for Ramsgate – though the journey was interrupted when *Pangbourne* was temporarily grounded on a sandbank, but luckily it caused no significant damage.

Pangbourne headed back to Dunkirk on 29 May, this time, though, her luck ran out. As she approached the beach at La Panne the Luftwaffe struck. 'A giant with a hammer smashes his weight against the ship's side four times in rapid succession. This is it! The storm is breaking,' continued the unnamed sub-lieutenant. 'The klaxons scream their warning, and before they stop I am at the gun. There high above us are the planes – Heinkels and Dorniers – and the bombs are screaming down … The world goes mad. The ship leaps in the air and cold salt water souses me as I shrink into the deck. The spanging of bullets and flying shrapnel is added to the explosion of the bombs.'

Pangbourne's hull was holed on both sides above and below the water line, resulting in the death of thirteen men and the wounding of nine others. With her compasses also out of action, her skipper had no choice but to head for home. Her part in Operation *Dynamo* at an end.

Opposite: The newspaper cutting from *The West Australian* in which the unnamed sub-lieutenant describes *Pangbourne*'s part in the evacuations. Main image: The Hunt-class minesweeper HMS *Pangbourne*. Having served throughout the Second World War with the pennant number J.37, *Pangbourne* was sold into merchant service in 1947.

French Anti-Aircraft Positions

Mentioned in Despatches, 28 May 1940

As Day 3 of Operation *Dynamo* progressed, the build-up of troops on the beaches exceeded the capacity of the ships, large and small, to recover them, and long lines of desperate, but patient soldiers, began to form. 'There they stood,' recalled A. Betts, the skipper of the small motor boat *Gypsy King*, 'lined up like a bus queue, right from the dunes, down the shore, to the water's edge, and sometimes up to their waists beyond. They were as patient and orderly, too, as people in an ordinary bus queue. There were bombers overhead and artillery fire all around them. They were hungry and thirsty and dead-beat; yet they kept in line, and no-one tried to steal a march on anyone else. Most of them even managed to summon up an occasional joke or wisecrack.'

Driver Benjamin Nickholds of the Royal Army Service Corps reached the Dunkirk area on the 28th, were he was to spend two days and two nights: 'I joined the queue which seemed to go on for ever. In it were servicemen from many different units. Most had abandoned almost their entire kit. I still had my rifle, ammo, a full water-bottle and some emergency rations. There was no water in town and very little on the beach. I had to survive with what I had.

'It was an orderly queue of very tired men who waited patiently to be rescued. They hoped to get a ship from the dock to take them to England. Dunkirk was in flames and a cloud of smoke hung over the dock. Periodically, a Stuka dive bomber would appear from behind this cloud. It was a terrifying experience as we saw them dive with screaming engines straight for us. They released a bomb which also screamed louder and louder until impact. We scattered as soon as we saw the approach of a bomber but took the same places in the queue when the raid was over …

'The bombs tended to penetrate a little into the sand and some of the blast was deflected upward by the sand. Some shrapnel did take a little flesh from my hand and dent my helmet. I may owe my life to my helmet …When the bombs landed on the beach or in the sea, the shockwave knocked the breath right out of us. Now and again one of the lads could stand it no more so he would dash into the town but it was no safer there. Some of them did not come back.'[23]

Amongst the guns in action defending the port and the beaches on 28 May were the French anti-aircraft positions seen here, the remains of which are located beside the D2 immediately south of Dunkirk and a short distance east from the Canal de Bergues. Constructed in 1939, this battery of four raised concrete emplacements was manned by the men of Batterie No.201 of the 406e Regiment d'Artillerie de DCA. It was one of eight such sites supporting the air defence system for the Dunkirk area. Equipped with 75mm guns on semi-fixed platforms, the battery was in action throughout the evacuations, but its service on the 28th was deemed worthy of recognition for it was on this day that the French gunners were Mentioned in Despatches by Admiral Abrial.

On 2 June Abrial ordered that the guns and emplacements be destroyed to prevent their use by the rapidly approaching Germans.

Opposite page: The remains of the French anti-aircraft positions near the Canal de Bergues.

23

Margate's Winter Gardens

Pressed Into Service as a Casualty Receiving Station

As the flow of evacuated soldiers across the Channel gathered pace, so did the need to put in place the necessary facilities to receive them. G.A. Abbott, an ex-Alderman of Margate, described how the town's famous Winter Gardens played its part:

'The Winter Gardens – one of the largest and finest concert halls on the coast – presented a strange sight when it was converted by the then Entertainments Manager, Mr. John Saxby, into an emergency first-aid station. Men were sitting about on chairs or the floor, some covered only with a blanket, being attended by nurses for minor wounds and injuries, and dozens were bathing their swollen feet in warm water while they drank a cup of tea.

'We collected a huge pile of wet clothing from men who had been in the sea. Working with the Liaison Officer, the re-clothing of the British troops was not difficult, as new uniforms, boots, and underclothes were constantly arriving from the Army Clothing Depot at Dover. We were particularly instructed, however, that none of the Allied troops were to be put into British uniforms. Consequently, an appeal was issued to Margate for civilian clothing, and the people responded magnificently.

'Day and night the work went on for over a week, and by that time we were getting short of clothing for our Allies. Then I got permission to broadcast over the relay system to Margate people for further help. Within half-an-hour we were receiving boots, socks, clothing of all description, and we were soon able to say we had enough. I remember hearing later that a certain J.P. missed his riding boots. His housekeeper had sent them as a contribution and they were given to a French officer. Not a man was sent away from Margate without medical attention, clean, dry clothing, good food, and, where possible, a wire or postcard to his relatives – but what a motley crowd they looked.'[24]

Dr G.L. Brocklehurst, Margate's Health Officer, was also involved in preparing for the arrival of the wounded:

'It was in the early hours of a morning late in May, 1940, that I was asked to provide a fast car to take two important passengers to London to see the Prime Minister. The Casualty Transport Officer took two officers to Downing Street and on his return told me that we could expect the landing of a large number of casualties. We presumed that they would be from Dunkirk, and probably most of us pictured the orderly disembarkation of wounded at the Jetty. None of us pictured the problems that were going to arise in transporting the wounded from an assortment of vessels, varying from a sloop to a mud-hopper. Fortunately, the sea was calm.

'The first aid services dealt with approximately 500 stretcher cases a day. The whole of the transport of the wounded had to be undertaken by them, as the only Army ambulances available were too heavy to go to the end of the Jetty. Towards the end of the period we were all wondering how long the Jetty would stand up to the strain of the procession of ambulances, as it was both mined and beginning to creak.

'One incident is worth recording from the humorous point of view. A party of Algerian troops came ashore from a sloop and were almost immediately followed by a stampede of sailors who seized them and removed their clothes. First aid workers saved the situation by rushing up blankets for them. It transpired that the native troops managed to get to the lockers of the sailors and had taken their spare uniforms. Two wounded being treated at the Winter Gardens next to one another found that they were brothers and had not seen one another since the outbreak of war.'[25]

An aerial view of the Winter Gardens in Margate, which were first opened to the public on 3 August 1911. (Courtesy of Simon Moores; www.airads.co.uk)

24

The Jetty at Margate

The Authorities Face An Unusual Problem

The first ship that arrivd at Margate at 14.30 hours on the 28th was *Sandown*, which landed 201 men. An hour later it was the turn of *Gracie Fields*, which disembarked 281 soldiers.

Superintendent H.B. Fleet, of Kent Constabulary's 'M' Division was amongst the many in Margate who had been involved in the resort's preparations. He recalled how he was first informed about Operation *Dynamo*: 'At 2.40 in the morning of Monday, May 27, 1940, I was awakened at the Winter Gardens, where some of the Police had taken up quarters since the outbreak of the war, as it was the location of the Civil Defence headquarters (then known as A.R.P.), by the night duty Inspector. He said that the local Military Commander, Lieutenant-Colonel B.C.T. Freeland, R.E., had received certain information which was of such nature that he desired to hold a conference immediately with certain senior Police Officers and the Mayor. This was held in secret at his office at Cecil Square at 3 a.m. It was actually the first information received in this town of what was to develop into the greatest evacuation ever known.

'Shortly after the conference I took up my duties on the Jetty Liaison Officer to the Royal Navy, which established its headquarters at the Droit Office, and also to the few military

personnel, who later occupied the Concert Pavilion at the other end of the Jetty.'[26] It was whilst he was at his post that Superintendent Fleet's attention was drawn to a problem that is rarely mentioned in accounts of Operation *Dynamo* – and which would almost certainly not have been confined just to Margate:

'It was not long after the first contingent of troops began to arrive when I was approached by a Customs Officer for instructions as to what to do with a couple of terrier dogs which were being closely held by two British Tommies. They had found them terrified by gunfire on the outskirts of Dunkirk, looked after them, waded out with them in the water and cared for them with great difficulty on a crowded boat. You can well imagine their feelings when told they would not be allowed to take them past the pier barrier. The parting was pathetic in the extreme.

'As the time advanced the question of the numerous dogs that came over became a serious problem for the Police. I was forced to use a second kiosk on the Jetty in which to place the animals. The numbers grew and it was only with great difficulty that the sliding door of the kiosk could be opened sufficiently wide to push one animal through and not permit a dozen to escape.

'It was found necessary to remove the animals frequently and this unpleasant job was done voluntarily by Mr. George Sayer (Corporation horsekeeper, well-known locally for his fondness of animals). He removed the dogs in a small van to the Town Yard, where they were humanely destroyed. Three hundred and thirty dogs of various breeds and sizes were so dealt with. In addition, 13 French Army dogs (with aluminium identity discs affixed to their ears) were put in quarantine and 12 days later placed on a French destroyer at Dover for return to France.'

An early postcard of Margate's jetty, or pier, surrounded by warships – scenes similar to that witnessed during Operation *Dynamo* some years later. Note the Droit Office in the right hand corner, this featuring in Object 16.

25

Naval Beachmaster's Photographs

Lieutenant J.G. Wells Served Ashore at Bray

Amongst the many unsung heroes of Operation *Dynamo*, of which there were undoubtedly many, were the Royal Navy personnel who served ashore, in the port and on the beaches, during the evacuation. One of the members of what became known as the Naval Beach Staff was Lieutenant J.G. Wells.

Having been 'selected for service at Dunkirk', and provided with the necessary orders 'for policing the beaches and expediting the embarkation as much as possible', Wells embarked on HMS *Esk*, for the journey across the Channel, at 20.00 hours on the evening of 29 May. Travelling with him on the E-class destroyer were another eleven officers, all twelve leading their own party that also consisted of one Petty Officer, one Leading Seaman, two Able Seaman and a Signalman. *Esk* sailed at 20.45 hours, Wells himself taking up the story in a report he penned on 6 June 1940:

'At 0125 [on 30 May], I was landed at Bray with three other officers and the parties of ratings. Commodore Hallett, who was in charge of the beach as a whole, remained afloat. We never saw him at all as I believe his boat broke down and he had to be towed clear of the danger area.

'It was obvious that naval personnel were needed for the embarkation of the large number of troops then waiting on the beach. They were all very tired and eager to get off the beach at any cost. Some had been waiting for 48 hours and all had witnessed the bombing that day by German aircraft. The system that produced the best results was to organize them into a long queue at each of the three embarkation points at Bray beach. The queues were three deep and were spaced out in groups of ten, this number being most suitable for the types of boat available.

'The following group could be used for shoving off a loaded boat, which took a good deal of moving at half tide owing to a bar running parallel to the sea. The Army pontoon boats proved most suitable owing to their draught, double ended construction and general handiness. Fortunately the weather was favourable for the operations, the sea remaining calm all day and a gentle Northerly breeze assisting in the recovery of drifting craft. An overcast sky and the presence of our fighter patrols seems to have deterred the enemy aircraft from bombing.'[27]

Opposite: The images taken by Lieutenant J.G. Wells whilst he was serving on the beach at Bray – images which he handed over to the Commanding Officer of HMS *Excellent* on his return. The top photograph is a close-up of some of the vehicles used in the construction of the improvised pier at Bray-Dunes. Above: Lieutenant Wells' handwritten comment on the rear of this picture states that it is a 'general view of Bray and pier'. Note the damage caused to the image by its immersion in the sea.

In his report, Lieutenant Wells went on to point out some of the issues that he and his colleagues faced at Bray: 'The main difficulty lay in the insufficiency of naval ratings to take charge of the outgoing boats and bring them back to the embarkation points. As a rule the soldiers detailed to return them did not carry out orders and it was neccessary [sic] to swim or wade out for drifting boats, causing a delay that was perpetually slowing up the operation. One can hardly blame them as it was clearly our responsibility. I asked for more ratings and a signal was made to this effect from outlying warships. However, none arrived.

'Another handicap was the bad communication between ships and shore. A motor cycle headlamp is a poor substitute for an Aldis Lamp. Semaphore was not easy and we failed to find the W/T sets that had been promised at Dover.

'It was necessary at one period early in the forenoon of Thursday [30 May] to get more ships to lie off Bray as they seemed to be concentrating on La Panne and Dunkirk. The signal asking for more support did not reach the right authority afloat for over an hour as the signalman had to bicycle for three miles along the beach and eventually send the message by boat. At no time during Thursday were there more than three warships off Bray until 2200, when the situation became much easier. Between 1300 and 1700 only 120 men were sent off, which was disappointing as we had plenty of small boats available.

Main image: Taken by a Luftwaffe airman in the aftermath of
Operation *Dynamo*, this picture provides an aerial view of an improvised pier
constructed on the beach at Bray-Dunes. The road along the seafront is now known as Digue de
Mer in Bray, whilst the bandstand in the centre of the promenade in this picture is today the location of
a memorial. Above: Photographed by a German soldier after the evacuation, a British Army lorry lies
abandoned on the beaches east of Dunkirk. Note the improvised pier in the background.

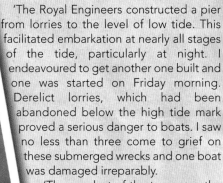

'The Royal Engineers constructed a pier from lorries to the level of low tide. This facilitated embarkation at nearly all stages of the tide, particularly at night. I endeavoured to get another one built and one was started on Friday morning. Derelict lorries, which had been abandoned below the high tide mark proved a serious danger to boats. I saw no less than three come to grief on these submerged wrecks and one boat was damaged irreparably.

'The conduct of the troops on the beach was splendid and their discipline and morale of the highest order. At times the sporadic embarkation was most disappointing but I never heard any complaints. Their behaviour under shell fire later in the day was a fine example to the sailors, who soon picked up the idea of lying flat on the stomach and singing: "Roll out the barrel", to pass away the time. Enemy 4-inch Howitzer shelled the beach at 2230 and thereafter at hourly intervals. Initially there was a number of casualties on the dunes, but as soon as the troops were organized on the beach, few received any injury. The effect on morale was more dangerous as it made one realise the proximity of the enemy, who was then about 5 miles distant.

'At 0100/31 I was informed that naval personnel would have to evacuate at dawn if the present shelling continued. Some officers, not in our original party, had already left, and at 0300, I swam out to fetch a boat for the Brigadier in command of the 42nd Division. Unfortunately I lost all my equipment in doing so but we managed to take him off at about 0330. The shelling of the beach then looked fairly effective and the order was passed from Headquarters that as the embarkation would probably be over at dawn the following day, all naval personnel were to embark forthwith. Accordingly I remained on board HMS *Halcyon* where we had taken the Brigadier.'

HMS *Halcyon* arrived at Dover at 08.45 hours on Friday, 31st May. Informed that he was no longer required, Lieutenant Wells duly returned to Portsmouth later that same day. Once there, he handed over some film containing pictures he had taken on the beach at Bray, though the camera or the film had been dropped and submerged, albeit momentarily, in seawater.

Opposite   page
top: An Army haversack, containing
various documents and books, that Wells encountered
lying on the beach at Bray. Opposite bottom: Venturing out on the
beach at low tide, a German soldier inspects some of the vehicles used in one of the
improvised piers on the beach at La Panne – note the 'Kursaal' building which can be seen in the
background. Above: With time, the effects of the tide gradually broke up the piers, one of which is being
examined here by German soldiers after the evacuation. Below: At least one abandoned ambulance can
be seen in this picture of one of the piers constructed at Bray.

26

HMS Wakeful's Tread-Plate

A Reminder of One of the Royal Navy's Losses

Six British and three French destroyers were sunk in the course of Operation *Dynamo*, along with nine other major vessels. In addition, a further twenty-three destroyers suffered serious damage.

It had already been a bad night for the Royal Navy when, just after midnight on 29 May, the destroyer HMS *Wakeful*, carrying 650 troops embarked from the beach at Bray, sailed for Dover by the northerly route Y. She had just cleared the North Channel and turned sharply to westward when two torpedo tracks were seen. One of the torpedoes fired by *E-30* was avoided; the other hit amidships.

HMS *Wakeful* was torn apart by the explosion. The two halves sank in just fifteen seconds, settling with their midships sections on the shallow bottom while bow and stern projected high above the surface. A number of vessels arrived on the scene to help with the work. Able Seaman Iain Nethercott was serving on HMS *Kelvin*, one of the ships that came to *Wakeful*'s aid: "She [*Wakeful*] was packed with soldiers at that time. Her sinking was a terrible tragedy with all those soldiers drowned below decks. There were a few groups of corpses still floating around in that area when *Keith* passed through.'

One of the first to reach the area was the drifter *Comfort*, which had been heading to La Panne. Its crew plucked *Wakeful*'s captain, Commander R.L. Fisher, alive from the water. Such was the scale of the disaster that only twenty-five of *Wakeful*'s crew and one evacuee were saved.

As the rescue work had been continuing, another explosion announced the fact that HMS *Grafton* (recently arrived on the scene with 800 troops on board) had been torpedoed by

The remains of HMS *Wakeful*'s tread-plate. A tread-plate is fitted to the deck of a warship at the gangway. At the time of writing, HMS *Wakeful*'s tread-plate was on display in the National Museum of the Royal Navy in Portsmouth Historic Dockyard, whilst the crest was held in the reserve collection.

Above: The W-class destroyer HMS *Wakeful*. Built under the 1916-17 Programme in the 10th Destroyer order, she served into the early years of the Second World War.

the German U-boat *U-62*. The Official History takes up the story: '*Comfort*, lying nearby, was almost swamped by the force of the explosion and the Captain of the *Wakeful*, whom she had rescued from the sea, was again washed overboard. Although sinking, the *Grafton* opened fire on a vessel which in the darkness she took to be an enemy torpedo boat and following the *Grafton*'s example the *Lydd* rammed and sank this dimly seen vessel. But in fact it was the *Comfort* moving in the darkness; only one of her crew and four of the men she had rescued from the *Wakeful* were saved … The Captain of the *Wakeful*, for the second time, was picked up, swimming, five hours after his own ship had been hit.'[28]

The corvette HMS *Sheldrake* sank the wreck the following day, leaving *Wakeful* as a war grave. In 2001, following an agreement by the British and Belgian authorities, work began to deal with the danger that *Wakeful*'s wreck, lying at a depth of just fifty-three feet, presented to the modern deep-draught ships that use the English Channel. It was eventually decided to remove part of HMS *Wakeful*'s superstructure, including funnels and navigation equipment, and secure them to the side of the wreck. It was during this sensitive operation that the tread-plate (seen here) and ship's crest were recovered by Belgian divers.

Right: HMS *Wakeful* pictured at speed off Dunkirk prior to her loss.

27

The East Mole is Damaged

Hit By Bombs During a German Air Raid

The fact that that the Mole at Dunkirk was proving instrumental in getting many of the men away from Dunkirk also meant that it was vulnerable to the German bombs and shellfire. It was on 29 May that disaster struck when the steam packet SS *Fenella* was lost when she came under aerial attack as she was loading troops from the East Mole.

Fenella had more than 600 on board when she was hit by three bombs in quick succession. The first hit her directly on the promenade deck, the second struck the Mole, blowing lumps of concrete through the ship's side below the waterline, and the third exploded between the pier and the ship's side, wrecking the engine room. *Fenella* was clearly unable to move, and likely to sink, so the troops were disembarked back onto the Mole. Luckily, the paddle-steamer *Crested Eagle* was nearby and the troops were re-embarked.

The Mole was also damaged by the steam packet turned-Armed Boarding Vessel, *King Orry*. As she moved towards the East Mole, bombs rained down on all sides. The ship was violently shaken and the steering gear was put out of action. All instruments, woodwork and the like were shattered. 'We were now attacked again but no direct hits were made,' reported Commander J. Elliott, 'bombs falling so close, however, as to give the impression of direct hits, especially as various debris flew up at every explosion'. With Elliott unable to steer the ship, he slammed against the Mole.

To bridge the gaps in the Mole, planks of wood, trestles, ladders and anything that could be found were placed across. These the troops then had to negotiate, very often in the dark, under aerial attack, with the waters of the Channel swirling far below them.

Jackie Taylor had enlisted in the Royal Artillery, but was transferred to the RAMC's 13th Field Ambulance. He was amongst the many that had to negotiate the damaged Mole: 'Near the Mole I came to the tail end of a queue of troops. There was a lot of tension amongst the men, if anyone attempted to strike a match they were shot at. Royal Marines were patrolling the queue to stop men sneaking ahead and causing a panic. In fact, I had a narrow escape. I had spotted one of my mates a few yards ahead of me and as I stepped out of the line to have a word I felt a bayonet prodding my back. I tried to explain that I only wanted a word with my mate just in front, but I had to get back in line smartly …

'We eventually shuffled to where the Mole had been bombed and some planks thrown across the gap. Military Police were telling them to run along the mole to find a ship tied up alongside and see if there was enough room for them. These ships had been bombed while waiting to be loaded … My turn to walk the plank came and when I got over I ran along with a few more men until I came to a large ship on the left. A group of men stood near a small gangway on top of the rails. It must have been high tide because the ship was level with the Mole rails.'[29]

Opposite: Troops on the East Mole boarding a Royal Navy warship. The poor quality of this image is due to the fact that it is an example of a 'Wirephoto', when images were sent, in this case to the US for immediate publication, by telegraph or telephone. Main image: The East Mole at Dunkirk, as it was in 1940, no longer exists, though this is the spot from where it reached out into the harbour. The Mole was not a stout stone wall with berthing places along its length, as might be imagined around a harbour. It was a narrow plank-way barely wide enough for three men to walk abreast. On either side was a protective railing made of strong timbers with, at intervals, taller posts which could be used by ships to secure themselves against the Mole in emergencies. At the far end of the Mole was a concrete 'nose' upon which stood a short lighthouse. The Mole was built in this fashion to allow the tides to roll in and out and therefore put less strain upon its structure.

28

Sea Scouts at Dunkirk

A Fictional Account That was Based Based on Fact

Few events in history have inspired a nation more than the 'miracle' of Dunkirk, which exemplifies the true resilient British character. The 'Dunkirk spirit' has become part of the English lexicon, with its own dictionary entry, meaning 'an attitude of being very strong in a difficult situation and refusing to accept defeat'. As a consequence, film-producers and writers have sought to encapsulate the essence of those dramatic nine days in the summer of 1940. Amongst these was a novel by Percy Westerman, *Sea Scouts at Dunkirk*.

The book is a fictional account of a tiny boat, manned by Boy Scouts, which went over with the 'Little Ships'. Long out of print, it is described by the publishers as 'an adventure story'. Unremarkable, one may think – except that Sea Scouts did indeed take part in Operation *Dynamo*.

The first mention of efforts by the Scouts was made in an issue of the Boy Scouts Association Weekly Newsletter in June 1940.[30] In this it was revealed that 'Sea Scouts played an important part in the epic of Dunkirk – A thrilling story is told by the Group Scout Master (GSM) of Mortlake Sea Scouts.' According to the GSM, whose name is given as 'Gill' in the bulletin, at 23.00 hours on 29 May 1940, the Admiralty issued instructions for the Sea Scout Vessel *Minotaur* to report 'down river' as soon as possible.

'Gill' was in fact a pseudonym given to Group Scout Leader Thomas Austin Towndrow. It was Towndrow who had responsibility for his group's training vessel, the former naval steam pinnace *Minotaur*. Built in 1915 for service as an Admiral's barge, *Minotaur* had been purchased by the Mortlake Scouts in 1929, the boat then being moored some ten miles upstream from London Bridge.

Towndrow went on to describe a little of the events that followed: 'By midnight [on the 29th] the crew was found, [Towndrow and a Rover Sea Scout engineer] and by 8.30 a.m. next day we were under weigh down river, refuelling and taking on stores and water as we went. At 8 p.m. we reported to our destination [Sheerness], and were given instructions to proceed to "a south-east port" [Ramsgate]. We made it by 9 o'clock the next morning.'[31]

A pair of armed naval ratings joined *Minotaur* at Ramsgate. Fuel and provisions were also taken on board and detailed operational instructions given to proceed to Dunkirk.

'By 10.45 a.m. we were on our way,' continued Towndrow. 'The crossing took five-and-a-half to six hours and was by no means uneventful. Destroyer after destroyer raced past, almost cutting the water beneath us, and threatening to overturn us with their wash. We approached the beach with great caution, at Dunkirk, because of the wrecks … and got on with the allotted job of towing small open ship's boats, laden with soldiers, to troop transports anchored in deep water, or off-loading our ship from the open boats and proceeding out to the transports.

'We were working about a quarter of a mile away from six destroyers. Suddenly all their anti-aircraft open fire. At the same time we heard the roar of 25 Nazis 'planes over head … After the raiders had passed, we shakily got on with the job. Eventually our fuel ran low and the engine made ominous noises so we were relieved. We took a final load to a trawler, returned to our East Coast base and turned in for a few hours' sleep.'

One of the naval ratings was 'Lofty' Christmas: 'Reaching the beach safely we proceeded to ferry troops to the transports lying some way of shore. The noise of the battle was deafening … add to this shell fragments and flaming onions that were falling around us, it was enough to send shivers down our spines.'

Minotaur made a second trip to Dunkirk, this time with instructions to work from the Mole. On the return, Towndrow and his engineer 'transferred to a naval cutter, full of troops, which was making the return journey. The officer in charge had lost his charts, but knowing the course back we were able to take over. After a nine-hours crossing we made our east coast base once more.'

Percy Westerman's fictional account was published in 1947, though clearly inspired by the adventures of *Minotaur* and GSM Gill, whoever he may have been. As for Westerman? Well, as you might expect, he really was a Sea Scout.

Opposite: The first edition of *Sea Scouts at Dunkirk* by Percy Westerman. Right: A group of 'Little Ships' being towed back up on the Thames on 9 June 1940. According to one account, the Sea Scout Vessel *Minotaur* may be the boat second from the right in the second row forward. In the row nearest the camera, second from the right, is the motor yacht *Ryegate II*. She had been commandeered from her owner, a Mr. A. Ryeland of Banstead in Surrey. In the middle of the furthest row, and identified from another image from the same series, is *Rapid 1*, which was owned by P.G. Broom.

The Ketch Reda

A 'Little Ship' That Completed Two Crossings

Now known as *Janthea*, the twin-screw ketch *Reda* was built in 1938 for her owner Austin Reed, a London publican. He took delivery of *Reda* in 1939 when Ron Lenthall, who was Tough's Waterman at Teddington (see Object 12), brought her from Suffolk to the Thames on her maiden voyage.

It was a few months later that Lenthall again encountered *Reda* when he embarked on his mission to gather together as many 'Little Ships' as possible for *Dynamo*. 'We knew where they were going, and what they would have to do,' Ron later recalled. 'We had to take down the masts as we knew most of the boats would be used for work off the beaches and not actually to bring men back – and take unnecessary gear off of them to make more space inside.' He

remembered taking down *Reda*'s mast and painting the name on its heel. He also remembered how Austin Reed visited his boat at Tough's yard and remarked on the full drinks locker: 'There's plenty of booze; leave it there, the chaps will have a greater need for it than me.'[32]

Reda was initially taken down the Thames to Sheerness, arriving there on 28 May. The following day she headed around the coast to Ramsgate, from where she set out across the Channel in company with five other yachts. It is possible that on this trip she was commanded by Sub-Lieutenant P. Snow RN, whilst Petty Officer R.W. Rawlings was the motorman.

Having endured a number of attacks by the Luftwaffe off Gravelines, the small flotilla arrived at La Panne beach at around 15.00 hours on the 29th. *Reda* was at once put to work towing whalers full of troops from the beach to off-lying ships. *Reda* then returned to Ramsgate with twenty-one soldiers aboard, her departure being the cue for the Luftwaffe to launch another air raid.

Reda's second crossing to France began at around, or just after, 14.30 hours on 31 May. At the time she was part of a massed flotilla of small craft, known to the authorities as 'Special Tows', which had set out from Ramsgate. It was undoubtedly one of the largest gatherings of 'Little Ships' ever seen. 'The event was unique,' notes the author John Richards, 'and was the result of the intensive work of the Small Vessels Pool, the naval dockyards, the Ministry of Shipping, the Port of London Authority and many others ... A post-war naval report on the Evacuation records that the small craft were "in hundreds". The line of small boats leaving Ramsgate on this Friday afternoon stretched almost five miles. The phenomenon was so extraordinary that it prompted the quip that it had become possible to walk to France!'[33]

During this trip *Reda* ferried fifty French soldiers to a larger transport, before bringing a further twenty-three men back to Ramsgate. In total, *Reda* brought forty-four men back to the UK.

After Dunkirk, *Reda* continued to serve as an auxiliary patrol vessel. At some point during the war her name was changed to *Columbine*. Having operated with the Harwich Patrol until June 1947, she returned to civilian ownership. In 1952 she was sold to Leeds businessman Arthur Kaye who re-named her *Janthea*. A very active member of the Dunkirk Little Ships Association, *Janthea* is well known on the Thames.

Janthea pictured crossing to Dunkirk during the Operation *Dynamo* anniversary in 2015. She is seen here in company with another evacuation veteran, MTB 102. (Courtesy of Lisa Larsson, www.flickr.com)

Medway Queen

One of the Vessels That Rescued the Most Men

The paddle steamer *Medway Queen* was requisitioned by the Admiralty in 1939, repainted in battleship grey, armed with a First World War-vintage 12-pounder gun, fitted out as a minesweeper and sent off with HMS in front of her name. Bearing the pennant number J48, HMS *Medway Queen* formed part of the 10th Minesweeping Flotilla.

On 28 May 1940, *Medway Queen* was anchored off the South Coast guarding against German aircraft laying mines when she was ordered to make for Dunkirk. Along with other paddle-steamers, such as *Brighton Belle* and *Gracie Fields*, she was amongst the first ships across the Channel. 'A long time before we got there,' recalled one of her crew, Bruce Sutton, 'we saw the flames and smelled burning oil. No person who was there will forget it.'

Medway Queen was ordered to head for the beach at La Panne. She had towed some small boats over and, as dawn broke on the 29th, the crew sent in the boats, time and time again, to

load up as many men as they could carry. By 07.00 hours *Medway Queen* had taken on board around 1,000 men before she set off back across the Channel.

On this first trip there was little danger from enemy aircraft, partly due to the cruiser HMS *Calcutta* standing by with her anti-aircraft guns. But there was drama as the paddle steamers approached Dover where a heavy air raid was underway. The crew of *Medway Queen*, which apart from her 12-pounder was fitted with a pair of machine-guns, claimed to have shot down a German fighter.

Brighton Belle, which was nearby, was less fortunate. She drifted over a submerged wreck which gashed a hole in her bottom. As she slowly sank, *Medway Queen* went alongside and took off as many of her evacuees and crew as she could. Fortunately there was not far to go to Dover because the ship, now carrying a double load, was dangerously low in the water.

By 17.00 hours on the second day, what was left of the flotilla lined up to cross the Channel once again. 'This time we had instructions to enter the harbour,' remembered the *Medway Queen*'s First Officer, Sub-Lieutenant John Graves RNR. 'Off the entrance the flotilla came under very heavy fire from shore batteries, and some of the ships hauled out of the line as the sea spouted columns of water around them. The scene was awe inspiring. Rows of great oil tanks were blazing furiously and the glare was reflected on the clouds.

A view of *Medway Queen* which shows the remarkable restoration work that has been carried out by the Medway Queen Preservation Society. (Courtesy of Tom Lee; www.flickr.com)

'Heavy shells plunged into the harbour which was littered with wrecks. It was enough to daunt the stoutest navigator but still the ships came and went, feeling their way past uncharted obstructions and avoiding each other.'

The ships tied up against the Mole, and men had to climb down ladders to reach the decks of the paddle-steamers, several feet below. 'It was while we were tied to the Mole that we were most vulnerable,' said the *Medway Queen*'s signaller, Eric Woodroffe. 'There was much more enemy activity then. I remember the bombs coming down, other

Top: HMS *Medway Queen* working as a minesweeper with the 10th Minesweeping Flotilla. In 1942 she was converted to a mine sweeping training ship, and served out the war in this capacity. (Courtesy of the Medway Queen Preservation Society) Left: One of *Medway Queen*'s crew pictured beside the 12-pounder gun. (Courtesy of the Medway Queen Preservation Society)

Above: A gun crew photographed during a training session on *Medway Queen*. (Courtesy of the Medway Queen Preservation Society) Below: HMS *Medway Queen*'s wartime crew pictured with the ship's dog. In view of *Medway Queen*'s remarkable achievement in rescuing so many Allied troops from France during Operation *Dynamo*, she was given the nickname of 'The Heroine of Dunkirk'. (Courtesy of the Medway Queen Preservation Society)

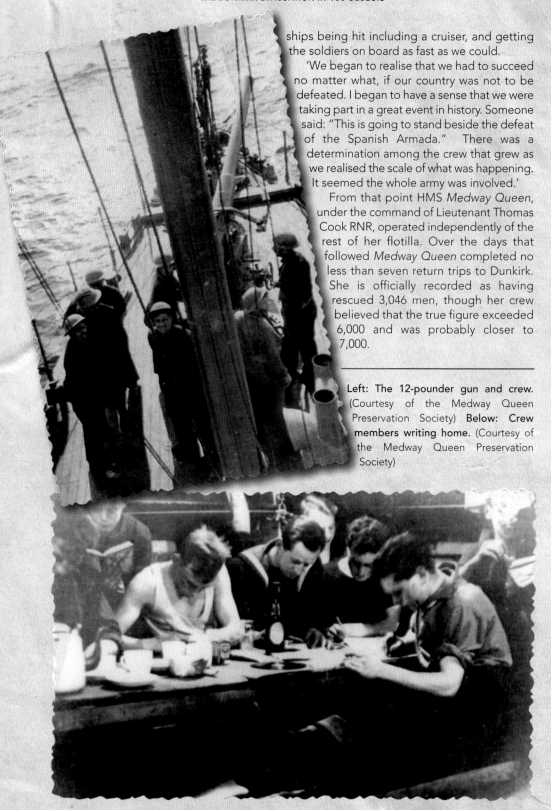

ships being hit including a cruiser, and getting the soldiers on board as fast as we could.

'We began to realise that we had to succeed no matter what, if our country was not to be defeated. I began to have a sense that we were taking part in a great event in history. Someone said: "This is going to stand beside the defeat of the Spanish Armada." There was a determination among the crew that grew as we realised the scale of what was happening. It seemed the whole army was involved.'

From that point HMS *Medway Queen*, under the command of Lieutenant Thomas Cook RNR, operated independently of the rest of her flotilla. Over the days that followed *Medway Queen* completed no less than seven return trips to Dunkirk. She is officially recorded as having rescued 3,046 men, though her crew believed that the true figure exceeded 6,000 and was probably closer to 7,000.

Left: The 12-pounder gun and crew. (Courtesy of the Medway Queen Preservation Society) Below: Crew members writing home. (Courtesy of the Medway Queen Preservation Society)

There were unexpected dangers. For example the paddles left trails of phosphorescence that were visible to marauding aircraft. This problem was dealt with by suspending oil bags from the bows to break up the waves. At one point sparks began flying from the funnel as deposits of soot caught fire. A bucket chain was formed across the deck and up ladders. The tallest member of the crew tipped water down the funnel to damp down the fire.

Alf George, of Ashford, Kent, served with the Royal Artillery during the Second World War, and remembers being brought into Ramsgate by *Medway Queen*: 'There were stretchers and bodies all along the Mole as we made our way along. We were given a tin of bully beef and a big packet of hard biscuits and told to share it among five of us. We'd been without food for three days.

'I looked over and there was this little paddle steamer about six feet below me. A sailor helped me down and I went to the after cabin and sat on a bench seat where I dropped off to sleep. Then I was woken up by an airburst of shell fire. I looked out of the window and there were all these flashes. The floor was completely covered with stretchers and injured men.

'I slept again and was awoken by a shuddering and a rattling, then everything went quiet. We thought we would be taken back across to France to continue fighting, but instead we were taken to Ramsgate Pier and unloaded. There were people at the end of the pier all cheering us.'

Despite being one of the first vessels to reach the beaches *Medway Queen* was one of the last to leave on 4 June – but only just. 'We berthed alongside the Mole for the last time at midnight,' remembered Sub-Lieutenant Graves. 'Machine-gun fire could be clearly heard. This time we took on about 400 French soldiers, all the BEF had by this time left. A destroyer astern of *Medway Queen* was hit and flung forward onto our starboard paddlebox, extensively damaging the sponson. The Captain nursed us away from the berth with difficulty and the *Medway Queen* made off very slowly down the harbour, with the familiar Mole still lit by blazing oil tanks falling astern.'

The battered paddle-steamer limped into Dover, her crew utterly exhausted, to be greeted by the sound of the sirens from all the ships in the harbour. To mark her final return, Vice-Admiral Ramsey signalled, 'Well Done *Medway Queen*'.

Having been threatened with destruction or the breaker's yard on a number of occasions since the Second World War, *Medway Queen* was finally saved by the Medway Queen Preservation Society. To find out about the Society's efforts to restore *Medway Queen*, which is normally berthed on Gillingham Pier, to her former glory, how to support this work, or to arrange a visit, please see: www.medwayqueen.co.uk

Medway Queen stands by the fatally damaged *Brighton Belle*. Fortunately, thanks to the efforts of the crew of *Medway Queen*, all the soldiers on board *Brighton Belle* were rescued, along with its crew and the Captain's dog. (Courtesy of the Medway Queen Preservation Society)

31

Princess Elizabeth

One of Only Two Surviving Dunkirk Paddle-Steamers

The paddle-steamer *Princess Elizabeth* was built in 1927 by Day Summers of Southampton for Red Funnel Steamers. She operated for most of her career between Southampton and Cowes on a mixture of excursion and packet sailings from Southampton and Bournemouth.

Princess Elizabeth was requisitioned in September 1939 by the Admiralty. Converted to serve as a minesweeper, she soon found herself operating, like *Medway* Queen, as part of the 10th Minesweeping Flotilla. When called upon to help with the evacuation of the BEF, her first task was to clear the mines from what was classified as Route X. The paddle-steamer's first crossing began at 13.00 hours on 29 May when she sailed from Dover bound for La Panne, arriving there at 20.13 hours. Her captain, Lieutenant C.J. Carp RNVR, later described what followed:

'Until dark we were constantly engaging enemy aircraft who were bombing the troops and boats. At 2103/29 I was ordered … to proceed to the assistance of the *Gracie Fields* off the Middlekirke buoy, later, however, on receipt of a signal from the *Gracie Fields* that she had been taken in tow and did not require our assistance, I returned to La Panne and resumed operations with the ship's boats.

'Sub-Lieut. J. Tomkins, R.N.V.R. who was in charge of our boats, rounded up three [more] and took them in tow. He reported that he had had great difficulty in getting the troops down the

Princess Elizabeth berthed in Dunkirk harbour. (Courtesy of Dunkirk Tourism)

Above:
A busy scene in the
English Channel as ships of all shapes and
sizes, military and civilian, make their way back to the South
Coast laden with their valuable cargoes of evacuated Allied troops.

beach to the boats owing to the surf and the fact that they were tired out, he continued to tow this flotilla to and fro between ship and shore until ordered to get his boat hoisted.

'At 0536/30 May weighed anchor and proceeded ... to Margate, arriving there and disembarking about 450 troops at 1420.'[34]

Having taken on board additional small boats for beach work, and four naval ratings to man them, *Princess Elizabeth* sailed from Margate at 15.18 hours on the 30th. She arrived off La Panne at 22.23 hours. During this trip, Carp noted that 'the situation ashore was now showing signs of organisation, although our embarkation was necessarily slow owing to the majority of the troops being wounded'. His ship duly sailed loaded with about 400 Allied soldiers.

Carp described his third crossing thus: 'At 1435/31 I left Margate and proceeded to Bray Beaches by X route, arriving there at 1950. When passing Dunkirk the vessel was attacked by a large number of enemy aircraft and opened fire on them. It was necessary to open fire on many occasions whilst embarking the troops. During the night operations the troops and boats at the beach were under ceaseless shell fire. Leaving Bray at 0115/1 June by X route for Margate the ship arrived there at 0735/1 and anchored whilst awaiting turn at Pier. At 0921/1 went alongside pier and disembarked about 400 troops.'

On 1 June, *Princess Elizabeth* headed to Sheerness for ammunition and coal. From there, Carp sailed for the beaches at Bray. However, due to thick fog and dense smoke he was ordered to return to Dover. It was there, at 17.03 hours on 3 June, that the paddle-steamer set out on its last crossing. 'Arriving off Dunkirk harbour entrance at 2330/3,' continued Carp, 'I berthed at East Pier 0015/4. After embarking about 380 French troops, I was ordered by the Pier Master to cast off and clear the harbour at 0220/4 June.' In all, *Princess Elizabeth* and her crew brought back 1,673 men.

In 1942 *Princess Elizabeth*'s role changed, to that of an Anti-Aircraft Vessel, before she was returned to her owners in 1944. She continued to sail until 1965, when she became a floating casino, then a restaurant and pub in the River Thames. She then went to Paris, becoming an exhibition and conference centre, before returning to Dunkirk for the last time in 1999, where she serves as a venue for city events and festivities.

32

The Crested Eagle Binoculars

Found in the Wreck of the Sunken Paddle Steamer

The General Steam Navigation Company's paddle-steamer *Crested Eagle* was requisitioned by the Admiralty at the outbreak of war in 1939. Along with two other paddle steamers, *Crested Eagle* was carrying out routine anti-aircraft duties with what was known as the Thames Special Service Patrol, when, on 25 May 1940, she was summoned to Sheerness. Three days later *Crested Eagle* sailed for Dunkirk, under the command of Lieutenant Commander B.R. Booth, being directed at first to the beach at La Panne and then to the East Mole.

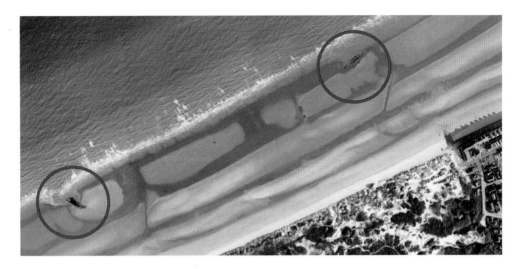

Above: The remains of both *Crested Eagle* (marked by the left hand circle in this image) and *Devonia*, another paddle steamer lost in the Dunkirk evacuation (the right hand circle), can be seen on the beaches near Bray-les-Dunes. Today, *Crested Eagle* is used as a mussel farm. The large building on the right is at the end of Boulevard Georges Pompidou in Bray-Dunes. (© 2010 Google-Imagery, ©DigitalGlobe, Aerodata International Surveys, Cnes/Spot Image, Geo-Eye, IGN France) **Opposite:** Having been recovered from the location of the wreck of this paddle steamer on the beach at Dunkirk, this pair of shipping line-issued binoculars is believed to have been used by the captain of *Crested Eagle*, Lieutenant Commander B.R. Booth. Today, the binoculars are one of the many exhibits in the highly-recommended Dunkirk 1940 Museum in what was Bastion No.32. (Courtesy of Jules Hudson)

At 14.30 hours on 29 May, *Crested Eagle* berthed by the seaward side of the East Mole immediately astern of the steam packet SS *Frenella*. Just as *Frenella* had completed taking on board the last of around 650 soldiers, the Luftwaffe attacked Dunkirk. In a devastating raid, *Frenella* was hit by three bombs in quick succession. The first bomb hit her directly on the promenade deck, the second struck the Mole, blowing lumps of concrete through the ship's side below the waterline, and the third exploded between the pier and the ship's side, wrecking the engine room. *Frenella* was clearly unable to move and likely to sink, but the men onboard were able to disembark and clamber onto the nearby *Crested Eagle*.

Now full, *Crested Eagle* set off back for England at around 17.55 hours. She was only about half a mile out when disaster struck, the paddle-steamer being hit by four bombs. One of those onboard was Private B. Fox who, attached to the 16th Field Regiment, Royal Artillery, had helped carry stretcher cases onto *Frenella*, only to be forced to quickly abandon the sinking steamer:

'We then carried the wounded on to SS *Crested Eagle* which a few minutes later was attacked by enemy aircraft, the engine room being bombed, causing an explosion, following which the ship caught fire. The ship's course was then altered towards the Bray-Dunes and was eventually beached there … the boat was now burning fiercely amidships …

'Upon reaching the top deck, we encountered Mr. Nublat, [a] French interpreter attached to the unit, who was lying on the deck badly burned and scalded. We made him as comfortable as possible and lowered him into a naval launch, which had been sent to pick up survivors.

'All rescue boats were filled with wounded and scalded men, and as it was impossible to stay on SS *Crested Eagle*, I proceeded to swim ashore.'[35]

Corporal P. Carman, with III Corps HQ Signals, recalled that when *Frenella* was hit, the men were ordered to 'drop everything and dash' to *Crested Eagle*: 'The boat finally sailed & had been under way about 10 minutes when we heard a stick of bombs coming, we knew they were ours & dropped flat, a second later a bomb seemed to burst right on the ship's bottom. The lights went out and there was a terrific scorching blast of hot air, then the room filled with choking fumes & smoke as though from the wrecked funnel. The boat kept going and was run aground in shallow water.

'There was a first blind rush for the one stairway & a fight to get out until someone started singing 'Roll out the Barrel' & amazingly enough it had the effect of bringing common sense to bear [and] it wasn't long before we were all climbing out – only to find ourselves in another saloon now well alight. However, an axe was found by the sailors & through the aperture we clambered to find 'planes still overhead & the sea dotted with men.'

Second Lieutenant F.E. McMaster of the Royal Signals had a fortunate escape: 'I was at the left and the bottom of the staircase when I heard the A.A. machine-guns firing and suddenly the explosion of the first bomb. Instinctively I bent myself as much as possible, protecting my eyes with my hands.

'Then I heard a terrific noise, saw a big flash, fell down on the back, and fainted. I recovered after a few seconds and was expecting the sinking of the boat. My hands and my face were terribly burnt. The staircase near me was destroyed and all around me some soldiers were killed or wounded trying to extinguish the flames off their burning clothes.

'Then I saw a window on [the] port side and managed to drop myself through it and fell down on a small triangular deck between the side and the left wheel of the paddler. There I recovered with the fresh air and saw that the *Crested Eagle* had been set on fire but the engine was still running. A short time later she was beached near the French shore.'[36]

Of the bombs that hit *Crested Eagle*, one struck aft of the bridge, and two more ignited the fuel tanks. *Crested Eagle* was a wooden vessel and she quickly caught fire, the after part of the ship being described as 'a blazing inferno'. Her engines, though, continued to run out of control. The destroyer HMS *Verity* signaled for the paddle-steamer to stop so that she could transfer her passengers, but *Crested Eagle* could not stop, and by this time, burning from fore to stern, her captain turned her and ran aground to on the beach at Zuydcoote, east of Dunkirk. It is there that she remains to this day.

Above: This memorial plaque on the remains of *Crested Eagle* was unveiled by Prince Michael of Kent, the Honorary Admiral of the Association of Dunkirk Little Ships, in May 2015. Main picture; The wreck of *Crested Eagle* can only really be viewed at very low tide. (Courtesy of Bruno Pruvost/Dunkirk Tourism)

The 200 or so survivors in the water were machine-gunned by the Luftwaffe, some being picked up by the minesweepers *Lydd* and *Hebe*.

A sequel to this story is that McMaster was really Lieutenant Lemettre, a French Army liaison officer with III Corps Signals. As he wrote in his report, he was badly burned on his face and hands. Despite the almost certain pain, Lemettre swam for about three-quarters of a mile to a Royal Navy destroyer. He was taken back to the UK and spent nine months in hospital being treated for his injuries. When he recovered, he was granted a commission in the Royal Corps of Signals, and changed his name to McMaster.

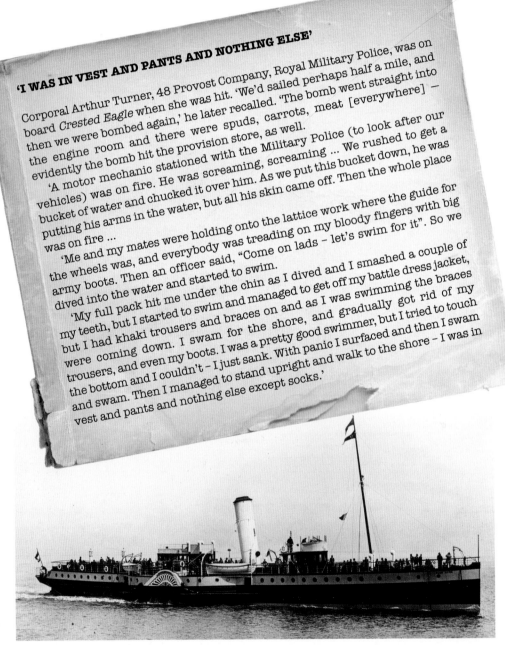

'I WAS IN VEST AND PANTS AND NOTHING ELSE'

Corporal Arthur Turner, 48 Provost Company, Royal Military Police, was on board *Crested Eagle* when she was hit. 'We'd sailed perhaps half a mile, and then we were bombed again,' he later recalled. 'The bomb went straight into the engine room and there were spuds, carrots, meat [everywhere] — evidently the bomb hit the provision store, as well.

'A motor mechanic stationed with the Military Police (to look after our vehicles) was on fire. He was screaming, screaming ... We rushed to get a bucket of water and chucked it over him. As we put this bucket down, he was putting his arms in the water, but all his skin came off. Then the whole place was on fire ...

'Me and my mates were holding onto the lattice work where the guide for the wheels was, and everybody was treading on my bloody fingers with big army boots. Then an officer said, "Come on lads – let's swim for it". So we dived into the water and started to swim.

'My full pack hit me under the chin as I dived and I smashed a couple of my teeth, but I started to swim and managed to get off my battle dress jacket, but I had khaki trousers and braces on and as I was swimming the braces were coming down. I swam for the shore, and gradually got rid of my trousers, and even my boots. I was a pretty good swimmer, but I tried to touch the bottom and I couldn't – I just sank. With panic I surfaced and then I swam and swam. Then I managed to stand upright and walk to the shore – I was in vest and pants and nothing else except socks.'

Opposite: Another of the paddle steamers that participated in Operation *Dynamo*. This is a pre-war image of *Glen Avon*, which made at least two trips to rescue a total of 888 men from the beaches at La Panne. Above: The wreck of *Crested Eagle* pictured in the aftermath of its sinking, gradually being broken up. Below: The graves of French and British troops, killed during Operation *Dynamo*, are examined by German troops. It is believed that this is the stretch of beach where *Crested Eagle* was beached and wrecked, the paddle-steamer being just out of view to the right.

33

Mona's Queen's Anchor

Recovered From The Wreck Site

The Isle of Man Steam Packet *Mona's Queen* was requisitioned as a troop ship on the very day that war was declared, 3 September 1939. She helped take men of the BEF over to France and she was the first ship to arrive back in the UK with troops from Dunkirk, reaching Dover with 1,200 men on board shortly after midnight on 26/27 May.

Many of the men of the BEF had marched and fought for days before reaching Dunkirk, with little food or water. When they arrived on the beaches to the east of Dunkirk they were in poor condition and desperately thirsty, having been told to abandon and disable their vehicles and destroy any items that might be of use to the enemy. A message was sent to Dover by Captain William Tennant at 07.58 hours on 28 May which read as follows: 'There are at present 2,000 men on Dunkirk beach, and 7,000 men on sand dunes for whom I have no ships. They are now in need of water which Army cannot supply … situation in present circumstances will shortly become desperate.'

So, *Mona's Queen* was loaded with hundreds of cans containing fresh water and sent back to Dunkirk. At around 05.30 hours on 29 May, but when she was only half a mile from the Mole, she had hit a mine, split in two and had sunk in two minutes. The explosion was seen by the Master of *Mona's Queen*'s sister ship, SS *Manxman*, P.B. Cowley: 'Mona's Queen was blown up by magnetic mine at approximately 1,000 feet astern of us and sank in four minutes. Two destroyers anchored close by sent two boats very quickly to the rescue.' Cowley concluded, with obvious relief, 'We had previously passed over the same spot.'[37]

The two destroyers were HMS *Vanquisher* and HMS *Intrepid*. They picked up Captain A. Holkham and thirty-one crew, but twenty-four men, most of them in the engine and boiler rooms, were lost. The captain of HMS *Vanquisher*, Lieutenant Commander Conrad Byron Alers-Hankey, later recalled his ship's involvement: 'While at anchor awaiting entry into Dunkirk on 28th May, S.S. *Mona's Queen* was blown up and sunk at about 0630 a short distance from the ship. As it was thought that this might have been due to an M.T.B. attack, cable was slipped and the ship manoeuvred to reduce the size of target presented. The starboard anchor and four shackles of cable were thus lost. The whaler was sent away to pick up survivors. 32 were recovered, including the Master. One of the survivors died on the return trip to Dover and was buried at sea.'[38]

Mona's Queen went to the bottom, but to mark the seventieth anniversary of her sinking, *Mona's Queen*'s starboard anchor was raised on 29 May 2010, and subsequently returned to the Isle of Man. Though the wreck is officially a war grave, the anchor had become detached and so the ship was not touched during its recovery. The anchor was raised by a French salvage vessel amid a twelve-gun salute from HMS *Monmouth* as the anchor was lifted from the seabed. It now forms the centre-piece of a permanent memorial at Kallow Point on the Isle of Man.

Opposite: The anchor from *Mona's Queen* at Kallow Point, Port St Mary in the south of the Isle of Man. *Mona's Queen* was one of the first vessels to make a successful round trip during the evacuations. (Courtesy of Richard Hoare)

Above: A dramatic shot of *Mona's Queen* breaking in two after striking the mine. Left: Survivors from *Mona's Queen* in HMS *Vanquisher*'s whaler about to be brought on board the destroyer.

34

Thames Sailing Barge Greta

One of the Oldest of the 'Little Ships'

The most notable aspect of the Dunkirk evacuation is unquestionably the myriad of small vessels that sailed across the Channel to help rescue the men from the beaches. They were a truly varied collection, with a number of them being formally chartered for the Royal Navy, and others simply commandeered without notice. Tugs accompanied some of the boats, often towing them, across the Channel but many made the journey alone, and made that journey two, three, or even more, times.

Odd though it may seem, and despite the official Small Craft Registration Order, the precise number of the small vessels that took part in Operation *Dynamo* is not known. Estimates given in various sources range from 700 to 1,300. The most detailed published record of the so-called 'Little Ships' has identified, with certainty, more than 1,000 vessels of all descriptions that took part in the Dunkirk evacuation.

These included sailing ketches such as *Angele Aline*, a beautiful sixty-five-foot yacht which had no engine and was towed out to sea where she could hoist her sails. There were also trawlers, like *Willdora* which was fishing off the south coast of England when the call came to help the troops stranded in France.

Main image: The sailing barge *Greta* today. *Greta* is now privately owned by Steve Norris. In the winter she is berthed at Standard Quay, Faversham, but spends the sailing season (April to October) based at the South Quay inside Whitstable Harbour. She is available for day trips. (Paul J. Martin/Shutterstock)

Ferries were employed in the rescue as well. These came in all shapes and sizes. *Southend Britannia* was a 107-foot-long ferry boat employed on the widest part of the River Thames to carry passengers from Southend to Sheerness. *Medway Queen*, which we feature in greater detail in Object 30, by contrast was nearly eighty feet longer and, as a large and powerful paddle steamer, could carry almost 1,000 passengers in her excursions along the Thames and the Medway.

There were, of course, many much smaller boats employed, like the twenty-five-foot motor yacht *Daphne* and the smallest of them all, at less than fifteen feet, the clinker-built open fishing boat *Tamzine*.

Amongst the oldest of the Little Ships was the Thames Sailing barge *Greta*. As the author Russell Plummer pointed out, the 'Thames sailing barges made up one of the more unlikely elements of the Dunkirk fleet and some historians believe it was the first occasion since the Anglo-Dutch campaigns that so many spritsail-rigged vessels had gone to war!'

The shallow draught of these vessels made them ideally suited for working off the beaches. Of the thirty or so barges that crossed the Channel, roughly one third failed to return, some being lost en route, others deliberately beached and abandoned after the supplies that carried had been unloaded. One that did return was *Greta*.

Built in 1892 at Brightlingsea, *Greta* was employed carrying grain, malt and building products along the river. Early in the Second World War *Greta* was chartered by the Ministry of Supply to carry ammunition from the Army depot at Upnor, near Rochester in Kent, to naval vessels anchored in the Thames estuary. After the war *Greta* returned to her duties on the Thames.

Opposite top: The sailing barge *Barbara Jean* is pictured on the beach at Dunkirk lying alongside abandoned Bren gun carriers. *Barbara Jean* was run ashore on 1 June 1940 by her skipper, C. Webb, and abandoned (some accounts state set on fire) after food, water and ammunition had been unloaded. Main image: Abandoned vehicles and equipment litter the seafront at Dunkirk – as pictured in the immediate aftermath of Operation *Dynamo*. Note the abandoned Thames sailing barge, believed to be *Ethel Everard*, in the centre background. *Ethel Everard* was towed across the Channel by the tug *Sun XII* in company with another barge, *Tollesbury*.

35

Bullet-Holed Lifeboat Relic

The RNLI Comes to the Rescue

It was not until 13.15 hours on Thursday, 30 May, that the Admiralty telephoned an obvious source of suitable vessels for use off the beaches at Dunkirk – the Royal National Lifeboat Institution. The RNLI was asked to send as many of its boats as possible to Dover at once. That was all that was said and the instruction was not queried, though the reason for the call was easily guessed.

As soon as the Institute received the order, it telephoned the eighteen stations around the south and east coasts within practicable sailing of Dover, from Gorleston in Norfolk, which is 110 miles north-east of Dover, to Shoreham Harbour in Sussex, eighty miles to the west. The lifeboat coxswains were ordered to make their way to Dover immediately for special duty with the Admiralty. They were told to take a full crew, full fuel-tanks and towing ropes.

The first boats arrived at Dover that evening and another three reached the port early the next day. Within twenty-nine hours of the summons all bar three of the lifeboats had reached Dover.

The Eastbourne lifeboat, *Jane Holland* (ON 673), was the oldest of the RNLI's fleet to serve at Dunkirk. She was also the one to survive the greatest damage. Taken across the Channel by a naval crew on 30 May, *Jane Holland* immediately set about ferrying troops. But things did not go well, and she was soon in trouble. A French motor torpedo boat had hit her forward in the confused melee inshore and, while the crew struggled to repair the damage, she was hit again. This time it was aft, and by a Royal Navy motor torpedo boat. She struggled on until, about half a mile offshore, the engine failed – a point at which *Jane Holland* came under heavy fire from German artillery onshore. She was also attacked by German aircraft.[39]

The crew finally 'abandoned ship' and was rescued by a passing boat. A French destroyer, considering the lifeboat to be a hazard, attempted to sink her with gunfire. As a result of all this attention *Jane Holland* was reported

Right: The damaged pipe in Eastbourne Lifeboat Museum. The Museum is housed in the 1898 RNLI William Terris Memorial Boathouse on King Edwards Parade, at the western end of Eastbourne Seafront. (Courtesy of the Andy Saunders Collection)

Above: The damage to *Jane Holland* being repaired after Operation *Dynamo*. Right: Un-named and undelivered, the lifeboat *Guide of Dunkirk* was sent to Dunkirk direct from her builders at Colchester in Essex. She sailed on 1 June. Once off the French coast, she was badly damaged by machine-gun fire, after which a rope then became entangled around her propeller. Having been towed back across the Channel, stern first, she was patched up and sent back into the maelstrom. On this trip she was extensively damaged by shell fire. (With the kind permission of the RNLI)

as lost, only to be found a few days later drifting, abandoned, in the Channel.

It is not known who penned this account, which is found in the Admiralty records: 'Started off in a lifeboat towed by *Sun II* … Cast off outside [Dunkirk] and told to go to a landing right up the other end of the harbour. Found they were under fire in the harbour.

'Shell struck the tug or drifter they were going alongside so they went on up harbour. Big enough hole in the lifeboat bows to crawl through. Drenched with spray caused by shrapnel. As proceeding up harbour saw a destroyer cut a small rowing boat down with two French sailors in it. They took these to the first destroyer.

'Went right up harbour: saw French troops but they refused to be taken off. So they came back out of the harbour to tug anchored outside. Then they were told to collect troops from anywhere. Engine stopped just before dawn inside harbour. Nearly every boat had gone by then. So they got up sail and tried to get out of harbour. Several destroyers passed, they waved and destroyers waved back: one hour after dawn when they were just about giving up hopes a M.T.B. came. Towed them out, engine started, then they were slipped and after about 4 miles the engine began to smoke and she caught fire. No one in sight and two M.T.B's came along to rescue.'[40]

The damage was extensive – her bows had been riddled by more than 500 machine-gun bullets, the fore-end box was badly stove in, and she was heavily water-logged. The object seen here, a bullet-riddled pipe from *Jane Holland*, stands testimony to the battering she endured. Incredibly, *Jane Holland* was repaired, returned to Eastbourne and continued to serve the RNLI until 1949.

36

An Airman's Letter

The Death of a Bomber Command Pilot

At 22.25 hours on the evening of 30 May 1940, Flying Officer Vivian Rosewarne and his crew took off from RAF Marham in a Vickers Wellington of 38 Squadron. Their aircraft, R3162, was one of ten from the squadron detailed to provide close ground support to the retreating Allied troops by attacking targets at Dixmude and Ypres – five Wellingtons being sent to each location.

The squadron's Operations Record Book notes that the visibility over the target area was fair, though there was heavy ground haze. It continues: 'Navigation satisfactory, both targets located and bombed from heights varying between 3,000 and 2,000'. Clouds were not used as cover owing to this height. No enemy fighters were seen, A.A. and searchlights activity was intense at Dixmude and Ypres. One aircraft was hit by S.A.A. [Small Arms Ammunition], one shot in starboard leading edge. One aircraft failed to return (F/O Rosewarne and crew) and reports indicate that he was probably shot down near Dixmude. 4 aircraft, not being certain of their target, declined to drop their bombs.' Along with Rosewarne, all of the other men on board R3162, Aircraftman 2nd Class J.C. Adams, Sergeant J. Knight, Sergeant D.D.G. Spencer, Sergeant J. Dolan, and Pilot Officer R. Baynes, were killed.

In the days that followed, RAF Marham's Station Commander, Group Captain Claude Keith, found a letter amongst Rosewarne's belongings. It was addressed to the young pilot's mother. Rosewarne began his last letter thus:

'Though I feel no premonition at all, events are moving rapidly and I have instructed that this letter be forwarded to you should I fail to return from one of the raids that we shall shortly be called upon to undertake. You must hope on for a month, but at the end of that time you must accept the fact that I have handed my task over to the extremely capable hands of my comrades of the Royal Air Force, as so many splendid fellows have already done … it will comfort you to know that my role in this war has been of the greatest importance.

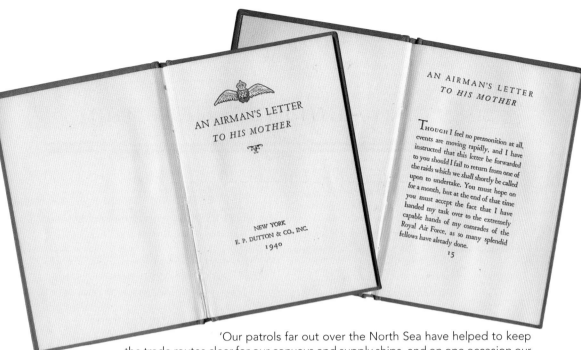

AN AIRMAN'S LETTER
TO HIS MOTHER

NEW YORK
E. P. DUTTON & CO., INC.
1940

AN AIRMAN'S LETTER
TO HIS MOTHER

THOUGH I feel no premonition at all, events are moving rapidly, and I have instructed that this letter be forwarded to you should I fail to return from one of the raids which we shall shortly be called upon to undertake. You must hope on for a month, but at the end of that time you must accept the fact that I have handed my task over to the extremely capable hands of my comrades of the Royal Air Force, as so many splendid fellows have already done.

15

'Our patrols far out over the North Sea have helped to keep the trade routes clear for our convoys and supply ships, and on one occasion our information was instrumental in saving the lives of the men in a crippled lighthouse relief ship. Though it will be difficult for you, you will disappoint me if you do not at least try to accept the facts dispassionately, for I shall have done my duty to the utmost of my ability. No man can do more, and no one calling himself a man could do less.'

Group Captain Keith was obviously moved, as the following comments he wrote testify: 'This letter was perhaps the most amazing one I have ever read; simple and direct in its wording but splendid and uplifting in its outlook. It was inevitable that I should read it – in fact he must have intended this, for it was left open in order that I might be certain that no prohibited information was disclosed. I sent the letter to the bereaved Mother and asked her whether I might publish it anonymously, as I feel its contents may bring comfort to other Mothers, and that everyone in the country may be proud to read of the sentiments which support "an average airman" in the execution of his present arduous duties.'

Rosewarne's mother consented, for his letter appeared in *The Times*, under the title 'An Airman to his Mother', on 18 June 1940. The public's response was remarkable; within days of its publication *The Times* received 10,000 requests from readers for reprints. Such was the level of interest that the letter was reprinted in book form around the world – including in the US where the edition seen here was released by the publishers E.P Dutton & Co. Inc. of New York. There had been twelve reprints by December 1940. In fact, by the end of the year more than 500,000 copies had been sold in Britain, the US and various Commonwealth countries.

Right: The Commonwealth War Graves Commission headstone that marks the last resting place of Flying Officer Vivian Rosewarne. He and his crew were buried in Veurne Communal Cemetery Extension, which is located in the north-east district of the town of Veurne (also known as Furnes).

37

Loss of Gracie Fields Telegram

Paddle-steamer Sunk on 30 May 1940

The Isle of Wight paddle-steamer *Gracie Fields*, which had been requisitioned by the Admiralty as a minesweeper, had made one successful round trip to Dunkirk and back, having taken off troops from the beach at La Panne on 27 May.

Two days later *Gracie Fields* returned to Dunkirk on her second trip and took off four British officers and some 800 other ranks, once again from La Panne. Four Belgian non-commissioned officers who were acting as liaison officers with the BEF were also taken on board. She set off back for the UK at around 18.00 hours fully loaded, but she did not get far.

Whilst still in sight of land she was attacked by enemy bombers and hit amidships. One bomb penetrated the engine room but did not hole the ship. Her steering was also jammed at 15 degrees starboard. As with *Crested Eagle*, her skipper, Captain N.R. Larkin, was unable to stop *Gracie Fields'* engines and she started going round in circles at six knots. Fortunately, the skoot *Twente* was on its way back from La Panne with 275 French troops on board. The Dutch skipper was able to secure his ship alongside *Gracie Fields* – an act of considerable skill – and received as many of the wounded and others as he could. Another skoot, *Jutland*, then secured itself on the other side of the paddle-steamer and took off some more of the men. Finally, the rest of the soldiers were rescued by the minesweeper HMS *Pangbourne*. It was at approximately 18.30 hours that the last man was taken off *Gracie Fields*.

The rescue of the men from *Gracie Fields* had taken just thirty minutes. What is equally astonishing is that, as we have discovered earlier, *Pangbourne* had been holed on both sides above and below the waterline whilst off Bray beach having had thirteen men killed and eleven others wounded in the same air attack that saw *Gracie Fields* damaged.

Opposite: The original telegram confirming the loss of *Gracie Fields* on 30 May 1940. Below: A pre-war picture of *Gracie Fields*. Captain Larkin, who had also been her master before the war, survived the sinking and after the war returned to serve with Red Funnel until his retirement in 1961. Amongst his post-war commands was *Princess Elizabeth*, another of the paddle-steamers that served at Dunkirk (see Obect 31).

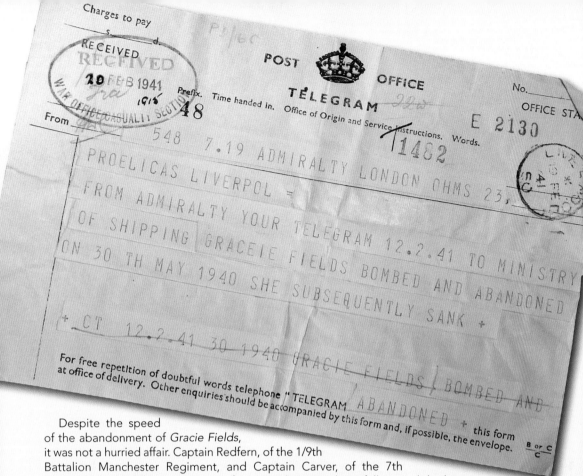

Despite the speed of the abandonment of *Gracie Fields*, it was not a hurried affair. Captain Redfern, of the 1/9th Battalion Manchester Regiment, and Captain Carver, of the 7th Battalion the Middlesex Regiment, for example, moved carefully round the boat to make sure that every survivor was taken off the paddle-steamer.

Private A. Turner, of 'C' Company 1/9th Battalion Manchester Regiment, was one of the many crammed on to *Gracie Fields*: 'I was with Sergeant Edward Pridham. I left him to go below to dry my clothes. About 5 minutes after, we were attacked by enemy aircraft, one of which scored two direct hits with bombs amidships. I hurried on deck to find it littered with dead and wounded. A tanker drew alongside to take off all available men. When we had transferred to the tank … she headed for England, arriving at Margate at 7 o'c. the following morning.'[41] On disembarkation, Turner searched for Sergeant Pridham, but failed to find him.

Private J. Mason also recalled having seen Pridham on the paddle-steamer: 'When a few miles out to sea [she] was attacked by a German bomber which scored two direct hits in the middle of the boat, resulting in a very large percentage of the passengers being killed or wounded. I was lying just behind the funnel at the time of the attack & from there I had seen Sergeant Pridham about five minutes previously trying to remedy a stoppage on the Lewis gun on the side of the boat. I did not see Sergeant Pridham again, nor was I able to find his body, but I did see the dead body of the young sailor who was in charge of the gun & he was only just recognisable.'[42]

After taking eighty men off *Gracie Fields*, *Pangbourne* took the paddle-steamer in tow, but she did not reach England, as she was clearly sinking. *Gracie Fields* was cut adrift and allowed to sink gracefully. The dead men were left on board *Gracie Fields* and went down with her at a point three miles west of the Middle Kirk Buoy near Ostend. One of those still on board was Sergeant Pridham.[43]

J.B. Priestly paid a famous tribute to *Gracie Fields*: 'This little paddle steamer like all her brave and battered sisters, is immortal. She'll go sailing proudly down the years in the epic of Dunkirk and our great grandchildren, when they learn how we began this war by snatching glory out of defeat and then swept on to victory, may also learn how the little holiday steamers made an excursion to hell and came back glorious.'

IN TRIBUTE TO THE
FISHERMEN OF LEIGH
WHO WENT TO
DUNKIRK 1st JUNE 1940
AND IN MEMORY OF
THOSE WHO GAVE THEIR LIVES
FRANK OSBORNE
LESLIE OSBORNE
HARRY NOAKES
HAROLD GRAHAM PORTER
GREATER LOVE HATH NO MAN THAN THIS
THAT A MAN LAY DOWN HIS LIFE
FOR HIS FRIENDS

The Cockle-Boat Heroes

Memorial Located in Leigh-on-Sea

In St Clements churchyard, Church Hill, Leigh-on-Sea stands a uniquely-sculptured memorial to four fishermen from the town who lost their lives in the waters of the Channel during the closing stages of Operation *Dynamo*.

Nothing could exemplify the nature of the 'Little Ships' more than the vessels taken over to France than the small fishing boats that were requisitioned by the Admiralty. The six boats that set off from Leigh-on-Sea just after midnight on 31 May – *Renown, Reliant, Endeavour, Leticia, Resolute* and *Defender* – proved invaluable. When they arrived off the beaches of Bray and La Panne, it was found that the swell was too great for the small boats to try and take men off the beaches. Instead, they operated a form of ferry service, taking troops off the East Mole to the larger ships waiting in deeper water. On board the cockle-boat *Leticia* was 'Jimmy' Dench, who recalled that, 'during the penultimate ferrying trip from the small fishing boats to the larger ships out at sea, a shell burst between the last boat and us. We turned back to go out, but the signaller that we had on board, and who had only been "out" for about six weeks and never been under fire, said, "We've got to go in again" (to rescue more soldiers). So we went in.'

Over the course of eight hours, as the evacuation was reaching its conclusion, these boats helped rescue hundreds of troops as the Germans closed in upon the Dunkirk perimeter. When there was no more that they could do, the Essex fishermen headed back to the UK – it was then that tragedy struck. Jimmy Dench described the incident: 'We saw another boat coming up behind us. It was the *Renown*, and, yelling that they had engine trouble, they made fast to our stern … We towed them 3.5 fathoms of rope being the distance between us. That was 1.15 am [1 June] … Tired out, the engineer, seaman and signaller went to turn in, when, at about 1.50 am, a terrible explosion took place, and hail of wood splinters came down on our deck. In the pitch dark, you could see nothing, and we could do nothing … except pull the tow rope which was just as we passed it to the *Renown* about three quarters of an hour before.'

Renown had hit a mine. The little fishing boat and all three fishermen from Leigh-on-Sea who were on board were blown to pieces, along with a young seaman from the Merchant Navy who had volunteered to join the crew.

Opposite: The Dunkirk memorial in St Clements churchyard, Church Hill, Leigh-on-Sea. Unveiled in 1972, the memorial depicts the prow of a sinking cockle boat with a large wave breaking over it to form a canopy. (Courtesy of Martin J. Smithson).
Right: *Endeavour*, photographed here in Leigh Creek, is the only one of the six Leigh Cockle Bawley boats that set out from Leigh-on Sea in June 1940 known to have survived. (Courtesy of John Winfield; www.geograph.org.uk)

The Dunkirk Challenge

The Only Surviving Steam Tug to Have Served at Dunkirk

The men stranded on the beaches to the east of Dunkirk were in poor condition and desperately short of food and water, Captain Tennant had put a call out for supplies to be sent from the UK. Admiral Ramsay responded by asking for craft to take these essentials to France. Amongst those pressed into service were the boats that worked along the Thames, and the Elliot Steam Tug Co. vessel *Challenge* was asked to tow a barge filled with fresh drinking water to Dunkirk.

Skippered by Captain Charles Parker, *Challenge* reached Dunkirk on 31 May. One of the tug's hastily-assembled volunteer crew was Charles William 'Mick' Wenban, a licensed Thames waterman and lighter-man. Wenban recalled what followed: 'We got to Dunkirk and received directions to put the barge ashore further along the shore. So we steamed along to the position they said, but instead of British troops we found Germans had occupied the ground.

'We quickly turned about back to Dunkirk harbour and this time we were told to go to La Panne. *Challenge* had just let go of the barge having run it at the beach at full speed ahead,

---

Below: The Steam Tug *Challenge* pictured leaving Shoreham-by-Sea on Saturday, 4 May 2013, en route to Southampton after a major refit. *Challenge* was built in 1931 by Alexander Hall & Co Ltd., Aberdeen, for the Elliot Steam Tug Co., London, and was the second tug to bear the name *Challenge* in the Elliot fleet. (Courtesy of the Dunkirk Little Ship Restoration Trust)

Above: One of a series of
images taken by the crew of *Challenge*
during Operation *Dynamo* – in this case a photograph of the
view that greeted the tug's crew as it approached Dunkirk and its surroundings.
(Courtesy of Mick Wenban) Below: Seen from the deck of *Challenge*, this is the Gravesend-based
Watkins tug *Tanga* pictured towing small boats towards the beaches at Dunkirk. The hospital ship in the
background, *Paris*, was sunk by German aircraft whilst crossing the Channel on 2 June 1940. (Courtesy of
Mick Wenban)

Above: A group of British soldiers which, having been plucked from the beaches at Dunkirk, is about to transferred to the decks of *Challenge*. (Courtesy of Mick Wenban) **Left:** One of two small plaques serve as reminders of *Challenge*'s part in the Dunkirk evacuation. This one is located on the bridge.

when we watched a dive bomber come in to attack. The 'plane went for the barge and dropped a bomb which blew the barge right out of the water. There were five Army men on the barge.' Wenban believes that there was only one survivor.

Challenge was then asked to help berthing vessels against the Mole. A description of Dunkirk at that time was given by anti-aircraft gunner Leslie Shorrock: 'A vast queue of men, three or four abreast, stretched from the top of the beach down to the sea, a distance of hundreds of yards. It was a very warm sunny day, with a clear blue sky, the sea appeared very calm and immediately in front of me, approximately one quarter of a mile from the beach, a large ship was sinking bows first … As I stepped onto the beach at the top I saw immediately in front of me, lying on his back on the sand, a dead British soldier, partly covered with a gas cape and on top of his chest his army pay book, with his name written thus, David Barraud RASC.'

After helping the Royal Navy, *Challenge* set back under orders for Dover. 'On our way back we found a damaged destroyer loaded with troops,'

Above: The dangers of participating in Operation *Dynamo* were exemplified by this view of a badly-damaged and sinking ship, pictured by the crew of *Challenge* off Dunkirk. (Courtesy of Mick Wenban)
Below: Another image taken from *Challenge* whilst en route to Dunkirk, this picture shows a passing a coaster full of rescued Allied troops. (Courtesy of Mick Wenban)

Above: A number of other tugs operated alongside *Challenge* at Dunkirk. In this case the tug *Persia*, operated by Messrs. William Watkins Ltd, was photographed with troops whilst en route to Ramsgate. (Courtesy of Mick Wenban)

continued Mick Wenban. 'We got a line to her and towed her back to port, where the troops were able to disembark safely.'

The versatile tug boats with their powerful engines were to prove very useful, particularly when the tide started to drop. The larger ships berthed along the East Mole found themselves grounding and, heavily loaded with troops, were unable to move off under their own steam. In stepped the tugs, who were able to pull the ships into clear water. Similarly, towards the end of the operation, with wrecks littering the approaches to the Mole and the harbour, the tugs were able to push and pull the ships through these obstructions to help them berth safely.

One of the tugs, *Lady Brassey*, was instructed not to load up with troops so that she was free to help any stranded or disabled ships. This meant that when an emergency call was sent to assist the SS *Prague* which had struck a mine off the Downs, she was able to respond immediately. Though severely damaged, *Prague* was still afloat and *Lady Brassey* took her in tow. It was evident, unfortunately, that *Prague* was not going to reach Dover. So to prevent her from sinking, *Lady Brassey*'s skipper, Captain F.J. Hopgood, towed her onto the Goodwin Sands.[44]

Challenge, meanwhile, arrived back at Dover on 1 June where further towing tasks were completed. One of these was to issue ladders around to Royal Navy ships in the harbour. These were later used to enable thousands of troops to embark from the Dunkirk harbour arm down to the deck of the rescuing destroyers.

Left: Charlie Parker, the Master of *Challenge* before, during and after the Second World War. (Courtesy of Mick Wenban)

Above: The crew of *Challenge*
pictured after their return from Dunkirk in 1940.
After the excitement of Operation *Dynamo* Wenban volunteered
for the Royal Navy. However, his eyes had been damaged when he jumped into the
oil-covered water to rescue the men from the *Maid of Orleans* and his application was turned down.
(Courtesy of Mick Wenban)

Challenge was back in Dover harbour when the destroyer HMS *Worcester* collided with the passenger ferry SS *Maid of Orleans* (see the section entitled 'Man Overboard'). At 20.00 hours, *Challenge*, along with the tugs *Crested Cock*, *Sun VII* and *Sun XIII*, took them in tow, hauling HMS *Worcester* to the Prince of Wales Pier. In the collision, some men had been thrown in the water and Mick Wenban jumped in and rescued one or two of them, helping them onto a nearby French pinnace.

Then at approximately 21.30 hours *Challenge* was ordered to steam back to Dunkirk and 'pick up or rescue anything'. At 23.00 hours, she was off North Goodwin in a line with *Ocean Cock*, *Crested Cock*, *Fairplay I*, *Sun VII*, *Sun XI* and *Sun XII*, all heading towards Dunkirk with the same orders. 'We were under command of a naval officer this time, although the vessel was still under the red ensign,' said Mick Wenban describing the tug's final trip across the Channel. 'When we got there, there was a lot of noise going on from German guns. There were many big fires.'

The great risk the ships faced at Dunkirk was in becoming stranded on the sand. To avoid this, the ships would drop anchor in deep water and then go astern on it, so that the vessel was facing out to sea, ready for a quick getaway.

Challenge was anchored in just such a fashion whilst Captain Parker scanned the shore with his binoculars. Mick Wenban junior recalled what he was told by his father: 'He [Charlie Parker] was looking on the quay and he was saying there are all these soldiers there. So Dad jumped up on the stern of the tug and he was shouting to them on the beach "come on lads we'll take you back", and they all start saying "*Achtung*" and they start firing at them and someone said, "Jesus Christ they're bloody Germans!"'

If the Germans were in Dunkirk harbour it meant that there were no more Allied troops left to save. 'It was obvious that our little tug could do no more, although we were told to try and bring back anything we could see,' Mick Wenban related. 'Our officer eventually ordered the tug back to Dover.' *Challenge* was one of the last vessels to leave Dunkirk.

Hurricane 'R' For 'Robert'

A Remarkable Dunkirk Relic

Perhaps one of the most unusual survivors of Operation *Dynamo* is a Hawker Hurricane that was not rescued from the beaches until 1988, having made a forced landing on the sands at Leffrinckoucke between Dunkirk and Bray-Dunes. Having been exposed, it was ultimately recovered by a team of enthusiasts from a local flying club; the story that emerged with the wreckage is a truly remarkable one.

With scarcely 300 aircraft and little more in terms of available pilots, Fighter Command faced a daunting task during the Dunkirk evacuation. Somehow the might of the *Luftwaffe* had to be opposed if the BEF stood any chance of being rescued from Dunkirk. Indeed, noted Vice-Admiral Ramsay after the end of *Dynamo*, 'it is unnecessary to stress the vital necessity for effective air co-operation in an operation of this nature. Not only did German air effort interrupt and reduce seaborne traffic, but it also prevented embarkation by suspending troop movement.'

Fighter Command, though, was operating under extreme conditions. Designed as a defensive force, it was expected to fight offensively many miles from its bases and often beyond

Main inage: Hurricane Mk.Ia P2902 emerges from the sand on the beach at Leffrinckoucke. (Courtesy of the Andy Saunders Collection)

radar and radio range. The time the aircraft had over the Belgian coast was limited and the enemy aircraft attacked in large formations, far greater than anything 11 Group's squadrons could hope to defeat. As the evacuation continued, some of the fighter squadrons made four and five sorties a day, flying and fighting until they were utterly exhausted.

It was a remarkable relic of the RAF's effort that was recovered at Leffrinckoucke. Once the wreckage had been excavated, contact was made with aviation historian Andy Saunders, asking whether he could provide any assistance as to the identity and story of the Hurricane. Andy explained that the engine numbers and part numbers the team had sent to him were, in fact, unhelpful and that a search needed to be made for the RAF serial number, hopefully located on the main constructor's plate in the cockpit. The recovery team was also advised to look out for four numbers that would probably be preceded by either the letter L, N or P.

It was not long before an engine cowling panel soon revealed the vital clue when the serial number P2902 was found stencilled on its inside. The wreckage was, therefore, the remains of Hurricane Mk.Ia; P2902.

Unravelling the rest of the story was more straightforward as RAF records showed that P2902 had been lost on 31 May 1940, whilst flying with 245 Squadron and with a Pilot Officer K.B. McGlashan at the controls. Clearly, if he could be found, McGlashan would have an interesting story to tell – and that was indeed the case when Ken McGlashan was tracked down to Collaroy Plateau, New South Wales.

Writing in 1988 he told how P2902 ended up on the beach near Dunkirk: 'On 31 May, having returned to RAF Hawkinge from Kenley the previous afternoon, it was a beautiful day and we could see the pall of smoke over Dunkirk from the airfield while we waited at full squadron readiness. We were scrambled at about 12.30 to counter German bombing activity over Dunkirk. I was leading the rear section with Pilot Officer Geoff Howitt and Pilot Officer A.L. Hedges, but halfway across the Channel, Hedges returned to Hawkinge with falling oil pressure.

'We arrived over Dunkirk at 25,000ft and almost immediately the first three sections dropped down to tackle Ju 87s and Me 109s. Soon after, I observed three Me 109s in wide formation passing below me. I was about to attack when an indistinguishable shout in my headphones warned me that my No.2 was concerned about something. As it turned out, with real cause! I

Above: This is believed to be the wreckage of Hawker Hurricane Mk.Ia P2902/RD-X of 245 Squadron on the beach at Dunkirk having been shot down on 31 May 1940. (Courtesy of Chris Goss)

then saw my No.2 peel off and dive across and under me and I thought he was about to precede the attack on the three 109s. I then broke left, and then right, to line up behind the 109s but there was no sign of my No.2.

'At the moment I opened fire there was a cacophony of noise and red tracers passed between my legs, coming in from the port side. Oil and glycol was thrown in my face and I was partially blinded. My reflex was to push the stick forward.

'All seemed relatively quiet, if not a little smoky, and I thought fire was imminent so decided to bale-out. I levelled off and was struggling with the canopy when the 109s obligingly shot out the rest of the Perspex and cleaned up the instrument panel. I felt a sharp blow on the outside of my left thigh and blood trickled down my calf. Later, I found this to have been a half-spent bullet that had crushed an AGFA film cassette in my pocket.

'I felt this was the end of me and as I had heard of Me 109s diving into the ground when following an aircraft down I went into another vertical dive – but there was no response from the motor. My sight began to clear and I saw the beach to the east of Dunkirk and decided I was more alive than dead after all and pulled out with the result that I totally blacked out from the 'G' force. When I came to I found that I was travelling very fast and low along the beach. I prepared for a crash-landing and turned the gun-button to 'safe', but my oily fingers slipped and I fired the guns for a split second before making safe. Eventually, the speed dropped, the propeller wind-milled and I selected flaps down and made an uneventful landing …

'I tried, rather nervously, to set fire to the aircraft by lighting a map and pushing it down the side of the seat. Then somebody started shooting at me and I beat a hasty retreat. Thinking that my parachute might save my backside, I slung it over my shoulder and hastened off, running up the beach as a battle raged around me and spent bullets and bomb and shell splinters rained down all around me, against a backdrop of utterly terrifying noise and beneath a sky where the sun was blotted out by oily black smoke. It was an apocalyptic scene.'

Ken McGlashan eventually made it to the Eastern Mole at Dunkirk from where he was evacuated back to the UK on board the Thames paddle steamer *Golden Eagle*, still lugging his

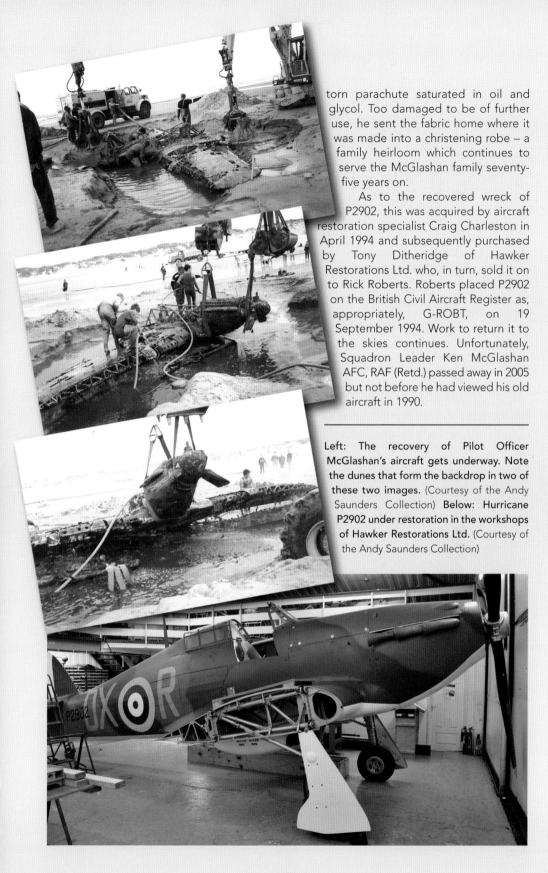

torn parachute saturated in oil and glycol. Too damaged to be of further use, he sent the fabric home where it was made into a christening robe – a family heirloom which continues to serve the McGlashan family seventy-five years on.

As to the recovered wreck of P2902, this was acquired by aircraft restoration specialist Craig Charleston in April 1994 and subsequently purchased by Tony Ditheridge of Hawker Restorations Ltd. who, in turn, sold it on to Rick Roberts. Roberts placed P2902 on the British Civil Aircraft Register as, appropriately, G-ROBT, on 19 September 1994. Work to return it to the skies continues. Unfortunately, Squadron Leader Ken McGlashan AFC, RAF (Retd.) passed away in 2005 but not before he had viewed his old aircraft in 1990.

Left: The recovery of Pilot Officer McGlashan's aircraft gets underway. Note the dunes that form the backdrop in two of these two images. (Courtesy of the Andy Saunders Collection) Below: Hurricane P2902 under restoration in the workshops of Hawker Restorations Ltd. (Courtesy of the Andy Saunders Collection)

The Fishing Boat Tamzine

The Smallest of the 'Little Ships'

Named after the 18-year-old wife of a sailing skipper who was drowned off the Isles of Scilly in an eighteenth century shipwreck, and who is said to be buried in the churchyard at St. Mary's, *Tamzine* is the smallest surviving open fishing boat to take part in Operation *Dynamo*. She is generally recognised as being the smallest survivor of the 'Little Ships'.

A clinker-built wooden-hulled open fishing boat, equipped with sails and a removable centre thwart, *Tamzine* had been designed for year-round fishing off the Birchington Shore. Built at the yard of Len C. Brockman and John Titcombe at Margate in 1937, she was the property of Ralph Bennett when she was requisitioned for use during *Dynamo*. Having been towed across the Channel, she was soon at work lifting troops off the beaches and ferrying them to the bigger vessels offshore. The difficulties involved in such duties were outlined by Vice-Admiral Ramsay:

'Having reached the coast the business of ferrying from the water line to the offshore craft was by no means easy. Apart from the surf, which was usually experienced for some hours every day, derelict lorries, which had been abandoned below the high tide mark, proved a serious danger to boats. Another source of much trouble close inshore was the large amount of floating grass rope which various craft had used and lost in their rescue work, and numerous articles of military equipment such as great coats jettisoned during the evacuation. A great number of small power boats were put temporarily out of action by such ropes and garments fouling the screws, usually resulting in broaching to and being swamped while they were thus unmanageable.'

As the evacuation drew to a close, *Tamzine* was taken in tow by a Belgian trawler and returned to the UK. It was her distinctive design that enabled her to be returned to her original owner, as the author Christian Brann reveals in his book *The Little Ships of Dunkirk*: '[Her builders] gave her their local peculiarity – a characteristic Viking-style straight stem. This enabled the Margate fishermen to identify and claim her as their own when, saturated with blood inside, but otherwise undamaged, she was towed back by a Belgian fishing smack … Though hundreds of similar small boats were used, few were recovered or could be traced back to their owners in the same way.'

Opposite: *Tamzine* can be seen today on display in the Imperial War Museum, London. She was donated to the IWM by her owner, Ralph Bennett, in 1981. Plaques bearing the Arms of Dunkirk and the Battle Honour 'Dunkirk 1940' can be seen by visitors affixed to her. Left: The remains of the stern of a 'Little Ship' photographed by a German soldier on the beach at Dunkirk after the end of Operation *Dynamo*.

The Wreck of Devonia

Paddle-Steamer Deliberately Beached After Being Bombed

Just a short walk along the beach from the wreck of *Crested Eagle* near Bray-les-Dunes (see Object 32) lies the remains of another paddle-steamer lost during Operation *Dynamo* – *Devonia*.

Commissioned at the end of 1939, *Devonia* was ordered to join the 7th Minesweeping Flotilla at Granton, taking up a role that she had filled with some distinction during the First World War. Sent south towards the end of May, coaling en route at Tynemouth and Harwich, *Devonia* crossed to La Panne on 30 May. There she launched her boat which made numerous runs to the beach and assisted in the loading of the Dutch skoot *Hilda*, which was closer inshore.[45]

Below: The wreck of *Devonia* on the beach near Bray-les-Dunes. (Courtesy of Christophe Bonte)

Above: Taken by a German photographer in the immediate aftermath of the evacuation, this is the wreck of the paddle steamer *Devonia* after it was deliberately beached having been damaged in an air raid on 31 May 1940.

At 10.35 hours on 31 May, Rear-Admiral Wake-Walker informed Ramsay that he would beach a ship in the hope of improving conditions for the small craft rescuing the men off the beaches. The task was allocated to Commodore Stephenson, then on the yacht *Bounty* off La Panne. Stephenson boarded *Devonia* at 16.00 hours to speak with the latter's captain, Lieutenant J. Brotchie, and orders were given for the vessel to be beached. The paddle-steamer, already badly damaged by near-misses during a German air raid at 12.30, was beached at full speed at La Panne.

The author Nick Robins notes that 'any idea of scuttling the vessel in the shallow water might not have prevented the Germans from repairing *Devonia* and putting it to service again. As the boilers were on standby there was enough steam available to point *Devonia* straight towards the beach and ram it hard into the shore. The objective was twofold: to create a short pier for uplifting troops from the beach, and to damage the integrity of the vessel to an extent that it could not be repaired. Still under shellfire, the crew calmly removed all useful and portable apparatus and ditched the remaining ammunition into the water.'[46]

At 19.30 hours she was finally abandoned. *Devonia*'s crew was initially transferred to *Hilda*, before being taken on board the destroyer HMS *Scimitar* and returned to Dover.

Devonia was the only Royal Navy ship to be lost on the 30th, though a number were damaged. The destroyer HMS *Vivacious*, for example, was damaged by a shell hit that left three men dead and twelve wounded; HMS *Hebe* received slight damage from a near miss; HMS *Wolsey* was in collision with the passenger vessel *Roebuck*; HMS *Impulsive* damaged a propeller on an uncharted wreck; HMS *Malcolm* collided with Dunkirk pier; and the destroyer HMS *Scimitar* was involved in two collisions, the first with a fellow destroyer, HMS *Icarus*, and the second with a drifter.

There were reports that *Devonia* had been salvaged by the Germans and put to work on the Elbe. These claims were unfounded, and the paddle-steamer was broken-up in situ – as the presence of her remains on the beach near Bray-les-Dunes testifies.

Grave of Sir Arnold Talbot Wilson

The Oldest and Most Highly Decorated RAF Casualty of the War

For its part in supporting Operation *Dynamo*, Bomber Command's losses continued to mount. Another Vickers Wellington which failed to return whilst carrying out a close ground support mission (see also Object 36) was L7791, a 37 Squadron aircraft flown by Pilot Officer William Gray.

Gray had taken off from RAF Feltwell at 21.35 hours on 31 May. In total, thirty-three Wellingtons had been detailed to attack German positions near the Dunkirk perimeter at Nieuwpoort. The cause behind the loss of L7791 has never been established, though it is known that Gray's bomber crashed at Eringham, a few miles to the south of Dunkirk. One of the crew members of L7791 killed that night was Pilot Officer (Air Gunner) Sir Arnold Talbot Wilson KCIE, CSI, CMG, DSO. Aged 56, Wilson is generally regarded as having been the oldest and most highly decorated RAF airman to be killed on bomber operations during the Second World War. He was also the third Member of Parliament to be killed since the beginning of the war. In an article published on 17 June 1940, *Time* magazine, on learning of the death of Sir Arnold, noted: 'Blue blood as well as red soaked the sodden plains of Flanders and the banks of the Somme last week as Britain's knights and lords fell with day laborers and farmers in the grim cavalcade of war.'

One of those who remembered Pilot Officer Wilson was Squadron Leader (later Wing Commander) Cyril Kay – his squadron, 75 (NZ) Squadron, was also based at RAF Feltwell: 'Another personality of those now somewhat shadowy days – at one perhaps with his more youthful colleagues in an inflexible determination, yet cast in a very different mould – was he who bore the honoured name of Sir Arnold Wilson. Wearing but the one thin stripe on his uniform sleeve and the air-gunner's brevet on the tunic breast, the tall, erect, angular figure looked strangely at odds with the noisy mess surroundings, as well he might, for at some sixty years of age he already had behind him a career as distinguished and brilliant as it was indeed remarkable. The slightly sallowed complexion common to many who have lived long in tropical climates was evidence of his extensive foreign service; and as was Lawrence with Arabia, so, too, will the name of Wilson be always associated with Persia.

'Soldier, explorer, civil administrator, author, and politician, Sir Arnold as a young man had won the Sword of Honour at Sandhurst and then joined his regiment in India, leaving shortly afterwards for service in Persia … Much later, as a roving Member of Parliament, he had interviewed and had discussions with both Hitler and Mussolini, and now here he was at Feltwell, the recipient of his country's highest honours and one of the most distinguished citizens of the land, fighting this latest war from the uncomfortable confines of a Wellington bomber's rear turret. In resigning his Parliamentary seat [of Hitchin, Hertfordshire, which he had represented since 1933] he announced to his constituents that "I have no desire to shelter myself and live in safety behind the ramparts of the bodies of millions of our young men", and his words were truly prophetic, for on the night of May 31, 1940, his plane was shot down over enemy territory, and he died as he would have wished – in the service of his country.'[47]

Opposite: Pilot Officer (Air Gunner) Sir Arnold Talbot Wilson was buried in Eringhem Churchyard, ten miles south-west of Dunkirk. He lies beside another member of L7791's crew, Sergeant (Pilot) James F. Brown. (Courtesy of Jean-Claude Graux and www.ww2cemeteries.com)

PILOT OFFICER
SIR A.T. WILSON, K.C.I.E.
C.S.I., C.M.G., D.S.O., M.P.
AIR GUNNER
ROYAL AIR FORCE
31ST MAY 1940   AGE 56

FOR RIGHTEOUSNESS
IS IMMORTAL.
WISDOM 1:15

44

Fire Float Massey Shaw

One of the Most Unusual of the 'Little Ships'

Without doubt, one of the most unusual craft to make the journey to Dunkirk was the Thames fire float *Massey Shaw*. Built by J. Samuel White of Cowes in 1935, the vessel met a fire fighting specification laid down by the London County Council, which called for the ability to pass under all bridges on the Thames and its tributaries at any state of the tide. She was named after Sir Massey Shaw, who commanded the Metropolitan Fire Brigade in Victorian times.

With a volunteer crew of thirteen under the command of Sub-Lieutenant Lucey RN, *Massey Shaw* soon found itself part of the armada of 'Little Ships' heading across the Channel. 'The *Massey Shaw* did not even possess a compass,' states a description of the vessel's subsequent actions on the Massey Shaw Education Trust's website, 'but they had bought one hastily from a chandler's in Blackfriars. There was no time to swing and correct it, which made it rather unreliable since the large steel hull of the fireboat caused a massive deviation. As a result, despite the excellent landmark of smoke from Dunkirk's burning oil tanks, they were well outside the swept channel when they got to the French coast. But their shallow draft enabled them to cross the hazardous sandbanks without grounding.

'The fires ashore were what the *Massey Shaw*'s crew were used to, but the bursts of shells, bombs and anti-aircraft fire were a new experience. As they steamed parallel to the beach, they

Opposite: The fire float *Massey Shaw* berthed in London's Surrey Quays. One of the 'Little Ships' she can be seen in the 1958 film *Dunkirk* starring John Mills and Richard Attenborough. For further information on *Massey Shaw*, the oldest operating fire-boat in Europe, please visit: www.masseyshaw.org. (Courtesy of Bill Scott). **Right**: Thames fire floats and fire-boats battle a major blaze in warehouses on the banks of the River Thames at the height of the Blitz.

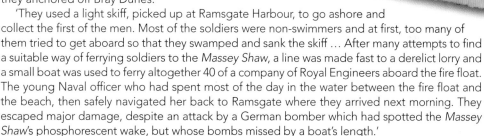

saw columns of men wading out in the shallows, waiting to be picked up by a host of small boats. Late that afternoon [31 May 1940], they anchored off Bray Dunes.

'They used a light skiff, picked up at Ramsgate Harbour, to go ashore and collect the first of the men. Most of the soldiers were non-swimmers and at first, too many of them tried to get aboard so that they swamped and sank the skiff ... After many attempts to find a suitable way of ferrying soldiers to the *Massey Shaw*, a line was made fast to a derelict lorry and a small boat was used to ferry altogether 40 of a company of Royal Engineers aboard the fire float. The young Naval officer who had spent most of the day in the water between the fire float and the beach, then safely navigated her back to Ramsgate where they arrived next morning. They escaped major damage, despite an attack by a German bomber which had spotted the *Massey Shaw*'s phosphorescent wake, but whose bombs missed by a boat's length.'

Having re-fuelled, *Massey Shaw* promptly set out to return to Dunkirk, though some of the exhausted firemen had been replaced by naval ratings (including two stokers and a beach party). The ad hoc crew also took with them a Lewis gun and a thirty-foot ship's lifeboat in tow as a tender.

'At 23:00 they arrived and anchored off Bray Dunes in 10ft. of water with their head towards the shore. The fires of Dunkirk gave them enough light to work by and the thick blanket of smoke provided some cover from air attack. But the shelling from German guns was relentless ... After four or five journeys, the *Massey Shaw* was full once more with troops pressed together in the cabin and standing shoulder-to-shoulder on deck. Her load of nearly 100 men was transferred to a troopship at anchor in the channel and she returned to be re-loaded.

'After some engine trouble ... stretcher cases began to arrive and these were hard to handle and transfer to the troopship. They made about five journeys from the beach to a paddle steamer and it was estimated that they embarked 500 men in this way. As dawn broke, the troopship was full and left for England. *Massey Shaw* returned to the beach and started loading again. At this point, on a falling tide, they began to bump on the sands and were in danger of damaging their propellers but, with their engines throbbing at full power, they just managed to get back into deep water. At 03:30 they were the last boat to leave that part of the beach. Halfway across the channel, the Naval skipper began to have doubts about the compass, but then, to his relief, came across a drifter towing two small boats packed with troops. They followed them into Ramsgate where they arrived at 08:00 on Sunday 2nd June, landing 30 or 40 more soldiers.'

Incredibly, *Massey Shaw* and her Fire Service crew returned to Dunkirk again the next evening, though on this occasion they headed to Dunkirk's jetty. There it proved difficult for soldiers to climb down to her decks and she came away empty. Eventually returning to Ramsgate, she was ordered back to London – a journey during which the fire float's crew rescued thirty French merchant seamen when their vessel, *Emil de Champ*, hit a mine.

45

An Air Gunner Casualty

Boulton Paul Defiants in Action at Dunkirk

One RAF squadron which suffered heavily during the aerial battles surrounding the evacuation was 264 Squadron. Based at RAF Manston, 264 Squadron was flying the Boulton Paul Defiant.

The Boulton Paul Defiant was designed in response to Air Ministry Specification F9/35 of 26 June 1935 calling for a two-seat fighter with all its armament concentrated in a turret. Due to production problems, the introduction of the Defiant had been delayed until December 1939 and its first operational sortie was not until 12 May 1940. On 29 May 1940, the squadron's aircraft were once again in action over Dunkirk, though two of 264's Defiants were shot down, a third badly damaged. The latter also involved the death of the gunner, 31-year-old Leading Aircraftman Evan John Jones. His RAF casualty file reveals a little about his fate: 'On 29th May, 1940, No.264 Squadron carried out two patrols of the Dunkirk area. During the first patrol the Squadron was attacked first by six Me.109s, two of which

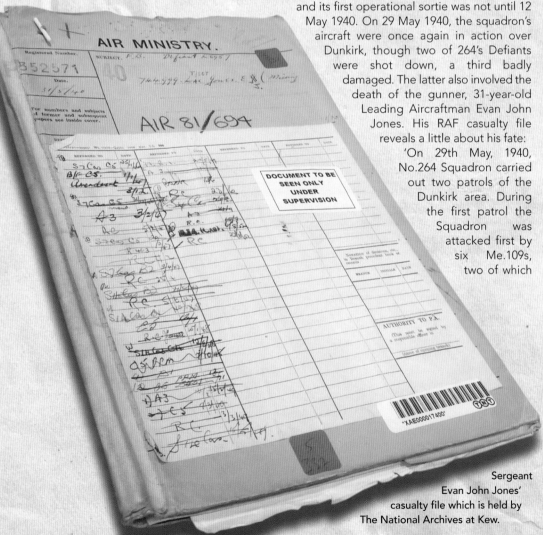

Sergeant
Evan John Jones'
casualty file which is held by
The National Archives at Kew.

Left:. Ground crew examine the damage to L6957 after the combat over Dunkirk on 29 May 1940. Below: Another view of a 264 Squadron Defiant.

were destroyed, and after reforming was again attacked by twenty-one Me.110s. Fifteen enemy aircraft were shot down and also a Ju 87.'[48]

One of the Messerschmitt Me 109s attacked the Defiant Mk.I of 'B' Flight flown by Pilot Officer Desmond Kay – L6957 – in which Jones was the gunner. 'His starboard aileron was torn to shreds and the hydraulics knocked out,' notes the author Norman Franks. 'Kay put his aeroplane into a dive and flew home, only to discover that his 31-year old Canadian gunner, Leading Aircraftman E.J. Jones (promoted to Sergeant after his loss), had bailed out and was missing.'[49] Despite its forced landing at Manston, L6957 (which was coded PS-T) was soon repaired and returned to service.

Pilot Officer Eric Barwell witnessed the attack on L6957: 'On 29 May we performed two patrols, and on the earlier one I managed to get a Me 109, the machine immediately bursting into flames and crashing into the sea. The sky over Dunkirk was one mass of aircraft of all shapes and sizes … Kay apparently did some very hearty evasive action and his air gunner must have thought he was out of control for he bailed out.'

In Jones' casualty file it is noted that he was seen to descend by parachute, before landing 'by BEF troops and fold up his parachute'. Despite extensive enquires, what happened to Jones in the hours that followed was never established, other than he was buried in the military cemetery at Zuydcoote on 30 May 1940 – though Jones' wife and family did not receive official confirmation of this until 1941.

Flying Officer V.A. Sawkins was involved in the RAF's investigation after the war: 'Inquiries in the area failed to establish exactly how he died. The only information being that he was picked up in the area and buried. Nobody in the area knew whether he was in an aircraft which might have crashed, or whether he was a victim of ground strafing enemy aircraft, as all the local population can remember is that at the time there was confusion due to the evacuation which was then in progress.'

Prior to his burial, a number of Jones' personal belongings, including a gold ring and watch, were removed from his body. These were collected by members of the French Red Cross and carefully archived at the Bureau des Successions in Paris, being finally returned to his widow in 1945.

Jones, who was posthumously promoted to Sergeant, today lies in Dunkirk Town Cemetery.

46

The Dunkirk VC

The Gallantry of Captain Harold Marcus Ervine-Andrews

Whilst there were countless acts of courage during both the retreat to Dunkirk and the astonishing evacuation that followed, one action stood out above all others. At the age of 28, Captain Harold Marcus Ervine-Andrews commanded 'B' Company, 1st Battalion, East Lancashire Regiment, which along with the rest of the 42nd (Lancashire) Division had fallen back towards Dunkirk in the face of the Germans advance.

Finally, the East Lancs reached Dunkirk, but there was to be no immediate evacuation for Ervine-Andrews or his battalion, as they were ordered back out to the perimeter where they were instructed to take over approximately 1,000 yards of the defences along the line of the Canal de Bergues. Ervine-Andrews later told of his experiences: 'I went up there on the evening of the 31st May to relieve one of my companies, D Company of my regiment. We knew we were in for a big attack the next day because all that day D Company had been having it pretty hard and at dawn on the 1st June the enemy attacked.'[50]

The Dunkirk perimeter was hardly distinguishable as a defensive line, being nothing more than an irregular chain of strong points. This meant that the intense artillery barrage put down by the Germans for some two or three hours had comparatively little effect and the East Lancs were able to hold back the enemy throughout the morning. One of Ervine-Andrews' forward posts, however, was running desperately short of ammunition. This was because during the retreat to Dunkirk, the men had been instructed to dispose of surplus ammunition and the supply dumps on the lines of communications

Right: Captain Harold Marcus Ervine-Andrews. Below: An artist's depiction of Ervine-Andrews firing at the advancing Germans, from the roof of the barn, during his VC action.

had been destroyed to prevent their contents falling into the hands of the enemy. The men of the East Lancs, in particular, had been ready to embark when they were 'whipped up' and ordered back to the perimeter, and they had to search amongst dead bodies around to try and find ammunition for their rifles.

Under mounting pressure, the East Lancs held on, but the shortage of ammunition became increasingly grave. The Germans had also succeeded in crossing the canal on both flanks and one of his sections was cut off, as Ervine-Andrews related: 'One of my sections was in a very, very, very, very, bad way. They had had a tremendous onslaught onto them, they were running very short of ammunition and they sent back and asked for urgent help and I looked round and I had no reserves whatsoever so I looked at the few soldiers who were with me in the company headquarters and said "look I am going up who's coming with me?" I said "give me that rifle" and I picked up a rifle and some ammunition and every single man there came forward with me. We went up, took over the position and the Germans had been lulled into a false sense of security and we were able then to hold up the attack on the position, and we held then for quite a long time until we ran out of ammunition.'

What Ervine-Andrews didn't say was that the strong point he and his few men held was in fact a small barn across from the canal. The terrain, according to Ervine-Andrews, was 'pretty good it was low lying, low land, intersected by dykes with very, very, few farm buildings here and there and a few folds in the ground but a very open area which gave me personally a very good field of fire'. Ervine-Andrews used that good field of fire to great effect by mounting the roof of the barn from where he could pick of the enemy with his rifle. It is believed that he personally accounted for seventeen Germans with his rifle before taking over a Bren gun in the barn and killing many more.

Though a company commander, Ervine-Andrews took it upon himself to fire most of the depleted stock of ammunition. He explained his reasons for his actions thus: 'We had the dominant position in that they were out in the open I was in a barn, they didn't know where I was and it's all very, very, quick. You are firing ammunition and if you fire accurately and you hit men they are discouraged it's when you fire a lot of ammunition and you don't do any damage the other chaps are very brave and push on, but when they are suffering severe casualties they are inclined to stop or as in this case they move round to the flanks because there is no point in going up and getting a bloody nose if you can avoid it by going round to a weaker position on either flank. Which is what the Germans did.'

The odds were too great for Ervine-Andrews' little band. The point eventually came when they could do no more; the burning barn having been all but blown to pieces and the men finally out of ammunition. It was 1 June, and Ervine-Andrews men had been in action for more than twelve hours without rest – effectively holding up the Germans for a full day.

Succumbing to the inevitable, Ervine-Andrews decided the moment had come to withdraw: 'I said I want all the ammunition you have here and I sent away all my surplus men and I kept 8 men with me and I kept a Bren gun carrier to get away on and I sent the others away. We then held the final little position, we held up the Germans for as long as we could and when I came to get away I had 2 wounded men and my intention was to tell them to stay there because the Germans could look after them better than we could, but they said they would like to be

Opposite top: Abandoned vehicles and equipment litter a similar river crossing to that defended by Captain Ervine-Andrews and his men. The street sign in the background in this view looking north indicates that this is the spot where the D302 crossed the canal to the immediate south of Zuydcoote – two bridges east from the East Lancs' position. In this view, the Allied defenders were located on the opposite side of the canal to the photographer, a German serviceman. Opposite: Looking over the canal from the south bank towards the positions held by the East Lancs on what is now known as the Canal de la Basse Colme, Nord, France. The road in this picture, and which crosses the canal at this point, is the D4. The barn from where Ervine-Andrews fired on the Germans is believed to have been located behind the white house in the foreground.

Captain Ervine-Andrews and his men finally escaped back to Britain on 4 June 1940. The last stages of their journey into Dunkirk had not been without incident, as he later recalled:

'There were some very big French tanks who withdrew under cover provided by my Bren gun carrier. At one stage on our way back to Dunkirk we were in defensive position and a couple of very smartly dressed Belgium officers came and told us that they had now left the war they had ceased hostilities and they were a neutral country and we had to be out of the area or they would come back and intern us.

'Well, luckily enough the company commander on my right was a splendid chap he had also been warned to get out so when the Belgium officers came back they found they were facing a couple of Bren guns and quite a number of men with fixed bayonets, were upon they promptly did a courteous retreat put it that way ...

'My company was extremely [orderly]. We marched along there, we really marched there ... We got back into Dunkirk itself we found a good safe cellar to sit in and we reported to the CO and we were told to wait and wait and in due course we were told that a destroyer was coming along and we were to go along to the end of the pier and get on it and that was it.

'[It was] rather disappointing when we got to the ship. I had told all my men in Dunkirk itself that every man must get either a Bren gun or an anti-tank rifle to bring back to England, when we arrived at the ship side the sailors quite rightly, although I was furious at the time, they took all these heavy weapons and threw them over into the sea on the grounds that it was more important to have men on the ship than waste carrying excess baggage. The ship was actually like a sardine box with men.'

That ship was the S-class destroyer HMS Shikari. On board, the Royal Navy provided a warm welcome for the weary East Lancs: 'They took us down they gave us chocolate and oranges, which were manna from heaven to us we hadn't had any organised food for several days only what we could scrounge.'

evacuated. So I said "alright", I looked at my men and I said "we will put them on the carrier".

'We put them on the Bren gun carrier which we had kept for ourselves and my men were quite happy they accepted that there were no qualms about it, I said we will make our way as best we can.'

By this time his party was cut off from the rest of the BEF and was all but surrounded. Taking advantage of any cover, they also had to swim or wade up to their chins in water along the canal for more than a mile to escape. Yet, thanks to Ervine-Andrews' determination, they made it through rough enemy lines to the blood-soaked beaches.

It is with little wonder that Harold Ervine-Andrews was recommended for the Victoria Cross. According to the words in his citation, 'Throughout this action, Captain Ervine-Andrews displayed courage, tenacity, and devotion to duty, worthy of the highest traditions of the British Army, and his magnificent example imbued his own troops with the dauntless fighting spirit which he himself displayed.'[51]

Of the award, Ervine-Andrews said the news was 'quite a bolt out of the blue': 'I was sitting in a restaurant about the 29th July some 6 to 8 weeks afterward and while sitting in the restaurant it appeared on the 9 o'clock news.'

Above: Looking east from the bridge over the Canal de la Basse Colme. The British positions were to the left; the advancing Germans to the right. Note the small boat which would have been of a similar size to those used by the Germans in their crossing of the canal. Below: A handwritten caption in German on the rear of this image states that it shows abandoned British military vehicles line a canal bank on the outskirts of Dunkirk during the evacuation in May and June 1940.

HMS Havant Memorial Window

Destroyer Sunk on Third Trip to Dunkirk

The H-class destroyer HMS *Havant* made its first trip over to Dunkirk on 29 May, returning to Sheerness with approximately 500 French troops. On her second trip *Havant* returned with four times that number of men. It was on her third trip that disaster struck.

She berthed alongside the East Mole at 07.30 hours on 1 June but there was only a trickle of men and after half an hour she had taken on board only about fifty men. Then, at around 08.00 hours, the Luftwaffe arrived overhead and the destroyer HMS *Ivanhoe* was hit amidships and appeared to be on fire. *Havant* cast-off from the Mole and went to *Ivanhoe*'s assistance. She went alongside and took off approximately 500 men, some of whom were wounded. Lieutenant Commander A.F. Burnell-Nugent, decided to make for Dover.

'On the way down the channel parallel to the beach to the west of Dunkirk we were subjected to intense dive bombing and high and low level bombing and also bombardment from shore,' wrote Burnell-Nugent. These were avoided by zig-zagging as much as the width of the channel permitted. *Havant* had just turned to the North Westward at the end of the channel when, at 09.06, we were hit by two bombs in the Engine Room which passed through the starboard side. Almost immediately afterwards a large bomb fell in the water about 50 yards ahead. This had a delay action and exploded right underneath the ship as she passed over it, momentarily giving the impression of lifting the whole ship.'[52]

Havant continued to steam at moderate speed, but out of control and gradually circling to starboard. Approaching the sandbanks opposite Dunkirk was finally brought to a halt by a mixture of the steam being let out of the boilers (a dangerous task completed by Chief Stoker M. Gallon) and the starboard anchor.

Though initially taken under tow, a further air raid helped seal *Havant*'s fate. With two large holes just above the waterline, and one beneath it, water was flooding in. As well as a number of fires raging, *Havant* had a heavy list to port – so much so that part of the upper deck was almost awash.

'The situation on board had deteriorated, and after a brief conference with some of my officers,' continued Burnell-Nugent, 'I decided that there was no hope of getting the ship back to England … after transferring the wounded, and then the rest of the ship's company, I left the ship.

'The ship being at this time in deep water I caused the magazines to be flooded to ensure that she sank before drifting onto the sandbanks. I circled round the ship in *Aegir* for about 5 minutes until she rolled slowly over and sank at about 1015 … The casualties sustained by *Havant* were 1 officer and 7 men killed and about 15 wounded, but in addition there must have been at least 25 soldiers killed or wounded onboard. The discipline of the soldiers was of the highest order.'

A memorial window, installed in the north side St Faith's Church in Havant, Hampshire, commemorates all those who served on HMS *Havant* at Dunkirk in 1940. A commemorative stone was also unveiled at the Royal British Legion's headquarters in Brockhampton Lane, Havant, in 1990.

The memorial window remembering HMS *Havant* and her crew in St Faith's Church in Havant. (Courtesy of Martin Baxter; www.hampshirechurchwindows.co.uk)

H.M.S. HAVANT

TO THE GLORY OF GOD
AND IN MEMORY OF ALL
WHO SERVED IN HER.
DUNKIRK 1940

48

Piece of Timber From East Mole

A Gift Presented to the House of Lords

The East Mole had been in almost constant use since the first full day of the evacuation, and on 1 June embarkation from its battered structure reached a peak. There is a big rise and fall of tide at Dunkirk, which meant that at high water the troops could step straight from the Mole onto the deck of a destroyer. At low tide, it was a different matter altogether, for there was then a fifteen-foot drop to be negotiated. Many ladders were sent over to help the evacuation continue at low tides, but the troops, loaded with their packs and rifles, took a long time to descend the ladders.

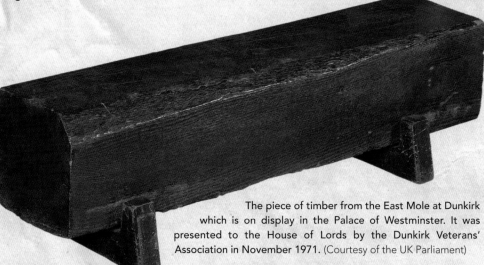

The piece of timber from the East Mole at Dunkirk which is on display in the Palace of Westminster. It was presented to the House of Lords by the Dunkirk Veterans' Association in November 1971. (Courtesy of the UK Parliament)

However, loading the troops from the beaches was proving even more difficult, as Rear Admiral Wake-Walker explained in a message to Vice Admiral Ramsay at Dover, at 10.35 hours on 1 June: 'Majority of boats broached to and have no crews. Conditions on beach very bad, due to freshening onshore wind. Only small numbers being embarked, even in daylight. Under present conditions any large-scale embarkation from beach is quite impractical. Motor boats cannot get close in … Dunkirk our only real hope.' Consequently, all vessels were directed to the East Mole, even though it was an inviting target for the Luftwaffe's bombers.

On what the Admiralty called 'this black day', thirty-one vessels were sunk, including three Royal Navy destroyers, and eleven were damaged. Yet these bleak figures hide the true story of the day, which was that almost as many men had been landed in England as had been on 31 May. From the beaches 17,348 men had been saved – a figure, though, that was dwarfed by the total of 47,081 men lifted from the Mole (giving a total of 64,429).

One reason for such success was that the rate of embarkation was considerably increased during the day due to improved organisation. The destroyer *Vivacious*, for example, spent only fifteen minutes at the East Mole to collect 475 men, and *Shikari* needed only twenty minutes to take on board 623 troops. Amongst those rescued from the East Mole on this day was Lionel

Tucker, who was serving as a motor engineer in the RAOC, being attached to the 1st Battalion Oxford and Buckinghamshire Light Infantry:

'After spending a day trying to get aboard a boat of any kind without success an officer with a pistol in his hand ordered a large number of us to leave the beach and make our way to the 'Mole' which we found already packed with hundreds of troops.

'The trek to the end of the "Mole" was disastrous, Jerry came over and made a direct hit causing many casualties, also a long delay in proceeding any further along.

'Eventually the gap was bridged and we were able to proceed, at that point I decided to remove all my webbing and equipment into the sea in case I had to swim for it. Eventually our savour was in sight, a fairly large ship which I learnt later was the *Maid of Orleans*. By this time, I had lost any idea of time and was thoroughly exhausted, got on board, flopped down on deck amongst the others and fell fast asleep, I remember nothing about the journey until I had a friendly kick from someone saying, "On your feet mate we are in Dover". I really couldn't believe what I was hearing was true. This was 09.45 hours on the 1st of June 1940.'[53]

Above: British troops boarding another of the many Royal Navy warships involved in Operation *Dynamo*, in this case the V-class destroyer HMS *Vanquisher*, from the Mole at Dunkirk at low tide. Below: Taken by a German soldier in the immediate aftermath of Operation *Dynamo*, this picture shows abandoned British and French vehicles on the quayside in the harbour at Dunkirk, with, in the background, the East Mole or jetty that proved so important during the evacuation.

49

The Motor Yacht Tom Tit

A 'Little Ship' Taken Without the Owner's Permission

On 31 May 1940, Ron Tomlinson and his brother Alan were at a cinema in Ramsgate when, halfway through, the film was interrupted by a newsflash. 'Anybody in Ramsgate trawlers, please report to the Admiralty Office at once,' was the message displayed. Both Ron and Alan answered the call and, within hours, were on their way to Dunkirk as part of the crew of the 95-ton trawler *Tankerton Towers*, of which Ron was the engineer.

Once off the beaches, *Tankerton Towers* repeatedly transferred men to the waiting larger vessels, despite a fouled propeller. Eventually admitting defeat, *Tankerton Towers* was taken in tow and returned to the South Coast with a group of fifty British and French soldiers. However, Ron's experiences on the opposite side of the Channel left him convinced that he needed to do more.

With his brother, Alan, he went down to the Admiralty office in the harbour and volunteered to go again. They sent them off in a tiny boat with a young Sub-Lieut. who made them turn back when he found that they were taking him, safely they protested, by the shortest route – straight across the Goodwin Sands.[54] As they re-entered Ramsgate harbour, Ron decided to act.

'As we neared Ramsgate West Pier,' he recalled, 'I said to Alan, "Get ready to jump, there's a boat moored on the end of the pier – we'll take that". As we approached the vessel, *Tom Tit*, Alan jumped aboard and started the engines; I followed him and let go of the ropes. As we came round out of the harbour, my elder brother Fred, who worked for Claxton Shipwrights at the time (as did Alan), saw us and shouted, "Bring it back – it's been brought in on fire", but we ignored him and went to Dunkirk.'[55]

Having got under way the pair was soon heading straight for the Goodwins once more. At this point they discovered a petrol leak – the cause of the fire during *Tom Tit*'s previous, and first, crossing. They quickly stopped the engine and repaired the leak, but lost precious time with the tide running out. They touched bottom a few times before they cleared the shallows, but reached Dunkirk safely.[56] Again, Ron takes up the story:

'I was concentrating on going into the pier [in Dunkirk harbour]. I didn't moor up; I just kept the engine running and let them jump aboard. As soon as I got a boatload, I went to the nearest ship, dropped them and came back in. I just keep filling up. I had them sitting in the cockpit and on the deck. I couldn't say how many, 40, maybe 50. One poor lad could hardly walk, so we took him down to our cabin and I thought he might as well have my bunk. But when I looked round, the cabin was absolutely full. We ran from the pier to any ship that we could get to, taking the troops off – I should think we made approximately 16 trips.'[57]

Whilst the two brothers had repeatedly filled up with soldiers, they encountered 'a Sgt.-Major on the jetty [who] told them not to come back because the Germans were on the pier. They told him they'd keep coming while he was there. On the last trip they persuaded him to join them.

'When they arrived in Ramsgate next morning, they expected to be arrested for stealing *Tom Tit*, but the Senior Naval Officer congratulated them and said he wished he could have had more like them.'[58]

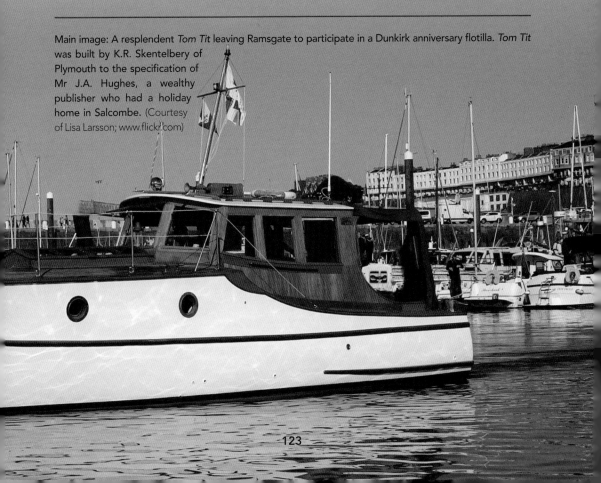

Main image: A resplendent *Tom Tit* leaving Ramsgate to participate in a Dunkirk anniversary flotilla. *Tom Tit* was built by K.R. Skentelbery of Plymouth to the specification of Mr J.A. Hughes, a wealthy publisher who had a holiday home in Salcombe. (Courtesy of Lisa Larsson; www.flickr.com)

50

The Lifeboat E.M.E.D.

Royal Navy Captain Killed in Action

Like the Eastbourne-based *Jane Holland* (see Object 35), the RNLI's Walton-on-the-Naze lifeboat *E.M.E.D.*, built by J. Samuel White & Co. at Cowes in 1928, was also ordered to assist with Operation *Dynamo* on 30 May. Much to the disappointment of her RNLI crew, the lifeboat, official number 705, was then immediately taken over by Royal Navy personnel. She duly sailed for Dunkirk under the command of Lieutenant Reginald Hounsham Mead RNVR.

At 07.15 hours on the morning of Saturday, 1 June, *E.M.E.D.* was taken in tow by the drifter *Thrifty*. The other craft in the same tow included the Aldeburgh lifeboat *Abdy Beauclark*, the ketch *Summer Maid*, and motor boat *White Bear*. At 07.25 hours, *Thrifty* set off from Dover to shepherd her small flock across the Channel.

The crossing was far from trouble free. At 14.04 hours, for example, the destroyer HSM *Esk* passed the small flotilla at speed, causing the last in the line to break its tow. At 15.17 hours the

The Dunkirk veteran *Capitán Christiansen*, formerly *E.M.E.D.*, on the quayside at Muelle Barón in Chile. (Courtesy of Robert Cutts; www.flickr.com)

ships were attacked by three German aircraft off Gravelines; five minutes later they were forced to avoid a floating mine. At 16.15 hours, a bomb exploded near *Thrifty*, broke the tow and threw men in to the water – though they were all quickly recovered. Undeterred, Mead and his crew battled on towards Dunkirk, encountering the Shoreham-by-Sea lifeboat *Rosa Woodd and Phyllis Lunn* on the way.

Having covered the conspicuous white parts of the lifeboat with oilskins, at 19.26 hours *E.M.E.D.* encountered the motor boat *Cairncorn* and received orders to proceed towards Dunkirk. At 20.30 hours, Mead encountered H.M. Tug *Sun IV*, commanded by Lieutenant J.E.L. Martin RN. The latter recalled that, 'the motor lifeboat *E.M.E.D.* hailed us and asked to be shown the way into Dunkirk. This boat remained with us for the remainder of the night.'

In company with *Sun IV*, *E.M.E.D.* arrived at Dunkirk at 21.35 hours. Petty Officer Telegraphist Cooley noted that there was, 'No one on piers. Picked up *Sun 4* [*sic*] one rowing boat to go to beach. Lieut. Mead killed. Boats in beach taking ratings from shore all night (run aground).'[59]

Though it is stated that 36-year-old Lieutenant Mead was killed by a shell (Lieutenant Martin of *Sun IV* writes that he was 'killed by shrapnel'), his crew continued their duties until ordered to sail from Dunkirk, which they did at 04.23 hours on the morning of 2 June – at which point *E.M.E.D.* was towed by *Sun IV*. The return crossing was no less problematic than the outbound journey. At 04.50 hours *Sun IV* ran aground; six minutes later a rope fouled the lifeboat's starboard propeller. Finally, at 10.10 hours, *Sun IV* and *E.M.E.D.* slipped into Ramsgate Harbour. Twenty minutes later some thirty-nine soldiers were landed by the lifeboat's crew, along with the body of Lieutenant Mead. The husband of Winifred Margaret Mead of Fulbrook, Oxfordshire, he was buried in Dover (St. James's) Cemetery.

Unlike Lieutenant Mead, *E.M.E.D.* survived the war and after being withdrawn in 1956, was sold to the Chilean Government. She was renamed *Capitán Christiansen*.

51

Damaged Over Dunkirk

The World's Oldest Surviving Hurricane

Hanging in one of the halls at the Science Museum in London is the world's oldest surviving Hawker Hurricane. With the serial number L1592, this Mk.I was the forty-sixth aircraft off the Hawker production line from the initial batch ordered for the RAF.

Initially issued to 56 Squadron, L1592 passed through the hands of a number of units before finally being allocated to 43 Squadron in the spring of 1940. As Operation *Dynamo* gathered pace, 43 Squadron, which had been based at Wick, was sent south to assist in covering the evacuation beaches, returning to its pre-war home at RAF Tangmere on 31 May. Within hours of their arrival in Sussex, 43 Squadron's pilots were airborne and heading out over the Channel, as the Operations Record Book reveals:

'No.43 Squadron were ordered to carry out an offensive patrol over Dunkirk in company with No.145 Squadron, No.245 Squadron and a Squadron of French fighters; the last two to rendezvous over Hawkinge. The Squadron took off at 0530 hours with the following pilots, Squadron Leader C.G. Lott (in command), Flight Lieutenant J.W.C. Simpson, Flying Officer J.D. Edmonds, Flying Officer W.C. Wilkinson, Sergeant Hallowes, Pilot Officer C.A. Woods-Scawen, Flying Officer M.K. Carswell, Sergeant Ottewill and Sergeant Gough.

'No enemy aircraft were sighted on this patrol and all returned to Manston to refuel. The French fighters were not seen.'[60]

It was Pilot Officer Charles Anthony Woods-Scawen who was at the controls of L1592 during this patrol, as he was during the one that followed: 'A similar patrol was ordered later and the same formations took part; on this occasion heavy enemy opposition was encountered in the shape of about 60 ME.109 and ME.110. A general melee ensued and pilots returned individually to Tangmere. Flying Officer M.K. Carswell and Sergeant Gough were missing and reported as such, but news was later received that Flying Officer M.K. Carswell had been landed at Dover from a destroyer, suffering from superficial burns and sent to hospital.'

Hawker Hurricane Mk.I L1592 on display in the Science Museum, London.

During the dogfight over the Channel near Dunkirk, Woods-Scawen, who was flying as Yellow 2 in 'A' Flight, tangled with a Messerschmitt Bf 109. In his combat report he recorded that the combat occurred at 11.35 hours at an altitude of 7,000ft:

'While on offensive patrol over Dunkirk with 145 & 245 Squadrons, we were attacked by several ME.109s. I engaged one in a dogfight and put two bursts into him [of four and five seconds respectively and from a range of 100-200 yards], which knocked pieces off his trailing edge, port wing. I was then shot at from below & a hit was registered in my radiator compelling me to retire. The resultant deluge of Glycol inside the cockpit prevented my seeing what had happened to my opponent. I returned immediately to Tangmere alone, having left earlier than the rest of our pilots.'[61] Because of L1592's rapidly overheating engine, Woods-Scawen was forced to make a wheels-up landing at Tangmere.[62] For his part in the engagement, Woods-Scawen was credited with a 'probable'.

The damage meant that L1592 was no longer serviceable. On 4 June it was collected from Tangmere and transferred to No.10 Maintenance Unit at Hullavington on the 27th of the same month. L1592 remained there, almost certainly under repair, until 23 July when it was allocated to 615 (County of Surrey) Squadron.

In the spring of 1944, plans were put in place to preserve a selection of historically important aircraft for future generations. L1592 was one of them. It was refurbished by Hawker in the early 1960s and first placed on display in the Science Museum in 1963.

Left: Whilst L1592 survived its time over Dunkirk, albeit damaged, many other Hurricanes did not – this being but one example. (Courtesy of Andy Saunders)

52

Man Overboard

British Army Casualty Buried in the Netherlands

It was HMS *Worcester*'s sixth journey to Dunkirk. Having taken on a full load of troops from the East Pier, Lieutenant Commander J.H. Allison ordered his crew to head for home. The Luftwaffe, however, was intent on preventing this, as Allison himself later recalled:

'During the next half hour the ship was attacked by successive waves of dive bombers consisting of three or four squadrons of about nine each. The first attack took place in Dunkirk roads where avoiding action was not possible ... In this attack about half the bombs dropped were time delay and the nearest appeared to be about 50 yards away. Although the ship was lifted in the water a number of times no structural damage was done. Succeeding attacks took place in the channel leading northward from No.5 buoy. In these attacks the majority of the bombs burst on impact with the water and caused great damage to personnel. Some of these dropped as near as 10 yards. In all it is estimated that over 100 bombs were dropped near the ship.'[63]

As a result of these attacks, forty-six men had been killed, a further 180 injured. HMS *Worcester*, though, finally made it to Dover. The destroyer, had not seen the last of its trials that day. 'Entering the inner harbour about 2030,' continued Allison, '*Worcester* collided with S.S. *Maid of Orleans* on the way out. I attribute this largely to the loss of manoeuvring power both of screws and rudder from damage sustained in recent operations.'

Thirty-three-year-old Sergeant Albert Edward Davis, 2nd Battalion Bedfordshire and Hertfordshire Regiment, had been standing near the bows when the collision occurred. With him was Company Quartermaster Sergeant W. McGann, who later recalled the following: 'On arrival in Dover Harbour the Boat we were on collided with a Boat leaving the Quayside & tilted, at that moment Sjt Davis was fully dressed wearing [a] greatcoat. When the boat righted itself I looked round and he [Davis] was gone.'[64]

Corporal J. Peck gave a similar account of the incident: 'Our boat came into collision with a Troopship which was leaving the harbour, and tilted to the port side. Previous to this I saw Sjt Davis in the company of C.Q.M.S. McGann; when the boat titled Davis was near the rails at the fore end of the boat and I saw him jump over the side and enter the water.

'I did not see him again, but a tug was close by and during the time we were standing still I did not see them pick anyone up, except one man, who was naked and had multiple injuries to both his feet.'

Sergeant Davis was never seen alive again. Listed as having died on 1 June 1940, he is buried in Jonkerbos War Cemetery near Nijmegen. How he came to be interred in a cemetery in the east of the Netherlands, not far from the banks of the Waal river, has yet to be established.

Sergeant Albert Edward Davis' Commonwealth War Graves Commission headstone in Jonkerbos War Cemetery. (Courtesy of Frans Ammerlaan)

53

The Little Ship with a Titanic Connection

The Motor Yacht *Sundowner*

On the night of 14 April 1912, Charles Herbert Lightoller, the second officer, was on watch on the bridge of RMS *Titanic*. It was the last watch he would undertake on the liner, for shortly after being relieved and preparing himself for bed, the ship collided with an iceberg. Pulling on a sweater and trousers, Lightoller went on deck to marshal the evacuation of the passengers. He was the most senior officer to survive the sinking. Twenty-eight years later Charles Lightoller would take part in another nautical evacuation – from Dunkirk.

In 1929 Charles Lightoller, who had earned the Distinguished Service Cross in the First World War, purchased a former Admiralty steam pinnace which was in poor condition and lying in the mud in Conyer Creek east of the River Medway. Over the course of the next two years the

Below: Since May 2012, *Sundowner* has been owned by The Steam Museum Trust who also manage the Ramsgate Maritime Museum. She can normally be seen berthed in Ramsgate Harbour – where this picture was taken. After Dunkirk, *Sundowner* continued to serve as a coastal patrol vessel, taking part in a number of other rescues – such as when a Walrus flying boat crashed in the sea and, on another occasion, when a Spitfire force-landed in the mud in the Thames Estuary.

Above: Both loaded with evacuated Allied soldiers, a tug tows a 'Little Ship' into a South Coast port during Operation *Dynamo*. The yacht has been identified as *Nydia*, which still survives under her original name.

boat was completely overhauled and was fitted with four-stroke engines. Named *Sundowner*, she was re-launched on 28 June 1930. Charles and Sylvia Lightoller then spent the next ten years cruising along the northern coast of Europe, taking part in many international competitions.

In 1939, with the threat of war in the air, Lightoller was asked by the Admiralty to secretly survey the Continental coast and, when the sudden need for boats to sail for Dunkirk was realised, the Admiralty came calling again. When he was told that *Sundowner* was required to help evacuate the BEF Lightoller insisted that he would take the boat over himself. So, on 1 June, with his eldest son Roger, and a Sea Scout called Gerald Ashcroft, Lightoller took *Sundowner* over to France along with five other vessels. On the way over, *Sundowner* encountered the motor cruiser *Westerly*, broken down and on fire. Lightoller went alongside and transferred her five-man crew, taking them on to Dunkirk, as Lightoller later explained: "We had been subject to sporadic bombing and machine-gun fire, but as the *Sundowner* is exceptionally and extremely quick on the helm, by waiting till the last moment and putting the helm hard over – my son at the wheel – we easily avoided every attack, though sometimes near lifted out of the water …

"The difficulty of taking troops on board from the quay high above us was obvious, so I went alongside a destroyer where they were already embarking … I now started to pack them on deck, having passed word below for every man to lie down and keep down; the same applied on deck. I could feel her getting distinctly tender, so took no more … They were literally packed like the proverbial sardines, even one in the bath and another on the WC."

Sundowner successfully reached Ramsgate at 22.00 hours that night with an astonishing 130 men on board. It was at this point that disaster nearly struck when the small craft was nearly sunk by the weight of troops moving to one side of the ship to disembark, forcing Roger Lightoller to shout at them to lie down and not move until told to do so.

54

Sergeant Jack Potter's Flying Goggles

Shot Down and Returned by Sea

By 1 June 1940, the air battle over Dunkirk had reached its climax. Already over the previous six days since the start of Operation *Dynamo* Fighter Command had lost more than ninety aircraft. Such losses were alarmingly high, but of even greater concern to Air Chief Marshal Hugh Dowding was the loss of experienced pilots – men could not be replaced as quickly as machines. Nothing was more important than getting downed pilots back to the UK.

One such airman was 19 Squadron's Sergeant Jack Potter, whose dramatic story on that Saturday, the first day of June 1940, began when he was up before dawn and soon heading out across the Channel in his Spitfire Mk.I, K9836. The squadron found itself over the Belgian coast at around 05.40 hours and immediately ran into a gaggle of German aircraft.

'On 1st June 1940, I was on patrol with Red Section … and shortly after reaching the patrol line we found twelve Me 110s over Dunkirk', Potter later recounted. 'We moved into attack, whereupon they turned very quickly back over the town as if trying to escape. However, we soon

---

Above: The flying goggles that Sergeant Jack Potter was wearing when he was shot down over Dunkirk on 1 June 1940. (The Andy Saunders Collection)

engaged them and they broke up and most of them appeared to turn steeply to the left. This appeared to be the only means of escape they knew and they became quite easy to shoot at.

'I fired at several without apparent effect and then engaged one which had just begun a steep diving turn to the left. I had a full plan view of the top of the aircraft and opened fire at about 400 yards. I held my fire for almost eight seconds and could see my bullets going into the front half of the fuselage. At about 150 yards my ammunition ran out, and I had to avoid the shell fire of another enemy aircraft which was firing at me from my port side.'

Right: Sergeant Jack Potter. (The Andy Saunders Collection)
Below: It was not only Fighter Command that was in action during Operation *Dynamo* – aircraft and crews from Coastal Command, Bomber Command and the Fleet Air Arm also played their part. Here, a Coastal Command Lockheed Hudson is pictured whilst patrolling over a burning Dunkirk during Operation *Dynamo*. The crews of these aircraft soon found themselves in the thick of the fighting. Hudson pilot Flight Lieutenant William 'Willy' Biddell of 206 Squadron, for example, was awarded the Distinguished Flying Cross for his actions on the evening of 31 May 1940, when he fought off several Messerschmitt Bf 109s over the port.

During the actions over Dunkirk at least two Spitfires are known to have landed wheels-down on the beaches there. One of them, N3295 (code letters ZD-G) had been flown by Pilot Officer Graham Davies of 222 Squadron – it landed on 31 May 1940 after its engine had been damaged by anti-aircraft fire. Davies set fire to his aircraft before joining the evacuating troops and reaching the UK by ship. Not far away, and on 25 May 1940, Pilot Officer George Gribble was flying Spitfire N3103 when it was damaged in combat with Messerschmitt Bf 109s of I./JG 76 and Messerschmitt Bf 110s of 6./ZG 76. Like Davies, Gribble also landed wheels-down and set fire to his aircraft. He also managed to make his way to the evacuation vessels and returned safely to England. Almost certainly this series of photographs illustrate the remains of the two Spitfires, but it is impossible to say with any certainty which aircraft is which. However, they became popular tourist attractions for German troops who visited the Dunkirk area to view the mass of wrecked and abandoned war materiel. (Courtesy of Chris Goss)

Potter tried to escape from the mêlée so that he could return home to re-arm. 'As I reached the outskirts of the fight a metallic 'bang' from my port side made me look at my port mainplane and I saw a hole about eight inches long and about two inches wide just above the position of the oil cooler … at about ten miles out from the coast the engine became very rough and oil and glycol smoke started to appear. Finally the engine seized up at about 4,000 feet and fifteen miles out from land.

'Looking around at the sea I saw a small boat and decided to land alongside it. I decided to stay with the aeroplane as the sea was very calm and I thought my chances of being picked up were greater if I landed alongside the boat than if I took to my parachute.

'I circled the boat at about fifty feet and then, being very close to the sea, straightened out to land … On first touching the water the machine skimmed off again, and after one more such landing it dug its nose into the sea. I was flung forward and my forehead and nose met the

Visible to all those
approaching Dunkirk by land, sea and
air, and from some distance away, were the palls of black
smoke towering over the port – seen here in an image taken by a patrolling
RAF aircraft. They were caused by the oil tanks in the harbour area having been set alight
to prevent their capture by the Germans.

Above: A Lockheed Hudson of Coastal Command's 220 Squadron pictured over the Dunkirk beaches on what the crews termed as 'Sands Patrols' – battle flights whose object was to protect shipping and attack any low-flying dive-bombers they might find.

reflector sight … I stood up in the cockpit and found the aircraft still afloat but it sank almost immediately … As the aircraft sank I tried to get out but the parachute caught on the sliding hood and I was taken down with the aircraft. However, I was soon released and pushed off with my feet only to be struck by the tailplane as it went past.'

Potter swam upwards and broke the surface to find himself just fifty yards from the boat. It was a French fishing boat called *Jolie Mascotte*. Potter was hauled on board by the crew of four – none of whom could speak English. Potter's appearance was a fortuitous event for the French fishermen, as they were lost! Potter, of course, knew exactly where he was and, with the aid of a chart was able to show the Frenchmen the bearing for Dunkirk.

As *Jolie Mascotte* approached the harbour, the men spotted a British destroyer and a naval motor boat was sent across to the fishing boat. A Royal Navy Lieutenant climbed aboard and he told Potter that his ship, HMS *Basilisk*, had already been bombed and that the engines and wireless were both out of action. The destroyer was loaded with soldiers and the officer asked if the little fishing boat could tow the destroyer out to sea away from the enemy bombers.

A line was attached and *Jolie Mascotte* began to pull *Basilisk* round when a mass of enemy aircraft filled the sky. 'There were about thirty Dornier 17s and Heinkel 111s,' Potter noted. 'Above them were about twenty-five Me 109s. I informed the Lieutenant that his ship was about to be bombed and we decided to cast off. At about three-quarters of a mile from the destroyer we watched the bombing operations.'

The enemy aircraft did not appear to adopt any particular formation, but at about 3,000 feet turned singly over the target and jettisoned all their bombs. The bombs left the aircraft in a string of about ten. There appeared to be very little attempt at precision bombing, but rather as if they let all their bombs go hoping that one would hit. 'As they bombed, others opened fire with machine-guns on the destroyer. During the course of the whole action they did not score a single hit despite the fact that the target was stationary and had only two pom-poms with no anti-aircraft shells.'

Undaunted, *Jolie Mascotte* returned, re-attached the line and began towing again. Yet soon afterwards, the fishing boat had to cast the line off again as about twenty Junkers Ju 87s dived from a height of around four hundred feet to deliver their deadly cargo – this time with the precision that was lacking in the earlier attack. The ship was hit by possibly four of the bombs.

When the Stukas flew off, *Jolie Mascotte* returned to the destroyer only to find that the ship was sinking and the order was given to 'abandon ship'. The little fishing boat rescued as many as 200 men from the stricken ship, but there were still many others stranded onboard. Luckily another destroyer then appeared and the remainder of the crew and soldiers were saved.

Jack Potter was one of eighteen pilots shot down that day, five of whom survived and were taken back by sea to the UK. In total thirty-eight pilots brought down during Operation *Dynamo* were either taken off the beach at Dunkirk or were rescued from the sea – almost the equivalent of three squadrons.

Below: One of the Royal Navy's most important contributions to *Dynamo*'s air defence was the deployment of the anti-aircraft cruiser HMS *Calcutta*. One of the largest warships to participate in the evacuation, she features in many accounts, her guns repeatedly firing on the Luftwaffe and thereby doing much to bolster morale. Though her commander, Captain Dennis Marescaux Lees, described *Calcutta's* involvement in the evacuation as a 'minor part', she remained in action, and under fire, for much of Operation *Dynamo*, weighing anchor at Sheerness for the last time in the early hours of 3 June. (US Naval History and Heritage Command)

Sub-Lieutenant Crosby's Photographs

Some of the Most Famous Images To Emerge From Operation *Dynamo*

Some of the most remarkable images of the Dunkirk evacuation, including iconic images that became familiar around the world during 1940, were taken by one man – Sub-Lieutenant John Rutherford Crosby. The son of a Glasgow bookseller, Crosby had enlisted in the RNVR in April 1939, being granted his commission as Sub-Lieutenant in December that year, at which point he was posted to HMS *Oriole*.

Built in 1910, *Eagle III* was the last Clyde steamer to be built with a single diagonal engine; she also had an outmoded haystack boiler. Having served as a minesweeper in the First World War, *Eagle III* was requisitioned by the Admiralty again in 1939. She left the Clyde in early 1940, having been renamed HMS *Oriole*, for wartime minesweeping duties at Harwich. She sailed for Dunkirk under the command of Lieutenant (Temporary) Edwin Davies RNVR, reaching La Panne with other units of her flotilla early on 29 May. Davies later wrote this account of his ship's work during *Dynamo*:

Opposite: The original wartime caption for this press image, dated 13 June 1940, states, as we can see, that it shows 'British soldiers helping comrades board a River Clyde paddle steamer in the early dawn during the evacuation of the BEF to England after defeat in Flanders'. Right: Soldiers wait patiently in line, up to their necks in the sea, to be hauled aboard HMS *Oriole*, which had been beached at La Panne, 29 May 1940. Though it is one of the most widely published pictures of the evacuation, rarely, if ever, has the photographer, Sub-Lieutenant Crosby, been credited. It has also, on occasion, been described as a fake – a montage – on the assumption that no ship could get so far inshore without running aground.

'You are aware that except for the seven words ("You will be required to embark troops") in F.O.I.C. Harwich's 1016/28 I was entirely unaware of what was required of me and I could therefore only be guided by the outstanding facts that there were many ships in the offing and many destitute soldiers on the beach. We had no power boats and those ships that had power boats seemed to be lacking in a sense of co-operation, but it was early evident to me that owing to the considerable surf and shoal character of the beach boat work would inevitably be slow and cumbersome and not devoid of danger. Consequently, and well knowing the virtues of a paddler for such work, I deliberately ran *Oriole* ashore making a clearing station of her by inviting all ships in the offing to collect troops through me rather than waste further time with their own lifeboats.

'I am aware that *Oriole* might have been utterly lost but I felt that I could satisfactorily answer such a loss. It is difficult to recount all that happened. The troops at first had to be held off at revolver point, but we soon initiated a modicum of organisation and then distribution went with a swing. Despite persistent bombing by the enemy I think we must have distributed some 2500-3000 troops between all types of ships in the offing and then as evening drew on I took on board *Oriole* the two or three hundred with whom I felt she would still float.

'As time for refloating approached I notified army officers that I would cruise about in the vicinity and would pick up all who could get out into nine feet of water by boats or any other means. I refloated about 6.00 p.m. and then cruised about in 8/10 feet of water until I had embarked an estimated 6/700 soldiers, nurses, mails, etc., the enemy bombing being simply torrential at this time.

'I submit that machines of our Air Force should be in constant attendance on these beaches until operations come to a close. I do not suggest that the enemy will be deterred from attacking such a fruitful target, but I am absolutely confident that a knowledge that our machines were harrying theirs as they were harrying us would give us heart to feel that we had support from quarters where support was most desirable.

'In all these operations the whole of my ship's company, without sleep, food or even water, used every endeavour to forward the work to the utmost of their abilities and consequently I would like to name every rank and rating as worthy of recognition.'[65]

In his report, Davies singled out seven members of his crew for particular mention. One of these individuals was Sub-Lieutenant Crosby: 'On several occasions very gallantly and at his own obvious imminent peril dove into surf and tide (strong) to render assistance to soldiers in difficulties and was thereby responsible in preserving many lives.'

The following transcript of a postagram, timed and dated as 18.00 hours on 2 June 1940, was attached to Lieutenant Davies' report: 'Arrived evacuation beach Belgian Coast 1st June in accordance with instructions. Complete absence of transport facilities. Service ships using own motor launches and whalers at very slow speed. *Oriole* having no power boat was beached to embark soldiers. It would have been feasible to have filled the ship in half an hour but many hundreds of soldiers attempted to rush and it was necessary to haul off shore with about 200 on board and another fifty hanging to exterior protections all round the ship.

'Ship was taken to a more sparsely populated portion of beach, army officers were posted with revolvers to keep order and ship was beached again. Ship was again rushed by such numbers as to imperil her chances and chances of all then on board and she was therefore again hauled off shore with a total of about 470. Throughout enemy fighters attempted to machine-gun ship and soldiers in the water (no bombs this day) and with about 470 on board I deemed it advisable to return to base. We shot down one enemy machine.'

Remarkably, as well as his photographic record, Crosby also wrote his own account of the events of Operation *Dynamo*. We pick it up his narrative at the point where *Oriole* had been beached: 'By this time, the Old Man had run the ship aground and she was in 10 feet of water or so. Many pongos tried to swim out, but hadn't the sense to ditch their gear. It is a wonder

Above: The original caption to this picture states that it shows 'British soldiers helping comrades board a River Clyde paddle steamer in the early dawn during the evacuation of the BEF'. It is almost certainly another of the images taken by Sub-Lieutenant Crosby from HMS *Oriole*. Main image: The scene on the beach at La Panne in a photograph taken from outside the l'Hotel Splendide by Sub-Lieutenant Crosby. Both *Oriole* (left of centre) and a Dutch skoot, seen above the back of the abandoned car, are beached; vessels standing offshore include the paddle minesweeper *Waverley* (on the right), another skoot and several Royal Navy destroyers.

Above: Sub-Lieutenant Crosby took this snapshot of HMS *Oriole*'s gun crew whilst the paddle-steamer was beached at La Panne. Below: Sub-Lieutenant Crosby was undoubtedly busy with his camera during HMS *Oriole*'s time on the beach at La Panne. Note the discarded clothing and equipment that litters the beach.

that many of them did not drown, but I never saw one. I saw one in the process of going down for the last time but fished him out alright. It was now about 6a.m. but felt more like four in the afternoon. Shortly the troops would wade out up to their necks holding on to the grass line. They came aboard and we acted as a pierhead for several ships anchored offshore. They sent in whalers and pinnaces and loaded from our sponsons. About 2,000 were sent out this way before the tide receded so much that they couldn't reach us with their boats. What a scene of desolation on the beach as the tide receded, leaving files, haversacks, coats, pouches lying on the wet sand … It was all rather tragic.'[66]

Crosby then went ashore, heading up the beach into La Panne. 'I kept my camera busy the whole time,' he noted. Eventually returning to *Oriole*, the ship then became the subject of a German air raid:

'The formation broke and the planes came at us every way, like a school of mosquitoes on a still summer evening. They seemed to single out a ship for themselves and went for it. We saw one plane dive vertically on us, and four bombs fell from it. They seemed to float down; they fell so slowly, or so it seemed to us. Somebody muttered: "For what we are about to receive … " But no, they were going to miss us. I fumbled for my camera even as the air all round was hideous with the screaming of the bombs. There was a roar and our four burst on the beach alongside. I got my photo as they burst.' That moment was, concluded Crosby, 'the last opportunity I had of using my camera, as we had our hands full after this'.[67]

Crosby remained with minesweepers as the war continued. He lost his life on 7 January 1943 when HM Trawler *Horatio* was sunk off the North African coast near Bizerta.

The last picture that Sub-Lieutenant Crosby took during Operation *Dynamo* – a remarkable shot of the beach at La Panne during a German air raid. It was taken from the decks of HMS *Oriole*, Crosby had turned and captured the very moment that four German bombs fell on the sands and exploded.

56

Avro Anson In Action

An Unequal Battle

On the morning of 3 June 1940, the Marshal of the RAF, Lord Trenchard, visited RAF Detling, his intention being to meet and chat with the aircrew of 500 (County of Kent) Squadron. Formed at RAF Manston on 16 March 1931 as a Special Reserve unit, 500 Squadron comprised half regular and half reserve personnel, all of whom were trained to operate twin-engine aircraft. On 7 November 1938, the squadron was transferred to Coastal Command, being equipped with Avro Ansons in March 1939. Shortly before the outbreak of war, 500 Squadron was mobilised and began flying patrols over the Channel and the North Sea – duties that continued throughout Operation *Dynamo*, during which period the flights were referred to as 'Thistle' patrols. Indeed, May was a busy time for the squadron which flew 1,286 hours with some crews flying at times twice a day, and up to five hours on each trip.

It is possible that one of the subjects discussed during Trenchard's visit, aside from the squadron's efforts and losses covering the evacuation, were the achievements of Pilot Officer Phillip Walford Peters and his crew two days earlier.

At 08.34 hours on the morning of 1 June, Peters took off from Detling

at the controls of the Anson Mk.V coded MK-V of 'B' Flight. His crew consisted of Sergeant Deryck Cobham Spencer, Aircraftman Pepper and Aircraftman Lewis George Smith.[68] The patrol of three aircraft was led by Flying Officer Whitehead in MK-T, the trio being completed by MK-H, which was flown by Sergeant Freetsone.

The formation, flying at a low level, had made searches along the coast and further out to sea looking for survivors in the water and in small boats, floating mines and for E-boats, when, at 10.40 hours, enemy aircraft were spotted. Whitehead immediately took the Ansons down to wave height and led them away from the coast. MK-V was about 50' above the sea near Ostend when a gaggle of nine Messerschmitt Bf 109s were sighted at an altitude of between 1,000 and 1,500 feet. The aviation historian Norman Franks provides the following account of what followed:

'Three of the German fighters broke away to attack the Anson, one coming in behind it, two others from the starboard quarter. Phillip Peters took violent evasive action, throwing the Anson all over the sky, successfully turning and twisting about so as not to present the aircraft as a steady target. As he did so, the air-gunner A.C. Smith and navigator Sergeant Deryck Spencer kept up a steady return fire as other 109s came in to assist their comrades. The gunners' fire was so effective that two 109s were shot down into the sea and another damaged in a fight which lasted for fifteen to twenty miles ...

'When the remaining fighters flew off, Peters continued his patrol, landing back at base at 12.37 hours. There the crew found two bullet holes in the wing, one through the flaps and a fourth through the cowling of the port engine.'[69]

For his actions during the combat, Peters was subsequently awarded the Distinguished Flying Cross. His citation concluded with the following: 'After the engagement this officer continued to carry out the patrol alone, having lost touch with the other two aircraft which had returned to the base.'[70] Smith and Spencer were both awarded the Distinguished Flying Medal.

Main Image:
A surviving Avro Anson – though not the one flown by 500 Squadron's Pilot Officer Phillip Walford Peters during his action on 1 June 1940. The aircraft seen here is on display in the Air Force Museum of New Zealand. (Courtesy of Bernard Spragg) Above: The Distinguished Flying Cross, as awarded to Pilot Officer Phillip Peters.

57

The Maritime Hospital, Zuydcoote

Scars of Battle That Can Still be Seen

Located amongst the dunes at Zuydcoote, near Bray Dunes to the east of Dunkirk, is the imposing structure of the Maritime Hospital. Known almost universally to those who were at Dunkirk in 1940, Army and Navy alike, as 'the Sanatorium', the construction of the Hôpital Maritime had begun in 1902, the first patients moving in during 1910. Following the outbreak of war in 1939, part of the site was requisitioned as a military hospital.

From the moment that the Blitzkrieg began on 10 May 1940, the hospital's five operating theatres were in use virtually non-stop, initially treating French and Belgian wounded, but, as the BEF withdrew, increasingly more British casualties. Indeed, when the Dunkirk perimeter was established, the hospital was immediately commandeered by the Royal Army Medical Corps. By 4 June, more than 1,400 men were being sheltered there, along with the members of the RAMC's skeleton staff.

The sheer size of the Maritime Hospital meant that it was a landmark used by many of the ships sent to the beaches east of Dunkirk. The destroyer HMS *Wakeful*, for example, anchored off the sanatorium at 15.00 hours on 28 May. 'During the next eight hours,' wrote her captain, Commander Ralph Lindsay Fisher, we 'embarked about 640 troops by ship's boats. Sub-Lieutenant Percival-Jones volunteered to go in the boats and did splendid work on the beach marshalling troops, at one time at the point of the revolver. All mess-tables and stools and other available timber was placed on the upper deck for life-saving purposes and the troops were stowed as low in the ship as possible to preserve sufficient stability for rapid manoeuvring in case of air attack. Engine-room, boiler rooms and store rooms were all utilised.'

The threat of air attack mentioned by Fisher was all too real, as Commander Francis Douglas-Watson of the minesweeper HMS *Pangbourne* (see object 21) recalled – his account detailing a little of the events on 29 May: '[We] anchored about half a mile off the beach opposite the Sanatorium. All available boats were lowered and sent inshore in charge of Lieut. W.K. Tadman R.N.R. and Mr. S.S. Rabbitts, Boatswain R.N. Between 1800 and 1900 the ship was subjected to numerous low diving bombing attacks, although no direct hits were made there were several near misses. The hull was holed on both sides above and below the water line and the D.G. [degaussing] coil cut in several places.'

One of Tadman's crew later recounted his memories of the Luftwaffe's attacks: 'What is that on the port quarter? – it looks like a tiny cloud. I strain my eyes through the glasses. It's Jerry again. I give the orders mechanically, and the gun swings on to the bearing. They come relentlessly on like great black vultures. No use opening fire yet; they are not yet within range. These are a different kind, with queer wings and fixed undercarriages. I rack my brain to think what they are.

'Suddenly the penny drops. They are Stuka dive-bombers. They wheel round in a circle and peel off one by one. Each has selected his prey, and here comes ours. In a screaming vertical power dive he is tearing down towards us at four hundred knots. The noise is terrifying … He starts to spit fire at us, and the tracer shells from his cannon blind me as I watch for the bombs to fall.'

The Maritime Hospital's location immediately adjacent to one of the beaches meant that it was literally on the front line, and was therefore hit during the Luftwaffe's attacks – both by

bombs and cannon/machine-gun fire. One account also states that some seventy shells fell on the site during Operation *Dynamo*. Whatever the actual cause, the scars of war can still be seen today throughout the complex.

Main image: Evidence of the bitter fighting in and around Dunkirk that can be seen on this building that formed part of the Maritime Hospital complex at Zuydcoote. It is on the main drive to the hospital. Left: A close-up of some of the damage inflicted on the buildings of the Maritime Hospital.

58

Admiralty Pier, Dover

A Welcome Return Home

Though other ports along England's south coast, from Falmouth to Ramsgate, were used to one extent or another during Operation *Dynamo*, it was Dover where most of the men were off-loaded. Indeed, of the 338,226 British and Allied troops evacuated between 26 May and 4 June, nearly 200,000 passed through Dover. Though the port's Eastern Arm and Prince of Wales Pier were used to take off the troops, the main disembarkation point was the Admiralty Pier.

Designed by distinguished marine engineer James Walker and his pupil partner Alfred Burges, construction of Admiralty Pier began in 1847. The intention was to create a large national harbour of which Admiralty Pier was designed to be only one part, in this case the western arm. By 1872 the structure was 2,100 feet long. In the beginning granite was used but later on concrete blocks were used below the water. The Admiralty Pier was the first marine structure in the country in which pre-cast concrete blocks were used.

Corporal George Edward Andow, of the 4th Battalion, Royal Tank Regiment, remembered arriving at the pier: 'When we got to Dover, we came off the boat and were sorted out. The Red Cross people were there with mugs of hot tea and sandwiches, then we got on board a train.'[71] The sorting out that Corporal Andow mentions was a complex exercise, as the various regiments had become inextricably mixed during the retreat and evacuation. Towards the end of the evacuation, when increasing numbers of French troops were landed at Dover, this process became even more complex, and there were officials posted at the end of the pier who called, 'British one side! French the other!'

Throughout the evacuation, the two Dover Harbour Board tugs, *Lady Duncannon* and *Lady Brassey*, were kept busy, pushing and pulling the ships from their moorings for either rapid repairs or essential refuelling. Such was the scale of the task, that at *Dynamo's* peak, the ships arriving from Dunkirk to berth alongside Admiralty Pier berths were often three abreast.

It was the welcome which the men received at Dover which left the strongest impression upon the returning troops. One such was Private Edgar Roberts of the 5th Battalion, Northamptonshire Regiment: 'In Dover. Ladies were there with cups of tea and bars of chocolate and cake. I got tea and a cake and got on the train.' Another soldier recalled that, 'People were lined up when we landed, and they were dishing out cups of tea for us.'

'The reception was tremendous,' an officer of the East Surrey Regiment related. 'When we arrived at Dover quay there were a hell of a lot of ships, [and] destroyers unloading wounded. It was organised chaos. The whole thing was done extremely well, and there was a great deal of activity and movement.'[72]

The skipper of HMS *Montrose* described his return to Dover on 27 May: 'The ship secured alongside the Admiralty Pier at 1817 and disembarked the soldiers. The latter were feeling much better after a rest, plenty of hot tea and food in the ship and went ashore in excellent heart. It was remarkable how good was their morale and behaviour from the time they arrived on the pier at Dunkirk until they left at Dover. It was computed by Military sources that *Montrose* had transported some 1,200 men and 28 stretcher cases, several of the latter being seriously wounded.'

Opposite: The view of the Port of Dover as seen from the wartime gun emplacements at St Martin's Battery on the town's Western Heights. On the right is the Admiralty Pier, where most of the men brought back to Dover were disembarked, though the port's Eastern Arm and Prince of Wales Pier were also employed. Right: Destroyers loaded with soldiers evacuated from Dunkirk pictured after their return to Dover, almost certainly berthing alongside Admiralty Pier. This image is believed to have been taken on 31 May 1940. The warship in the background with the pennant number D-94 is the destroyer HMS *Whitehall*.

DUNKIRK

By the early summer of 1939 I had graduated from cadet training into the Royal Air Force and had a long course of advanced flying training at Kinloss in Northern Scotland. By the time that war broke out I had already been posted to a fighter squadron equipped with obsolete aircraft totally unsuited to face the German Luftwaffe.

These machines were very soon replaced though by Spitfires, much to our delight. it took a little while to get accustomed to them as their normal airspeed was more than double that of anything we had handled before, but we soon settled down.

Hurricanes, another splendid fighter of its epoch, were in a majority then as they were soon afterwards in the Battle of Britain, but they were withdrawn from service some years later, whilst the good little Spitfire saw the war out right to the end and I was lucky enough to keep on flying them.

Well, we had the phony war from September 1939 onwards and life seemed pretty good until May 1940 when the Germans suddenly invaded Belgium, over-ran Northern France and became a definite menace to our own country. Hitler's troops forced the collapse of Belgium and came sweeping down the coast towards Dunkirk.

The evacuation of that port with the greater part of our British Expeditionary Force and very many french troops has long since passes into British history and added yet another glorious page, although a retreat.

Anyway, the whistle blew for us, and at that moment our squadron was stationed at Hornchurch in Essex. Like all other units of Fighter Command, apart from the few still stationed

Left: The account written by Squadron Leader Graham Davies DFC recalling his part in Operation *Dynamo*. Below: Squadron Leader Graham Davies DFC's logbook in which he recorded being shot down over Dunkirk. (Images courtesy of Geoff Davies)

			PUPIL GER		DUTY (INCLUDING RESULTS AND REMA
					TOTALS BROUGHT FORW
M					FORMATION + ATTACK
M					ATTACKS.
MA					DIGBY TO NORTH COATES F
MA					NORTH COATES FITTIES TO DIG
MA					NIGHT RECCO.
MAY					DIGBY TO NORTH COATES FIT
MAY					NORTH COATES FITTIES TO DIG
MAY				SELF	ATTACKS
MAY		SPITFIRE	J	SELF	SECTOR RECCO.
MAY	26	SPITFIRE	J	SELF	KIRTON TO SUTTON BRID
MAY	26	SPITFIRE	J	SELF	AIR FIRING.
MAY	26	SPITFIRE	J	SELF	SUTTON BRIDGE TO KIRTON
MAY	26	SPITFIRE	J	SELF	ATTACKS.
MAY	28	SPITFIRE	J	SELF X	KIRTON TO MARTLESH OPERATIONAL PATROL OV
MAY	28	SPITFIRE	J	SELF X	DUNKIRK. LANDED DUXFO
MAY	28	SPITFIRE	J	SELF X	DUXFORD TO HORNCHUR
MAY	29	SPITFIRE	G	SELF	OP. PATROL OVER DUNK
MAY	30	SPITFIRE N 3295.	G	SELF X	OP. PATROL OVER DUNK OP. PATROL OVER DUNKIRK.
MAY	31	SPITFIRE	G	SELF X	LANDED ON BEACH. DESTROYED A/C. RETUR
MAY	30	SPITFIRE	G	SELF X	OP. PATROL OVER DUNKI

SUMMARY FOR MAY 1940   Sp
UNIT No 222 SQDRN.
DATE 1-6-40
SIGNED

APU. OC A.
R7

S/LDR. OC 222 SQDRN.

GRAND TOTAL [Cols. (1) to (10)]
307   Hrs.   Mins.

TOTALS CARRIED FOR

Squadron Leader Davies DFC's Logbook

Shot Down Over Dunkirk

Moving to RAF Hornchurch late on 28 May 1940, the pilots of 222 Squadron soon found themselves in the sky over Dunkirk, the first aircraft taking off at 04.15 hours the following day. One of the pilots who participated in that patrol, as well as two on the 30th, was Pilot Officer Graham Davies.

With little respite, the squadron was airborne from Hornchurch at 10.51 hours on the 31st. The Operations Record Book provides the following brief summary: 'The Squadron (ten aircraft) took off on patrol. While over Dunkirk the formation became broken owing to layers of cloud. Pilot Officer Vigors reported engaging a Heinkel 111 at a height of 2,000 feet between two layers of cloud. The E/A [enemy aircraft] dived into clouds, apparently hit. Pilot Officer Davies failed to return after the patrol.'[73]

At the controls of Spitfire N3295, Davies later recorded the following account: 'When my own queer adventure started we were flying at something between 6000 and 8000 feet, but intensive anti-aircraft fire obliged us to climb into cloud cover. The stuff came up not only from the enemy but even from our own batteries and those of the French …

'We got into cloud at about 10,000 feet, but just at that moment my engine caught a bit of shrapnel and went out of action for good. One's first impulse was to bail out, but dropping rapidly out of the cloud and looking down that appeared to mean falling into the sea or into the middle of a terrific group battle going on, with the prospect of certain death in either case. I decided to stick to the ship and land it if possible on the beaches we still held.

'My good little Spitfire carried on quite well with its dead engine although it was not exactly a glider but a heavy fighting machine with a small wing surface for its weight. Nearing ground I put my wheels down, although very doubtful about that, not having the slightest idea as to what the beach surface might be like. However, the tide was half way out and the sand proved to be hard, on which I managed to make a satisfactory touch-down. Had it been soft, a belly landing would have been the only possibility.

'I had hoped to land if possible within our own lines and this proved to be the case as I was close to Marsdyck some four miles from Dunkirk.

'The beach here seemed utterly deserted, nothing in sight anywhere, but things kept falling into the sand from time to time and going off with an unpleasant crump. I got out of the Spitfire and walked towards some sand dunes behind which their appeared to be some sign of life, heads peeping over.'

The heads turned out to be those of French soldiers. Through them, Davies eventually made it into Dunkirk: 'Down in the harbour I saw at the end of the long mole there were still two of our ships, a destroyer and what looked like a paddle steamer. Thus, I set out along that extensive jetty to reach them if possible. If you happen to know Dunkirk you may remember that the mole is a very long one, something like Southend pier. At the time it seemed to me endless.

'The thing was deserted but littered with bodies of French and British troops, over which one had to step. In actual fact, the mole was already under German rifle and machine gun fire, which explained its unpopularity as a means of escape. How I got to the end of that thing, walking, dropping, skipping and dodging goodness alone knows, but one made it somehow.'

A Lifeboat Coxswain's Gallantry

Edward Parker's Award of the Distinguished Service Medal

A number of the nineteen RNLI lifeboats that crossed to Dunkirk did so at the hands of their own crews. One of these was the Margate lifeboat *Lord Southborough*. It was at around 18.00 hours on the evening of 30 May that *Lord Southborough* departed from Margate, being towed across the Channel by one of the requisitioned Dutch schuits. Coxswain Edward Drake Parker's ten-man crew was supplied with steel helmets and food and cigarettes.

Lord Southborough did not reach the vicinity of Dunkirk until after midnight, the schuit towing her having run aground on a sandbank. Under its own power, the lifeboat approached the beaches at Malo-les-Bains where a call from the shore diverted the boat to the dark masses of the waiting lines of troops.

The lifeboat drew over four feet of water and the troops had to wade out until the water was up to their arm-pits. As the soldiers stood beside the lifeboat her rail was four feet above their heads and the sailors had to haul the weary troops, heavy with water, over the rail and into the boat. It was terribly exhausting work.

The first troops to be dragged on board were eighty Frenchmen. When these were loaded, Edward Parker took them out to the stranded Dutch barge and returned to the beach for more men.

The next batch of troops was from the Border Regiment. But by the time *Lord Southborough* was full the tide had retreated and the heavily-laden lifeboat was stuck on the beach. Fully exposed to aerial attack and utterly defenceless, the men could do nothing but sit and wait for the tide to turn.

Eventually the tide flowed and *Lord Southborough* floated free. Parker's crew made a third trip to the shore and back to the barge before dawn.

Main image: The Distinguished Service Medal.

Edward Parker was then instructed to take no more rescued soldiers to the barge but further out to the destroyer HMS *Icarus*. This *Lord Southborough* did time and time again, watched by the captain of *Icarus*, Lieutenant Commander E.G. Roper: 'The magnificent behaviour of the crew of the Margate lifeboat who, with no thought of rest, brought off load after load of soldiers from Dunkirk, under continuous shelling, bombing and aerial machine-gun fire, will be an inspiration to us as long as we live.'[74]

On one occasion, the officer on the bridge of *Icarus* cried out to Parker to cast off immediately. The moment that the lifeboat pulled away from the destroyer, a flight of German aircraft broke through the clouds. For a few seconds the lifeboat-men were conscious only of stunning detonation of bombs and the paralyzing stammer of machine-guns.

A freshening wind had raised a swell so heavy that by 07.00 hours the lifeboat could no longer go near the shore. Instead, Parker was ordered by *Icarus* to cruise up and down outside the surf and search for any men in the water swimming or clinging to wreckage.

At this stage the shore-line presented a sorry sight: 'The lifeboat-men saw a whaler and a motor-boat turn over and sink. Boats lay wrecked all along the line of surf. Others were half-buried in the sand and soldiers were labouring to dig and drag them out … as far as the lifeboat-men could see not a boat except their own was afloat. She was alone, and men were wading out to her. Some of them were knocked over by the surf, struggled, and failed to rise. Others stepped suddenly from the shallow water covering the many sand-banks into the deeper channels between them, and disappeared. The lifeboat crew saw men drowning close to her, and could not reach them.'[75]

By 09.00 hours it had become clear that there was little more that *Lord Southborough* could do. With a few of the survivors rescued from the water still on board, Parker turned the boat round and sailed back to Margate.

For his actions, Parker was awarded the Distinguished Service Medal, which he received from the King at an investiture at Buckingham Palace.

Top: Edward Parker DSM.

Right: The crew of the Margate lifeboat, equipped with steel helmets, standing by outside the boathouse during the war. Left to right they are D. Price, E. Parker, A. Ladd, H. Sandwell, A.C. Robsinon (Hon. Sec.), T.D. Harman (second coxswain), H.E. Parker (the coxswain's brother, and bowman), E. Barrs, A. Morris and A. Lacey.

61

Admiral Sir William Frederic Wake-Walker's Statute

Memorial to one of the Key Individuals of Operation *Dynamo*

On 29 May, Rear Admiral William Frederic Wake-Walker returned to the Admiralty to be told that Vice Admiral Phillips wanted to see him. Wake-Walker went to Phillips' room and found him with the Naval Secretary. He was asked if he would like to go to Dunkirk to try and help with the organisation of the embarkation. Wake-Walker said that he would be 'delighted'. By 16.00 hours a car had been arranged and Wake-Walker, along with Lieutenant-Commander Wynne-Edwards and Commander Norfolk, were on their way to Dover. He sailed from there at 20.00 hours on the destroyer HMS *Esk*.

It was not intended that Wake-Walker would supersede Captain Tennant, who would remain ashore as Senior Naval Officer Dunkirk. Wake-Walker's role would be that of Senior Naval Officer Afloat, organising the movement of the ships and other craft to and from the harbour and the beaches.

He reached Dunkirk in the early hours of the 30th, to see the beaches lined with troops. He decided to place a Royal Navy officer in a motor boat off each of the beaches with Wake-Walker himself operating off Dunkirk harbour. He saw that the harbour was not being fully utilised whilst the beaches were over-crowded.

Wake-Walker's aim was to ensure that there were always vessels off each of the beaches and alongside the East Mole to enable the embarkation to proceed continuously. He was soon personally involved in the embarkation. At one point, he saw a small pontoon boat lying unused. He called some men of the 12th Lancers over and placed four of them at each corner of the pontoon and together they waded out into the water, where he got them Noah-like onto the pontoon two-by-two.

He flitted about on Motor Torpedo Boat 102 (see Object 86) in order to keep in touch with the movement of all the vessels. At various times, he operated from the destroyers *Worcester*, *Express*, *Hebe* and *Keith*, until this last one was sunk when he transferred permanently to MTB 102.

Wake-Walker also kept in touch with Admiral Ramsay at Dover to advise on the movement and requirement of vessels, just as he was with Lord Gort on the situation of the troops on the beaches. It was on 30 May that he first saw the collection of Little Ships, the organisation of which presented a unique challenge for Wake-Walker and his officers: 'I saw for the first time that strange procession of craft of all kinds that has become famous – tugs towing dinghies, lifeboats and all manner of pulling boats – small motor yachts, motor launches, drifters, Dutch scoots, Thames barges, fishing boats, pleasure steamers.' As the tows of boats appeared each had to be directed to the beaches where they were most urgently required.

Wake-Walker remained at Dunkirk until the very last stages of the evacuation. When he returned to England, he had found that he had lost 7lbs in weight. For his role in the evacuation he was appointed Companion of the Bath.

The statue of Admiral Sir William Frederic Wake-Walker which is located on the Pier Head in Liverpool. By the sculptor Tom Murphy, the statue was unveiled by HRH the Duke of Edinburgh in 1998. (Chris Dorney/Shutterstock)

62

Dynamo's 'Traffic Policeman'

Described in a Letter by Dr Basil Smith

Owned by Dr Basil Smith, the motor cruiser *Constant Nymph* was one of the first Thames vessels to be ready to sail for *Dynamo*. She was taken to Sheerness by Smith himself on 27 May, and from there to Ramsgate. Smith himself takes up the story:

'We left Ramsgate about 3.30 p.m. on 30th May, 1940, in tow of HMS *Jutland* (A Dutch boat [schuit] taken over by Navy) after lying outside the Harbour from 9.30 a.m., during which time we had done a little ferrying work between ships. We were towed with a whaler and cutter on same tow.

'Arrived at our station some miles east of Dunkirk Harbour about 9.30 p.m. and towed whaler and cutter to beach as soon as *Jutland* had anchored – slight mist. At first we could only find Frenchmen on the beach and took off several boat loads, then a British Officer waded and swam to *Constant Nymph* while running slowly up and down the beach line in about 3 feet 6 inches waiting for the boats to be filled and keeping a look out for British troops.

'In spite of darkness and slight mist, the fires on shore and fine night made bodies of men show up against the sand. On hearing from British Officer that thousands of our men were a little nearer Dunkirk, we worked

---

LEGG & SMITH.
CHARTERED ACCOUNTANTS.

GROVELAND HOUSE,
BOW LANE,
LONDON, E.C.4.

18th October 1940.

H. B. Louard Esq.,
14 Wood Lane,
FALMOUTH.

Dear Louard,

Little Ship Club, Dunkirk.

In reply to your letter of 7th October, the Ministry of Shipping paid for the repairs to "Constant Nymph" and also paid my claim for lost gear, such as compass, etc. Of course the claim had to be at cost and there is a very considerable loss as everything is costing more to replace and some of the more expensive things, such as compass, were now in the summer of 1939.

No Article on Dunkirk would be complete without referring to our traffic policeman whom I mention in my Notes. He was an elderly man in his shirt sleeves, smoking a pipe and reading a newspaper, sitting on a kitchen chair outside the wheel house of a naval Drifter off the North Foreland. I presumed the Drifter was in wireless communication with the shore, and every ship, this did not affect motor boats carrying only a few troops, closed with this Drifter and asked the shirt-sleeved gentleman where this lot should be taken, and the shirt-sleeved gentleman took the pipe out of his mouth, looked up from his paper for a moment, and gave them the name of the port to receive their packet.

I should like to have been able to show Hitler and Goering of Air Force fame this terrified gentleman!

Yours sincerely,

B Smith

further up and got mainly
British for some time; not many wounded.

'One nice fire which was a leading mark was blown out by
another bomb later on in the night, but we were fairly well at home by then
and it caused no delay. Having filled *Jutland*, the motor boat with whaler and cutter turned
over to *Laudania*, a similar ship, and filled that. *Jutland* left about 3 a.m. I am informed by
Captain of *Laudania*, that these ships hold about 450 men each, making a total of 900 men taken
off.'

At about 08.00 on the 31st, with *Constant Nymph* out of fuel and her propeller fouled by a
rope, Smith turned his boat over to the crew of a drifter. He was taken on board *Laudania*,
returning to Margate at 17.00 hours.

In a letter dated 10 October 1940, seen here, Smith recalled the vital part one unidentified
individual played in the evacuations: 'No article on Dunkirk would be complete without referring
to our traffic policeman … He was an elderly man in his shirt sleeves, smoking a pipe and reading
a newspaper, sitting on a kitchen chair outside the wheel house of a naval Drifter off the north
Foreland. I presumed the Drifter was in wireless communication with the shore, and every ship,
this did not affect motor boats carrying on a few troops, closed with this drifter and asked the
shirt-sleeved gentleman where this lot should be taken, and the shirt-sleeved gentleman took
the pipe out of his mouth, looked up from his paper for a moment, and gave them the name of
the port to receive their packet. I should like to have been able to show Hitler and Goering of
Air Force fame this terrified gentleman!'[76]

Opposite: The letter written by Dr Basil Smith recounting the 'traffic policeman' who was positioned on
a drifter off North Foreland. Above: The vessel that towed *Constant Nymph* across the Channel was the
requisitioned Dutch schuit, or schoot, *Jutland*. This image shows one of *Jutland*'s sister schuits, *Horst*,
entering Dunkirk during the evacuations. Lying at Poole prior to *Dynamo*, *Horst*, commanded by
Lieutenant Commander G. Fardell RN, had transported 1,150 men before she ran aground near the West
Mole on 3 June and was abandoned.

63

Dynamo's Youngest Casualty

John Atkins Was Aged Just 15 When He was Killed

On 29 May 1940, the London and Rochester Trading Company's Thames barge *Pudge* was in Tilbury docks waiting to take on board a cargo of wheat for Ipswich, when she was requisitioned by the Admiralty. Her skipper was told to sail to Dover, along with other Thames barges, where the crew learned of the task that awaited them.

'When they got to Dover,' notes one account, 'the naval officer in command asked for eight or ten volunteers from among the skippers and their mates to take their barges to Dunkirk. There were 17 barges in Dover harbour that day, lying alongside the Prince of Wales Pier and every one of the skippers was ready to take his barge across. They drew lots and six were selected for immediate service, the three engined/auxiliary barges *Pudge*, *Thyra* and *Lady Rosebery*, and the three sail only barges *Doris*, *H.A.C.* and *Duchess*. The three auxiliary barges proceeded out of the harbour with the sailing barges in tow.[77]

In due course, *Pudge*, along with the two other barges – *Thyra* and *Lady Rosebery* – were taken in tow by the steel-hulled tug *St. Fagan*, not only to keep them together as they crossed the Channel, but to save fuel and time. They arrived some three miles to the east of Dunkirk in the early hours of 1 June, and were cast-off from the tug.[78]

As they set their sails to make their way to the shore, there was a tremendous explosion – *St. Fagan* had hit or set off a mine. The 97-ton *Pudge* was lifted out of the water by the blast, but she fell back 'the right way up', according to her skipper, Bill Watson. When the dust and smoke settled, there was nothing left of *Lady Rosebery*, *St. Fagan*, or another barge, *Doris*. The tug had crew of twenty-five. Only six survived. *Pudge* picked up what survivors the crew could find.

Opposite: John Edward Atkins' name on Panel 63 of the Tower Hill Memorial in London. He is officially listed as having the rank of Ordinary Seaman. The Tower Hill Memorial commemorates the men and women of the Merchant Navy and fishing fleets who died in both world wars and who have no known grave. It stands on the south side of the garden of Trinity Square, close to the Tower of London. (Courtesy of Robert Mitchell) Above: The Thames barge *Pudge* today. (Courtesy of Lisa Larsson; www.flickr.com) Right: A newspaper cutting detailing John Atkins' death. (Courtesy of John Grehan)

15, Gave Life at Dunkirk

BRITAIN'S youngest war victim is believed to be John Edward Atkins, 15-years-old barge hand of Denton, near Gravesend. His parents have been officially informed that he as died after being seriously wounded in the Dunkirk evacuation.

One of those who lost their lives on *Lady Rosebery*, which had been skippered by W. Ellis, was the barge's cook and third mate, John Edward Atkins. John was born in 1925 to John William and Lilian May Atkins of Shamrock Road, Gravesend, Kent; he was one of five children. John's education was initially at Chalk School and later at the Gordon School. On leaving Gordon, he started his working life in a factory, before joining the Thames barge Lady Rosebery

The fifteen-year-old from Gravesend was excited at being involved in the operation to save the BEF, and had written a letter to his parents before setting off across the Channel. This they received on 1 June, the day he died. It read: 'We are under the Navey [sic] now we are going to France today an[d] we might never come back. Don't worry'. His words were tragically prophetic. At the time of his death, John Atkins was believed to have been Britain's youngest fatality of the war.

Returning to the events of 1 June, leaking badly from the shock waves from the explosion, little could be achieved by *Pudge* remaining off Dunkirk. A destroyer relayed the order for her to make for home with her rescued survivors. Whilst heading back for the UK, the tug *Tanga* took *Pudge* in tow and three hours later arrived safely in Ramsgate.

159

64

The Cassel Gate, Bergues

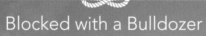

Blocked with a Bulldozer

Opposite: The Porte
de Cassel at Bergues. The town's
ramparts, some four miles in length, are partly medieval
and partly constructed by Vauban. Above: A remarkable photograph
showing the bulldozer being removed from the Porte de Cassel by the Germans after the
town's capture in 1940. Note the damage visible on the gateway – much of which can still be seen.

One of the key positions in the Dunkirk perimeter was the town of Bergues. Some seven miles directly south from the port itself, Bergues was, in 1940 at least, 'an old country town built on the side of a hill at the junction of three canals and was entirely surrounded by the 17th century ramparts which were pierced by four gates'.[79] The roads that passed through these formidable gateways were vital to both sides and for this reason they were heavily defended by the Allies.

One of the solid brick archways, the Porte de Cassel (or Cassel Gate), was defended in an unusual manner, having been blocked by a disabled Army bulldozer, the blade left facing the German advance. This was recounted by one of the first reporters into Bergues after its capture – John Fisher, *Life Magazine*'s Berlin correspondent who had been allowed to accompany German units to the outskirts of Dunkirk:

'Shortly before Bergues, last strong Dunkerque fortification, we had to leave our cars. Picking our way through a swamp, we stopped to watch German Stukas trying to force their way through a barrage of French anti-aircraft fire … Along railroad tracks, through a mine-infested wood, we entered Bergues in Indian file. Trucks, tanks, vehicles of all kind had been hastily pushed together in a futile effort to barricade the road. The town gate was blocked by a huge American caterpillar snow plough, behind which a French machine-gunner had left an unfinished meal.

'I squeezed past and entered a scene of complete ruin. For four days German Stukas and artillery had rained a shower of steel upon the town leaving no house untouched. Flames were still licking their way among the debris, while charred wood and burning cloth filled the air with stifling smoke …

'German shells were whistling overhead. And underneath these sounds I could hear the rapid staccato bark of German machine guns, answered by the slower *tak tak* of French gunners. To the north we could see the billowing smoke clouds of burning Dunkerque.'[80]

65

Porte De Bierne, Bergues

Battle Damaged Gateway

Despite a stout defence by both British and French troops, Bergues was entered by German troops on 2 June, the British defenders pulling back to positions along the canal in the town's north-western corner. The defence of the Dunkirk perimeter had, however, taken its toll on Bergues.

By daybreak on 1 June, for example, 'fires had taken hold near the church and town hall and whole rows of residential buildings were in flames. The heat was so intense that even the troops dug in around the ramparts were feeling its effects, while terrified horses galloped up and down the streets into which debris from burning buildings was falling.'[81]

For Captain W.R.S. Doll, the Medical Officer with the 1st Battalion The Loyal Regiment, his evacuation from Bergues was far from straight-forward: 'The town was so shattered that we were unable to recognise our way about. We made one false attempt to get out, being halted by a blown-up bridge, when to our delight we found a soldier who was apparently still on duty; he turned out to be a Royal Engineer who was dealing with the last bridge, and he redirected us to it. Once again we lost our way, and, following a dispatch rider, we came out near the crest of the hill well in sight of the enemy. We turned at full speed and tore back over heaps of bricks and rubble into the town.'[82]

Whilst Doll finally succeeded in escaping from the battered streets of Bergues, many of its residents had not, as the reporter John Wilson noted having clambered past the bulldozer blocking the Cassel Gate: 'As we walked through the streets I notice people here and there creeping out of their cellars. Two thousand had remained through the six-day bombardment. A French tank car exploded while nearby a horse leisurely grazed stray bits of grass surrounding a World War monument. Swallows were flying about the empty street looking for their homes.

'The war had swept across Bergues and in its wake left nothing but ruins. While the German advance was breaking French resistance barely a mile to the north, soldiers here were already emptying French warehouses … Allied trucks and motorbikes [were] already doing their bit for the German Army. Again I saw a litter of abandoned matériel, ping-pong sets and golf clubs among it.'[83]

Such was the scale of destruction wrought upon Bergues during May and June 1940 that some eighty per cent of its buildings had been damaged or destroyed by the end of Operation *Dynamo*. Even today, parts of the ramparts, such as the Porte de Bierne seen here, still have visible scars that stand testimony to the fighting in the Dunkirk perimeter.

Opposite: The Porte de Bierne at Bergues, with the repairs to a shell hole clearly visible. Above: A pair of photographs of Bergues taken by a German soldier after its capture, both of which show the scale of the damage inflicted on the town.

66

A Dunkirk Rifle

One of the Pieces of Equipment Left Behind

As soon as it became apparent that the British Expeditionary Force might have to be evacuated from the Continent it was understood that it would be impossible to recover the vast amount of equipment that had been sent to support the army in France. A meeting at the Quartermaster-General's Department, before the start of Operation *Dynamo* saw the evacuation would be 'on a scale unprecedented in the history of war'.[84]

Even at this preliminary stage, the difficulties that were likely to be experienced were understood, particularly if troops were to be lifted from beaches. This meant that any items that could not be carried by hand would have to be left behind – and of course such valuable war materiel as artillery, trucks and tanks, could not be allowed to fall into the hands of the enemy intact, and would have to be destroyed.

Orders to destroy, or render unserviceable, everything other than personal equipment were therefore issued to the troops. Dennis William Black of the Royal Army Service Corps recalled receiving those orders on 25 May when his company drove into Armentières: 'On arrival we were told to destroy our stores and equipment and all our vehicles, except one open black truck with a Lewis gun mounted on the back, and two staff cars. Then we had to proceed to Dunkirk as best as we could. Our rations were one small tin of bully beef and one packet of hard biscuits between two men ... We had to reach a river bridge before midnight on the 27th May because the bridge was being blown up by the Royal Engineers. We made this by a few minutes, and then we had to destroy our remaining vehicles, and proceed on foot to La Panne.'[85]

Main image: The Infantry and Small Arms School Corps Weapons Collection's Dunkirk rifle. Below: When the rifle was x-rayed, it was discovered that it was loaded.

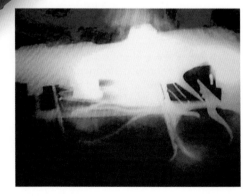

A tiny fraction of the huge losses suffered by the British at Dunkirk is the British .303 SMLE rifle seen here. It was discovered in 1999, buried at a depth of six feet in the sand below the low water mark just off the beach at Dunkirk.

When uncovered, and having been cleaned and conserved, it was discovered that the rifle was cocked and that the sights were set at 700 yards. Further, when subjected to x-ray examination, it was found that an unfired round was in the chamber with another two or three in the magazine. From this, notes the original caption, 'we may surmise that the soldier concerned was firing at aircraft. He was then either killed, wounded, or abandoned the weapon when embarking on a rescue craft.'

Arthur Joscelyne was a civilian aboard one of the 'Little Ships' – in his case, the Thames barge *Shannon*: 'The soldiers were not used to boats – and they all rushed to get aboard. We could have capsized at any moment. An officer stood up in the bows and got his revolver out. He said, 'I'll shoot the first man who makes a move before I give you permission to board – you will do it in an orderly manner!' He stood there with his revolver, while we got about fifty of them on board. They were in such a state that they just lay down anywhere. A couple of them threw their rifles overboard and said, 'We shan't want these anymore!'"[86]

One can only contemplate whether the rifle seen here was abandoned in such a manner. It is on display at the Infantry and Small Arms School Corps Weapons Collection at Warminster, an instructional collection that forms part of the British Army's Land Warfare Centre.

Right: It was not only small arms that were abandoned during the evacuation. Here a British 3.7-inch anti-aircraft gun is pictured by a German war photographer having been left behind on the seafront at Malo-les-Bains.

67

Blue Bird at Dunkirk

Little Ship Once Owned by
Land and Water Speed Record Holder Malcolm Campbell

Built in 1932 by J.N. Miller & Sons, Fife, the twin-screw schooner *Chico* was originally launched as *Frebelle III*. She was then sold to Sir Malcolm Campbell in 1933, the third of four motor yachts he was to own between the wars, each in turn called *Blue Bird*.

On 28 December 1939, *Blue Bird* was requisitioned for service with the Rear Admiral, Minelaying Squadron. She was fitted out with echo sounding gear at Gosport and in January 1940 was re-named *Chico*.

On 30 May 1940, *Chico*, commanded by Sub-Lieutenant J. Mason RNVR, left for Dunkirk where she embarked 217 troops before returning to Dover. On the 31st she ferried nearly 1,000 troops from the Dunkirk shore to ships, disembarking a further estimated 100 troops herself on her return to Dover. On 2 June, she was transferred to life-saving duties on Route X.

Colonel Harold Barnard TD, RA, was onboard *Chico* at Dunkirk. A famous yachtsman himself, Barnard later recalled the following: 'Conditions in and around the harbour were appalling and proved difficult enough even for experienced crews to navigate. The sea had turned to a black, treacly oily mixture; the air as dense and fume laden as a man could tolerate with difficulty.

'The harbour was full of sunken wrecks; the advancing Germans had got their range and shrapnel from shells was flying about. Stray tow ropes, the debris from vessels blown out of the water and reduced to pieces, fuel drums, floating human bodies and limbs, and innumerable discarded items of clothing including heavy great coats were all potential hazards. The boats themselves, jostled for position, were being over-run and occasionally overturned by too many eager evacuees who were sometimes just as much a danger to each other.'[87]

Opposite: The Dunkirk 'Little ship' *Chico* in Oban Bay. (Courtesy of The Carlisle Kid, www.geograph.org.uk)
Above: *Chico* pictured at Oban's North Pier. (Courtesy of The Carlisle Kid, www.geograph.org.uk)

One of many rescued by *Chico* was Fred Sherrington. Fred had joined the Territorial Army in 1939 and, in due course, was sent to France with the BEF. 'After being harried across France and Belgium,' recalls one his children, 'his motorised unit, part of the Lancashire Fusiliers, was ordered to support a defence of the Dunkirk perimeter by the Guards. His role was to ferry fuel and ammunition to Bren-carriers in a 3-ton lorry. Returning from one such duty, well into the evacuation of the beaches, his vehicle was mortar-bombed and destroyed on the coast road to the north-east of Dunkirk.

'Trying to walk, back to Dunkirk, he and his friend "Cooper" were forced onto the beach at La Panne by the attentions of the Germans. A motor boat was some way off the beach and my father and Cooper waded out but the motor boat sailed off leaving them up to their chins in the sea.

'Cooper could not swim and my father found himself supporting his friend. My father remembers being in the sea for hours until they were spotted by a "converted gentleman's yacht". By now, Cooper was unconscious and my father was unable to even raise a hand to lift himself from the sea. A deckhand hoisted him with a boathook under the collar!

'They were landed, twelve hours later, on the Isle of Sheppey. The boat still exists … and is called *Chico*.'[88]

German Propaganda Leaflet

Brought Home as a Souvenir of Operation Dynamo

The distribution of propaganda leaflets dates back before the First World War and they were first used in the Second World War by Britain, with the RAF dropping leaflets over the German port of Kiel in September 1939. Their value in affecting the attitude and morale of the enemy has always been questionable, though it was believed that they were most effective when the morale of the troops was low. This, no doubt, is what inspired the Germans to try and undermine the British troops as they sought shelter amongst the sand dunes at Bray and La Panne or queued patiently, if fearfully, along the beaches and the East Mole.

Certainly, the men of the BEF, in many cases, had not washed or eaten for some days and water was in short supply. They were also all too painfully aware that they had been forced to retreat and were facing the ignominy of defeat. Their morale should certainly have been at its lowest ebb, but the Germans had yet to learn of the Dunkirk spirit, and their leaflets made little impression upon the troops.

Apart from the example shown here, other leaflets were dropped within the perimeter, needling the men over the lack of RAF air cover and saying that the British generals had gone back to England and had abandoned them. Even if such observations had been true, and that was certainly the belief amongst some of the troops, did the Germans really expect the troops to surrender and become prisoners of war when there was a real prospect of being evacuated?

One of the leaflets read as follows: 'British soldiers! Germans around! You are encircled! German troops invaded Courtrai, Tournai, Valenciennes, Lillers … why do you fight further? Do you really believe the nonsense, that Germans kill their prisoners? Come and see yourselves the contrary! The match is finished. A fair enemy will be fairly treated.'

Thousands of the leaflets were dropped and could be seen blowing along the roads, amongst the dunes or across the open beaches. As for their true value, the leaflets were welcomed by the troops – as a souvenir that they could take home.

Right: An Allied solider examines a propaganda leaflet dropped by the Germans during Operation *Dynamo*.

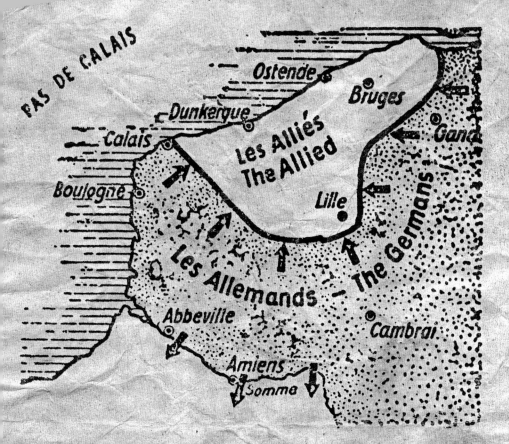

Camarades!

Telle est la situation!
En tout cas, la guerre est finie pour vous!
   Vos chefs vont s'enfuir par avion.
A bas les armes!

British Soldiers!

Look at this map: it gives your true situation!
Your troops are entirely surrounded —
   stop fighting!
Put down your arms!

69

Account by the Master of Tynwald

Reveals the Strain Imposed by Operation *Dynamo*

The strain placed on many of those involved in the evacuation from Dunkirk, in this case personnel from one of the rescue ships, is clearly illustrated in an account written by Chief Officer J.H. Whiteway of *Tynwald*. Formerly operated by the Isle of Man Steam Packet Co., *Tynwald* had initially sailed to Dunkirk under the command of her master, Captain W. Qualtborough, the orders to sail coming at 20.30 hours on 28 May.

'The ship arrived at 2.00am Weds 29 May after a passage uneventful except for the amount of traffic and the difficulty of identifying green lighted buoys from starboard lights,' wrote Whiteway.[89]

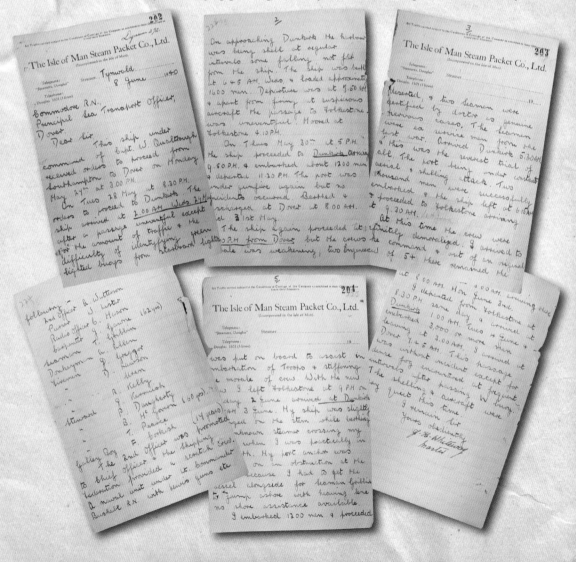

'On approaching
Dunkirk, the harbour was being
shell[ed] at regular intervals, some falling not far from
the ship. The ship was berthed at 6.45am Weds and loaded
approximately 1600 men. Departure was at 7.50am and apart from firing at suspicious
aircraft the passage to Folkestone was uneventful. Moored at Folkestone 4.10pm.

'On Thurs May 30th, at 5pm, the ship proceeded to Dunkirk, arriving 9.50pm and embarked
about 1200 men and departed at 11.20pm. The port was under gunfire again, but no incidents
occurred. Berthed and discharged at Dover at 8.00am Frid. 31st May.

'The ship again proceeded at 10.00pm from Dover, but the crew's morale was weakening,
two Engineers deserted and two seamen were certified by doctor as genuine nervous cases.
The seamen were servicemen from the last war.

'Arrive Dunkirk 5.30am, and this was the severest trial of all. The port was being under
constant aerial and shelling attack. Two thousand men were successfully embarked and the ship
left at 6.15am and proceeded to Folkestone, arriving at 9.30am 1st June.

'At this time the crew were definitely demoralized. I arrived to take command and out of an
original crew of 54 there remained [just 15] … The 2nd Officer was promoted to Chief Officer
and the Shipping Federation provided a scratch crew. A naval unit under Lt. Commander Bushell
RN with Lewis guns etc was put on board to assist in embarkation of troops and stiffening the
morale of crew.

'With the new crew I left Folkestone at 9pm on Sunday 2 June, arrived at Dunkirk 1.40am on
3 June … I embarked 1200 men and proceeded to Folkestone.'

Tynwald completed one further crossing to Dunkirk, embarking, Whiteway noted, '3,000 or more
men'. In total, she transported some 8,953 men, the largest total of any personnel vessel. It is also
stated that one in every fourteen of the troops landed in Britain during Operation *Dynamo* was
rescued by a vessel from the fleet of the Isle of Man Steam Packet Co.

Opposite: The account written by Chief Officer J.H. Whiteway. Above: The personnel vessel *Tynwald*
passes the wreck of her Steam Packet sister, *King Orry*, as she approaches Dunkirk on 29 May 1940.

70

German Soldier's Tug Photograph

Tug *Fossa* Pictured on the Beaches After the Evacuation

The steam tug *Challenge*, Object 39, was just one of a number of tugs that ventured across the Channel during Operation *Dynamo*. Another was *Fossa*, which would be, as we can see here, the subject of a number of photographs taken in the aftermath of the evacuation.

Built in 1929 by A. Hall in Aberdeen, *Fossa* was delivered to Gaselee & Son Ltd., London. She was requisitioned by the Admiralty on 3 October 1939. According to the historian Russell Plummer, *Fossa*, previously operated by Gaselee & Sons, towed a number of vessels across the Channel, including the ketch *Jeanette* with which *Fossa* then worked loading troops from the East Mole. When *Jeanette* developed a steering fault, *Fossa* herself went in, towing *Jeanette* and a naval cutter. *Fossa* then ran aground and cast off the tows, the men on board being transferred to another boat.

Fossa's master was Captain G. Finch. His entry for Dunkirk, presumably for the night of 1-2 June, reads as follows: '0001 Arrived Dunkirk, three hundred troops on to the *Fossa*. 0350 Outside the harbour entrance the *Fossa* grounded. The *MLC 21* unsuccessfully attempted to tow the tug off and then embarked about one hundred of the *Fossa*'s troops and crew and proceeded to Ramsgate.'[90]

Though efforts had been made to refloat *Fossa*, she is generally recorded as having been lost on 2 June. Lieutenant Ackroyd Norman Palliser Costobadie RN was the commander of the Dragonfly-class river gunboat HMS *Locust*. At 03.50 hours on 2 June, he noted that the 'tug *Fossa* signalled she was ashore and required assistance. In attempting to close, *Locust* took the ground but came off again, and I decided it was impracticable to close *Fossa*. A Motor Landing Craft was therefore hailed and brought alongside and her troops, 51 in number were transferred to *Locust*, and the M.L.C. was sent to rescue the crew of the Tug, and any troops she had on board.'[91]

Having been abandoned on the beach at Malo-les-Bains *Fossa* was later salvaged by Kriegsmarine personnel and allocated to the Port Commandant at Dunkirk. Her subsequent fate is not known.

Above:
The Tug *Fossa*, with a Thames
sailing barge beyond, lies stranded east of
Dunkirk. Note the two German soldiers pictured standing in front
of the bridge. Main image: The scene on the beach at Malo-les-Bains, near the
Malo Terminus Casino (visible on the far left), in the immediate aftermath of the evacuation. From
right to left, the ship wrecks are the tug *Fossa*, the steamship *Lorina*, and two Thames barges, *Aidie* and
Ethel Everard. The remains of an improvised pier can also be seen.

71

Ramsay's Signal to his Whole Command

'The Nation Looks To the Navy'

By the early hours of Sunday, 2 June 1940, it was becoming clear to Ramsay and his staff that Operation *Dynamo* was rapidly coming to a conclusion. Plans were made for what it was hoped would be the last night of sailings across the Channel.

NAVAL MESSAGE.

S. 1320d.

FROM:

V A DOVER

To:

DESTROYERS AND MINESWEEPER

THE FINAL EVACUATION IS STAGED FOR TONIGHT
AND THE NATION LOOKS TO THE NAVY TO 'SEE THIS THROUGH.
I WANT EVERY SHIP TO REPORT AS SOON AS POSSIBLE
WHETHER SHE IS FIT AND READY TO MEET THE CALL WHICH HAS
BEEN MADE ON OUR COURAGE AND ENDURANCE.
=1052

Main image: Rear Admiral W.F. Wake-Walker, CB, OBE's copy of Vice-Admiral Ramsay's 'The Nation Looks to the Navy' message. It is on display in the 'HMS – Hear My Story' exhibition which is situated in the Babcock Galleries at the National Museum of the Royal Navy in Portsmouth Historic Dockyard.

Right: Dunkirk fell to the Germans on 4 June 1940, the first German troops entering the town between 07.00 hours and 08.00 hours. Here some of the early occupiers are pictured on the beach beside a camouflaged dug-out with a Union Flag still flying. The wreck in the background is that of the French destroyer *L'Adroit*, which was bombed and sunk by German Heinkel He 111 bombers in shallow water off Dunkirk, at Malo-les-Bains, at 12.00 hours on 21 May 1940.

In his despatch, Vice-Admiral Ramsay wrote the following: 'Considerable doubt existed during the forenoon [of the 2nd] as to the numbers remaining to be evacuated in Dunkirk. It was thought that 2,000, plus the 4,000 rearguard British troops, might well be found in Dunkirk. The number of French troops remaining was increasing from the 25,000 quoted the previous evening to figures in the region of 50,000 to 60,000.

'The Rear Admiral, Dover, arrived back from the coast in a M.T.B. and during the forenoon a joint Naval and Military conference was held to devise a plan for the forthcoming night's evacuation. The fact that evacuation traffic was suspended in daylight hours enabled all transport resources to accumulate during the day and to be held available for a massed descent upon Dunkirk Harbour during the night.'

This plan provided for as many as 37,000 men to be evacuated, plus whoever the 'Little Ships' still making the journey might pick up. In addition, the French would use their vessels to lift troops from the beaches and the west pier of the outer harbour. This, Ramsay hoped, would finish the job.

At 10.52 hours on the morning of the 2nd, Ramsay sent the message seen here to his whole command: 'The final evacuation is staged for tonight, and the Nation looks to the Navy to see this through. I want every ship to report as soon as possible whether she is fit and ready to meet the call which has been made on our courage and endurance.'

At 17.00 hours that afternoon the massed armada of evacuation ships set off for Dunkirk. It consisted of thirteen personnel vessels, two large store carriers, eleven destroyers, five paddle minesweepers, nine fleet sweepers, one special service vessel, nine drifters, six skoots, two armed yachts, one gunboat, and a large number of tugs, lifeboats and the like. The smaller craft were either formed into organised tows or travelled under their own steam and at their own pace.

Generally speaking, the operation proceeded well. At 22.00 it was reported that loaded vessels were leaving Dunkirk. Then, at 23.30 hours, came the message, from the Senior Naval Officer Dunkirk, which everyone had been striving for: 'BEF evacuated.'

Despite such welcome news, the sheer number of French troops in and around Dunkirk suggested that *Dynamo* should continue. 'As a result of the night's operation ...,' wrote Ramsay, '[the French] Admiral Nord agreed that the operation should be considered as completed, observing that all ammunition at Dunkirk had been expended and that the numbers left behind were small consisting principally of non-combatant troops. This decision was agreed to by the French Admiralty at II.00, and the operation 'Dynamo' [was] terminated by Admiralty Message I423/4.' The last of the evacuation ships had sailed for Britain on the morning of 4 June 1940.

72

Safely Home Letter

‘The Evacuation from Dunkirk was Surely a Miracle’

In his official despatch written on 18 June 1940, Vice-Admiral Ramsay noted by the end of 4 June 1940, a total of 338,682 men had been disembarked at British ports. Such a figure had exceeded the expectations of most. Little wonder, therefore, that an editorial in *The New York Times* at the beginning of June declared, 'So long as the English tongue survives, the word Dunkirk will be spoken with reverence'.

The recently-elected Prime Minister, Winston Churchill, had words of warning in his speech to Parliament on 4 June: 'We must be very careful not to assign to this deliverance the attributes of a victory. Wars are not won by evacuations ... Our thankfulness at the escape of our Army and so many men, whose loved ones have passed through an agonising week, must not blind us to the fact that what has happened in France and Belgium is a colossal military disaster.'

For many who had been brought back from France, their evacuation was more than likely met with relief. H.R. Pratt Boorman was the proprietor of the *Kent Messenger*. Whilst *Dynamo* was underway, he chose to visit one of the Kent ports, Ramsgate, to observe the situation for himself: 'The front was crammed with people. They were watching the ... arrivals ... As they arrived they gave their names in, dropped their rifles, if they still had them, in a heap, and climbed into waiting buses or trains. They had been through hell. Tired, hungry and wet to the skin, they came in a steady stream for a week. Always cheerful – glad to be home again.'

For many of these men, their first action was to get a message off to friends or family. Corporal Frank Hurrell, serving with the 3rd Field Army Workshop, RAOC, recalls his return:

'When we got to Dover we were put into old customs sheds. In there were these ladies from the women's services – the Red Shield Club – all the various ladies' associations. I had no tunic – I'd lost it – and one of the elderly ladies took off her fur coat and put it round me whilst I sat down, and gave me a cup of tea. Then she produced a stamped envelope – stamped and sealed – and she said, "Right. Address it to go to your wife or whoever. Put the message on the back. Use it like a postcard – it will get there quicker."'

Signaller Alfred Baldwin, 65th Field Regiment Royal Artillery, had a similar experience during the train journey following his arrival in the UK: 'On the way we stopped somewhere around Redhill, at a small village station, and all the village ladies came out. They gave us each a postcard, on which we wrote our home address, and they posted them for us ... It just let our parents know that we were in England again. Back at home I think they realised that we'd been beaten, and we'd had a real hammering, but, nevertheless, they treated us as heroes, You'd have thought we'd won a battle instead of lost one.'

Opposite: The letter that one member of the 1/6th Battalion South Staffordshire Regiment wrote to his parents on 3 June 1940, following his evacuation from Dunkirk, informing them that he was safely 'back in England'. Right: Taken on 31 May 1940, this picture, captioned with the title 'Still Smiling', shows 'some of the BEF arriving back in London' following their evacuation from Dunkirk.

73

Newspaper Coverage

The *Daily Express'* Front Page, 31 May 1940

Through an inferno of bombs and shells the B.E.F. is crossing the Channel from Dunkirk – in history's strangest armada,' proclaimed the *Daily Express* on 31 May 1940. To fully appreciate what Operation *Dynamo* was achieving, the paper's editor, Arthur Christiansen, despatched one of his roving reporters, Hilde Marchant, to one of the South Coast ports.

Above: A copy of the *Daily Express* of Friday, 31 May 1940.

Described as 'a trail-blazing journalist', Marchant had already made a name for herself whilst reporting on the events of the Spanish Civil War. Her account on the progress of the evacuation was published on the *Express'* front page on 31 May:

'The Army is coming back from Belgium. It is a dirty, tired, hungry army. An army that has been shelled and bombed from three sides, and had to stagger backward into the sea to survive … There was a touch of glory about these returning men as I saw them tramping along a pier, still in formation, still with their rifles. For this army still had a grin on their oily, bearded faces.

'They were exhausted. They had not slept or eaten for days. Many tramped off in their stockinged feet. Others were in their shirt-sleeves. Many had wounds. Many had torn uniforms, and their tin hats blasted open like a metal cabbage …

'The men came ashore in heaps, scarcely able to stand. Yet they pulled themselves into straight lines and walked to the harbour gates. I saw one man with a handkerchief tied over his head wound. Another with a torn trouser-leg soaked in blood. Another with his arm tied up in a scarf. There had been no time for bandages.'

Despite the state many of the arrivals were in, Hilde noted that 'their eyes, bloodshot and half-closed, still mirrored the spirt and cause of their fight.' The editorial in that day's issue reinforced this message:

'No country has a right to ask for such heroism as our fighting men have freely given. The B.E.F. carry out the greatest rear-guard action ever fought in history. Brave men face an overwhelming mass of metal and machinery. Yet such is their valour that Hitler has to throw a million troops against them.

'When the battle is over, and our last soldiers reach these shores, they must be treated as a victorious army. Today there is no time for bands to play or for fighting men to make ceremonial marches. But if the circumstances were not so serious, if the men were not needed at other points for our defence, they would have deserved the same welcome as London gave the conquerors of the *Graf Spee.'*

Below: French and British troops on board ships berthing at Dover, 31 May 1940.

Rescuing the French Soldiers

Operation *Dynamo*'s Last Effort

Though by 3 June 1940, the newspapers could proudly boast that the BEF had been saved and that Operation *Dynamo* had been completed, there was still a large number of French troops in and around Dunkirk. These were Britain's allies and could not simply be abandoned, many had also stoutly defended their sector of the Dunkirk perimeter and the 'miracle' of Dunkirk was in part only made possible because of the sacrifices of the French troops under General Fagadle, and, in particular, those of General Barthélémy's rear guard. So, there was one more rescue effort to be made by the ships on the night of 3-4 June.

The actual final lift was to take place between 22.30 hours on the 3rd to 02.30 hours on the 4th. The destroyers, personnel ships, corvettes, skoots and paddle-steamers would operate from the East Mole. The ships were to use the full length of the Mole, being sent in and despatched as quickly as possible. There would be no time to hang around. The drifters and small craft were to go directly into Dunkirk harbour, and any other British craft were to use the West Mole (called the New Avant Port). French vessels, of an unknown number, were to pick up any soldiers they found at Malo-les-Bains beach, the Quai Félix Faure and the West Mole.

At Ramsay's disposal were nine passenger ferries, nine destroyers, four paddle minesweepers, seven fleet minesweepers, nine drifters and two corvettes. The Dragonfly-class river gunboat HMS *Locust* would also accompany the flotilla and would wait off Dunkirk where it would receive men ferried out to her from smaller vessels.

The French were to send craft to Dover during the day where they would be organized into flotillas for the crossing to Dunkirk for the night-time evacuation. In addition to this, four French torpedo boats were available.

This was enough shipping to embark the 30,000 French troops who the British Naval Liaison Officer at French Naval Headquarters had told Ramsay were at Dunkirk. Such a number was estimated to be around 5,000 more than could be taken from Dunkirk harbour, the rest would have to be lifted from Malo beach. In reality, there was around double that number of French soldiers in and around Dunkirk. Many would be left behind.

That last night of the evacuation from Dunkirk resulted in the rescue of a little less than the number hoped for, with just 26,175 Frenchmen being transported to England on that final effort.

Opposite: One of the many evacuated Allied soldiers, in this case a French infantryman (albeit wearing a British helmet), rests his weary feet during the journey across the Channel. Above: A wounded French soldier is disembarked at Dover having been successfully evacuated from Dunkirk.

A FRENCH VETERAN REMEMBERS

One of the 139,997 French soldiers brought to the United Kingdom during the Dunkirk evacuations was Paul Dervilers. Speaking in 1989, at which point he was 87-years-old, he recalled that his rescue had been possible through the work of the paddle steamer *Medway Queen*.

'I was on the beach walking up the coast towards Belgium', he remembered, 'when I saw some Englishmen getting into a dinghy and I joined ten of them who tried to get aboard'. Perhaps overloaded or damaged, the dinghy soon became waterlogged. 'We all began bailing hopelessly with our helmets,' continued Dervilers. 'Fortunately, half-way to an off-lying ship, we picked up an abandoned little skiff in good shape and we got into it. It was 23.00 when we climbed up the ladder of the *Medway Queen*.'

75

Aerial Combat Drawing

'Where was the RAF at Dunkirk?'

During and since Operation *Dynamo* there has been much discussion about the perceived absence of the RAF over the beaches in May and June 1940. In his autobiography *Enemy Coast Ahead*, Guy Gibson, for example, recounts how he was confronted by an Army officer who kept on repeating 'Where was the RAF at Dunkirk?' To some in the Army, the RAF became known as the 'Royal Absent Force'.

Ramsay himself went on to write: 'To both Naval and Military observers on the coast, the situation at times was extremely disheartening. Rightly or wrongly, full air protection was expected, but instead, for hours on end the ships off shore were subjected to a murderous hail of bombs and machine gun bullets.

'Required by their duty to remain offshore waiting for the troops, who themselves were unable to move down to the water for the same reason, it required the greatest determination and sense of duty, amounting in fact to heroism, on the part of the ships' and boats' crews, to enable them to complete their mission. In their reports, the Commanding Officers of many ships, while giving credit to the RAF personnel for gallantry in such combats as were observed from the ships, at the same time express their sense of disappointment and surprise at the seemingly puny efforts made to provide air protection during the height of this operation, though the gallantry of our out-numbered airmen was the admiration of all.'

Though many viewed the RAF's involvement as weak, ineffective or virtually non-existent, the reality, however, could not have been more different. The effectiveness of the RAF can be seen in that during Operation *Dynamo* the Luftwaffe was only able to seriously threaten the evacuation on two and a half days – 27 May, the afternoon of 29 May and 1 June. Even then, the war diary of the *Luftwaffe*'s II *Fliegerkorps* describes 27 May as having been a 'bad day'. By the end of the evacuation, every squadron in Fighter Command, except three in Scotland, had seen action at some time or other.

The truth was that, in many cases, the RAF was in operation many miles from Dunkirk – inland or along the coast – attempting to halt the German aerial attacks before they reached the beaches, or at such high altitudes that those on the ground would have found it hard to distinguish friend from foe. To see a Spitfire or Hurricane as low over, or close to, the beaches as depicted in the Ministry of Information drawing seen here would have been the exception rather than the rule.[92]

The historian and author Norman Franks once wrote that 'the Dunkirk operation severely tested Fighter Command – not only its fighter pilots, but also radar operators, controllers and ground crews. Fighter Command had been primarily designed for a defensive war; however, throughout the evacuation it was asked to operate many miles from its bases over sea and, at times, outside radar and radio range ... it was also the first time many senior airmen – squadron and flight commanders – saw action and discovered that their tactics were outdated.'[93]

Above: The Ministry
of Information drawing
depicting a Fighter Command
Spitfire shooting down a German bomber
over the beaches to the east of Dunkirk, with the port
itself in the distance. Below left: Some of the detail on the
drawing – a paddle steamer at work on one of the beaches. Below
right: Men queue on the beaches to be picked up by one of the armada of Little
Ships.

76

Headcorn Railway Station

An Improvised Feeding Centre for Evacuated Troops

Though the biggest challenge of Operation *Dynamo* had been to evacuate the troops from the beaches and port at Dunkirk, this was only part of the story. Once disembarked in the South Coast ports, the issue of how to move the men on to their final destinations remained. As the Director of Movements at the War Office, Major-General M.G. Holmes CBE, MC was ultimately responsible for solving this thorny issue.

'The classic example of improvised large-scale movement is, of course, Dunkirk,' he once recalled. 'The first warning of the impending evacuation from Dunkirk was given by my Directorate to the railways on the 21st May, 1940. Certain movements followed at once, but exceptionally heavy movements started on 27th May, and during the period 27th May to 4th June, 569 special trains were run from the South-East coast of England, conveying nearly three hundred thousand men'.[94]

As the disembarkation ports lay within its area, the burden fell chiefly on the Southern Railway. Unable to cope with the expected demand, Southern Railway sought the assistance of the other main line railway companies, requesting an additional 160 trains, each formed of eleven or twelve carriages.

By the time that Dynamo was terminated, 325 special trains had departed from Dover, eighty-two from Ramsgate, seventy-four from Margate, sixty-two from Folkestone, sixteen from Sheerness, fifteen from Harwich and one from Newhaven. On average, each train transported 546 men.

Below: Headcorn station today. (Courtesy of Stacey Harris; www.geograph.org.uk)

Two principal routes were used from the Kent coast. Trains from Dover and Folkestone travelling west via Ashford and Tonbridge to Redhill, whilst trains from Ramsgate, Margate and Sheerness were, for the most part, sent via Chatham, Kensington and on to Reading, thus by-passing Redhill. Such was the scale of the movements that Redhill alone served as the transit point for 351 troop trains and twenty-six ambulance trains.

To deal with the increase in traffic, as one account notes, a 'Movement Control function was established at the War Office with overall strategic responsibility for the operation. However, regional control was devolved to Movement Control Points at Redhill, Reading and Salisbury, which controlled all troop and ambulance train traffic. Landing and Distribution Control Centres were established at the ports involved, to organise the loading, dispatch and reporting of trains to the Movement Control Point at Redhill. Each train was allocated a specific code based on the station of departure and a sequence number …

'transport of the troops was only part of the requirement. Many of the men had not eaten for a number of days and official refreshment stops were set up at Headcorn, Paddock Wood and Faversham [railway stations]. However, because of the need to keep to a tight schedule, the trains were only permitted to stop for a maximum of 15 minutes. Additional ad hoc feeding stations are known to have been established at Tonbridge, Guildford, Woking, Basingstoke, Salisbury and Redhill.'[95]

Above: Refreshments being served to evacuated troops aboard a train standing at Headcorn Station, before continuing on its journey to London from the Kent coast, 31 May 1940. Left: Evacuated soldiers board a train to taken them inland away from the port where they landed.

77

Great Western Railway Account

Describes Service on Land and at Sea

Operating in a geographic area that bordered the Southern Railway, the Great Western Railway found its heavily committed to supporting the so-called 'Dynamo Specials', as the trains carrying the troops away from the disembarkation ports came to be known. Despite this, the greater part of the company's commemorative Dunkirk publication – seen here – is devoted to 'its effort at sea'.

As the book's author, Ashley Brown, notes, 'in the epic rescue of the British Expeditionary Force from the French coast in 1940, Great Western ships played an honourable part, the *St. David*, the *St. Andrew*, and the *St. Julien* as hospital ships, and the *St. Helier*, the *Roebuck*, and the *Sambur* as transports.'

Under the command of Captain W.Y. Larbalestier, *Roebuck* had sailed from Dover in the early hours of 31 May, her orders to make for La Panne. 'This was,' noted Brown, 'well off the beaten track of *Roebuck*, and Larbalestier had on board nothing in the way of a map or chart that was likely to be of the slightest service to him.' Despite an encounter with a destroyer which collided with the steamer's stern, causing minor damage, *Roebuck* eventually reached the evacuation beaches:

'The scene at La Panne was one that stamped itself on the memories of those who witnessed it,' continued Brown. 'On the beaches the waiting troops were to be seen stretching in broad, dark files to the sea. Beyond the water line the waves were breaking against an improvised jetty of abandoned tanks and lorries, and, round about, small boats were making daring, and for the most part, futile attempts to come to the jetty and load. For at La Panne on that day the Fates were not propitious.

'A freshening north-east breeze had sprung up and one after another the small craft, risking everything in the attempt to get the men from the beaches, were being smashed or capsized. To the Master, Officers and men of the *Roebuck*, the situation was maddening. "It as agonizing," Captain Larbalestier subsequently reported, "to watch the thousands of our men on the beaches and find we could not do anything."

'For an hour or so the *Roebuck* lay as close to the shore as she dared go, but she might as well have been in the middle of the Channel. Communication between the beaches and the ships for the moment was at a standstill. From this misery she was rescued by an order to proceed immediately to Dunkirk.'

Once the hospital ships *St. Julien* and *Paris* had left the port, Larbalestier guided his vessel in. At last, his ship's part in *Dynamo* could begin in earnest. In all, forty-seven stretcher cases, seventy-two wounded and 570 troops were embarked over improvised gangways before *Roebuck* sailed for home at 03.35 hours.

Opposite page: The cover of the Great Western Railway's Dunkirk commemorative booklet. Above: The Great Western's Hospital Ship *St David* at Dunkirk during Operation *Dynamo*. Note the East Mole in the foreground. Right: A view of one of one the improvised jetties, or piers, recalled by *Roebuck*'s crew. Note how an improvised hand rail has been laid out along the pier's length.

78

A Little Ship's Red Ensign

Flown on the Cutter *Polly* During Operation *Dynamo*

This Red Ensign, inscribed with the legend 'Dunkirk May-June 1940 "Polly"' along the hoist, is a reminder of one of the Little Ships participation in the evacuation.

The twenty-eight-foot cutter *Polly*, a sloop of wooden construction with an auxiliary Hyland four-cylinder engine, was built by Cockerel Cruisers, Rochester, in 1931. Originally owned by Leslie Knopp, *Polly* was sold to J.D. Shanahan of Seven Kings, Essex, from whom the vessel was called up for service in *Dynamo*. Solicitor George Saunders was among the crew of four, his job being to attend to the stubborn inboard engine — he was given the name 'Stinks' by his shipmates because of his interest in the engine.

Polly made two trips to the shores of France, during which it rescued thirty-eight British soldiers. Because of her wooden hull, after the evacuation *Polly* was used as a minesweeper until she was struck by another naval vessel, whilst tied up, and sunk.

Not all of the Little Ships sailed under a civilian crew. The launch *Silver Queen*, for example, was commanded by Able Seaman Patrick Sullivan when it left Sheerness on 29 May:

'We finally reached Dunkirk at 0800 on Thursday. We proceeded to ferry troops to HMS *Esk* and then the German artillery started shelling us, we carried on and after we had been working for about two hours, the planes came over and started to bomb us, one coming so close, it lifted us out of the water (roughly 25' off the starboard beam).

'We managed to take about 1,000 troops to the big ships, and then on our 10th or 11th trip, we had about 100 French soldiers on board, took them to a Trawler, who told us to go to Dunkirk harbour for another ship. We got there but found no ship, so we decided to come home. We had no charts or compass, but trusted to our sense of direction. Halfway over we found a soldier's field compass and used that.

'Then we sighted land, and thinking it was Ramsgate or some other Port, we turned towards it, and got about half a mile off, when the Germans opened fire, we then discovered it was Calais. They pounded away at us with six batteries for roughly 20 minutes, one round hitting us in the stern and another on the starboard bow. The *Yser*, in company with us, was also hit and she started to draw water badly. She had a Verey's Light pistol and fired it, whereupon a Destroyer came up and covered us.

'We reached Ramsgate at 2100, managed to tie up and disembark the troops, then she was slowly sinking. We lost everything we set out with'.

Opposite: *Polly*'s Red Ensign. (Courtesy of Alexander Historical Auctions; www.historyauctioneer.com) Below: *Polly* (circled) was one of the Little Ships that featured on a set of sixteen stamps issued by the Republic of Palau, an island nation in the Pacific.

79

La Place de Minck Information Panel

Dunkirk is Badly Damaged

Located near the bottom of Dunkirk harbour, the information panel at La Place de Minck points out that, somewhat predictably, 'the port and surrounding areas were particularly targeted' by the enemy during the course of the evacuation.

On his arrival at Dunkirk, Captain William Tennant RN noted how the Luftwaffe appeared to be 'chiefly occupied in wrecking Dunkirk and the port. It was quite out of the question to use the harbour at all, and my first reaction was that evacuation would have to be done from the beaches. It soon became obvious, however, that they were not including the pier in their attentions. At times they were held off by a fine morning mist which sometimes persisted until afternoon. At times, when the wind was favourable, a heavy pall of smoke from burning oil tanks, to the westward, largely obscured the pier.'

Commander Hector Richardson, who served as the Senior Naval Officer at Bray, also recalled the efforts of the Luftwaffe in his subsequent report: 'When being bombed in daylight and at night it is apparently the Army training for the men to lie over on their faces in a huddled heap and to await the completion of the air raid. I consider that if one lies over on one's face during an air raid, one gets the impression that the bombs when falling with very horrid shrieking noises are each and all coming to land right in the small of one's back.

'There is little doubt that the Army were considerably cowed by the bombing and I do feel that this form of inactivity during a raid is psychologically bad. I would have thought it better that the men be trained to stand up and take cover and loose off their rifles and anyhow look at the bomber, especially by day. It appeared to us obvious which aircraft was going to be anywhere near us and which was going to be miles away, while to watch the Army lying down with their faces to the ground with the bombs shrieking, one could see that they were going through a tricky time by being in such a position. I saw no sign, except in one very isolated case, of any of the Naval ratings being at all genuinely upset by the bombing. Machine-gunning, though, was quite embarrassing.'

Approximately 1,000 civilians in Dunkirk and the surrounding suburbs lost their lives during the evacuation.

Left: Some of Dunkirk's residents pictured leaving the town during Operation *Dynamo*. Opposite: The information panel at La Place de Minck.

6

1940-1945
L'esprit de Dunkerque
2015

La place du Minck sous le feu ennemi

Durant la bataille de Dunkerque, le port et ses abords sont particulièrement visés. Ici la place du Minck est assombrie sous les fumées des incendies.

The « Place du Minck »
under enemy fire

During the Battle of Dunkirk, the port and surrounding areas were particularly targeted. Here the « Place du Minck » is darkened from the smoke from the fires.

Place du Minck onder
vijandelijk vuur

Tijdens de slag om Duinkerke liggen vooral de haven en de omringende wijken onder vuur. Hier wordt de place du Minck verduisterd door de rook van de branden.

Ville de Dunkerque

80

Souvenir German Photographs

Vivid Evidence of the Equipment Left Behind

That the British Army suffered almost debilitating losses in terms of equipment and materiel during Operation *Dynamo* is beyond dispute. Amongst the items left behind in France, much of it to be re-used by the German Army, were 2,472 guns, 63,879 vehicles, 20,548 motorcycles, 76,097 tons of ammunition and 416,940 tons of assorted stores, whilst 162,000 tons of petrol and fuel were destroyed. Only thirteen light tanks and nine cruiser tanks were brought back to the UK from a total of 445.

The historian Basil Liddell Hart once wrote of the situation thus: 'Although the British Army … escaped from the trap in France, it was in no state to defend England [*sic*]. It had left most of its weapons behind, and the stores at home were almost empty. In the following months Britain's small and scantily-armed forces faced the magnificently equipped army that had conquered France with only a strip of water between them.'

The historian Sean Longden described the scene that met the eyes of the retreating soldiers as they approached Dunkirk: 'Burnt out trucks littered the verges on the outskirts. The entire town was surrounded by the wreckage of vehicles. It seemed bizarre to the arriving soldiers that drivers, who had so lovingly tended these vehicles, should now be destroying them. Soldiers stood in front of trucks smashing windscreens with rifle-butts, as others removed vital engine parts and threw them into ditches and canals. Lorries stood with their bonnets open, tangled wires, holed sumps spilling oil onto the road.

'Everywhere were cars with smashed windscreens and slashed tyres. Motorcycles, their petrol tanks cracked open by axe blows, lay in heaps alongside twisted bicycles. The ground was

---

Main image: A number of abandoned British Mk.VI Light Tanks, and a lone Universal Carrier, on the beach between Malo-les-Bains and Dunkirk pictured surrounded by German troops immediately after the end of *Dynamo*. The wreck in the background is, once again, that of the French destroyer *L'Adroit*.

littered with the remains of smashed car batteries abandoned on the roadsides along with the sledgehammers that had destroyed them. One soldier saw an officer seated upon a packing crate. The forlorn man was holding his head in his hands, unable to watch the destruction. The soldier realised it was his own brigade commander. Utterly dejected, the brigadier could not watch as his driver battered his staff car with a pick-axe.

'Vehicles were not the only victims of this destruction. Like hideous metal trees, the ruptured barrels of wrecked artillery pieces pointed skywards, as if taunting the natural world with man's ability to wreak havoc.'[96]

One officer from the British 1st Division's 3rd Brigade recorded the scene at Bray Dunes: 'The scenery provided ... a picture of the abomination of desolation ... vehicles abandoned, many of them charred relics of twisted metal on the roadside and overturned in the ditches. Light tanks and guns poking up out of the [water]. Horses dead or dying from want of water. Here and there civilian or French Army corpses lying in the open. An unforgettable spectacle.'[97] The pictures seen here, all taken by members of the German armed forces, stand testimony to these descriptions.

Top right: German personnel examine a pile of equipment that was left on the beaches to the east of Dunkirk. Middle right: A view of the French Navy's *Chasseur 9* stranded on the beach at Malo-les-Bains at the end of Operation *Dynamo*. Note the Universal Carrier in the foreground. In similar photographs it is possible to see the Regina Hotel and the Guynemer statue in the background. Bottom right: A further view of Mk.VI Light Tanks on the beach between Malo-les-Bains and Dunkirk, the tanks proving a centre of attention for camera-wielding German servicemen.

81

Battle Damage on the Church of Saint-Éloi

Scene of a British Bayonet Charge

As the evacuation reached its conclusion, the Germans closed in on the few troops left as a rear guard. Bregues was taken and the Germans pressed on north towards Dunkirk, capturing Fort Vallères. They were temporarily halted by the French General Fagalde, who scraped together every man he could find to mount a counter-attack.

During the night of 2/3 June, Fagalde's men slipped northwards towards Dunkirk and the much hoped-for evacuation. General George von Kuechler's Eighteenth Army did not press hard upon the retreating French, having been ordered to conduct a 'systematic attack' so as not to incur unnecessary casualties now that the battle was all-but won. There was no interference either by the Luftwaffe, for which Dunkirk was no longer of any interest. Göring's men were preparing themselves for the next big objective, the assault on Paris, the first big raid upon the French capital being planned for the next day.

Though the Germans only moved slowly the shrinking Dunkirk perimeter was clearly crumbling and, according to one account, news was received that some of the enemy had managed to infiltrate into the centre of the town.[98] Knowing that this could spell the end of the evacuation, several hundred Guards decided to drive the Germans out of Dunkirk and launched a bayonet charge. Taken by surprise, the Germans were driven back for three-quarters of a mile as far as the Church of Saint-Éloi and Place de Jean Bart in the very heart of Dunkirk.

One of those who took part in the charge was Edgar Rabberts of the 5th Battalion, Northamptonshire Regiment: 'I only used my bayonet on one man. My short legs found it hard to keep up with the Guardsmen and I just used the bayonet on the first German I came across. I got him right in the middle. There was no messing with those big bayonets. When you jab one in and twist it, they don't live. The charge was a complete success, as the Germans obviously hadn't expected anything of this sort to happen. We managed to clear the whole area which got everybody in the docks a little bit of breathing space.'[99]

The end, though, was not delayed for long. At 03.40 hours on the morning of 4 June HMS *Shikari* pulled away from Dunkirk in the final act of Operation *Dynamo*.

Opposite: Evidence of the bitter fighting in 1940 can be seen on the walls of the Church of Saint-Éloi in Rue Clemenceau, Dunkirk. Above: The Church of Saint-Éloi is next to the Place Jean Bart – a view of which, including abandoned Allied military vehicles and equipment, is shown here. Note the statue to Jean Bart, which can still be seen in the square to this day, in the centre of the picture. The Church of Saint-Éloi is a short distance from where the photographer was standing.

82

A German Officer's Report

❦

"This Place of Terror"

For days the BEF and various French units in and around the French port of Dunkirk had endured bombardment from land and air. That was until the last ship had departed and the fighting ceased. Then all was indeed quiet on that part of the Western Front, to the amazement of a young German officer, *Oberleutnant* Heinrich Braumann of Sturmgeschütz-Abteilung 210.

In a report he subsequently submitted to his commanding officer, Braumann vividly described the scenes and the sounds on the morning of 4 June: 'On the beaches of Bray-Bains, the guns

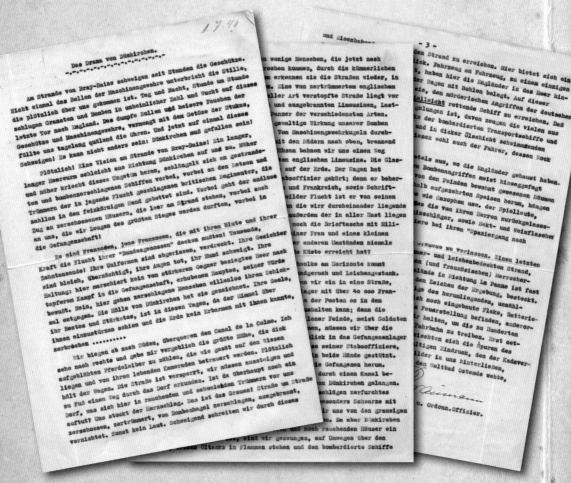

Above: The report written by *Oberleutnant* Braumann which he submitted to his commanding officer.

Above: To accompany his account of the events during the capture of Dunkirk, *Oberleutnant* Braumann attached a number of photographs to his report. He captioned this image, one of the first that he had taken during his unit's approach to Dunkirk, as 'Countless destroyed English vehicles clog the village streets'.

and cannons have been absolutely quiet for hours. Not even the loud noise of the machine-guns disturbs the total silence that has now come over us. Day and night, hour after hour, grenades and bombs had fallen in frightening numbers and with brutal force on this last gateway to England. The muffled rumbling and throaty growling of artillery and machine-guns mixed with the roars of the Stukas had painfully filled our ears for days on end. And now – nothing but silence! Surely, this cannot mean anything other than Dunkirk must have fallen![1]

'Suddenly! A vision on the beaches of Bray-Bains! A very long, worm-like line of soldiers is creeping slowly in our direction, from Dunkirk. This monster creeps closer and closer, it passes by the stranded and bombarded shipwrecks, past the countless left-overs and debris embedded in the fine sands after having been left behind in a mad rush by the defeated British regiments. Past walks this endless train of soldiers; past the crumbled houses, which now stand empty on the beach; also past us, who have been allowed to be witnesses of the biggest victory. Past they go, into captivity!

'These are the French soldiers, those Frenchman, who had to cover their fellow-Frenchmen at the cost of their lives and with their blood. Thousands; tens of thousands! Their uniforms torn to pieces, covered with dirt. Their faces look pale, tired from lack of sleep, their eyes seem dead and their mouth are shut in silence.

'We are turning south and cross the "Canal de la Colme" … Suddenly the vehicle stops. The road is closed. We must get out of the vehicle and explore a way through the village by foot. Is there a village left at all, we wonder, based on what we see in front of us, in between burnt wreckage and smouldering debris. We catch our breath. This is bloodcurdling! Street after street smashed up, broken, destroyed by the bombs, burnt out, demolished. Not a single sound can be heard …

'In front of us lies a blocked street, densely covered with demolished French and English munitions of various kind, shot and burned out cars, vans, radio- and equipment vehicles, in-between a range of tanks … Painstakingly we cleave ourselves a way through.

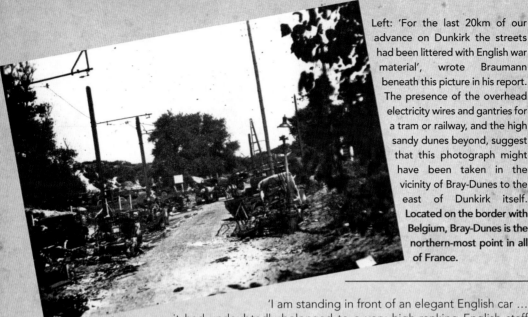

Left: 'For the last 20km of our advance on Dunkirk the streets had been littered with English war material', wrote Braumann beneath this picture in his report. The presence of the overhead electricity wires and gantries for a tram or railway, and the high sandy dunes beyond, suggest that this photograph might have been taken in the vicinity of Bray-Dunes to the east of Dunkirk itself. **Located on the border with Belgium, Bray-Dunes is the northern-most point in all of France.**

'I am standing in front of an elegant English car ... it had undoubtedly belonged to a very high-ranking English staff officer, because it still contained maps of Belgium and France, as well as recently-written orders. In a hurried escape, the vehicle had been deserted by its passengers; scattered clothes and equipment stand witness to that – especially the uniform of the driver left behind in all haste, which still contained his wallet with military pass and the worn-out picture of a woman and a little girl, which under different circumstances, he would have certainly never left behind. I wonder whether he ever made it to the English coast.

'We continue our journey. The smoke cloud on the horizon is getting closer and closer but with it also comes the smell of burnt material and of dead bodies. We walk past a machine-gun post and turn into a street, on both sides of which sits a prison camp with over 40,000 French soldiers. It is incomprehensible how the watch post can bear the overwhelming cadaver stench, because the whole street is covered in dead bodies of the enemy; most of the soldiers were from the French colonies. In order to move forward we must drive over the dead bodies. We also throw a quick glance into the camp and we could see a French General surrounded by his staff officers. He sits at the table crestfallen, holding his head with both hands. The captured lie around exhausted, motionless and apathetic.

'On the other side, the prison camp borders a canal. We cross it and reach the city boundaries of Dunkirk. Here spreads out a battlefield furrowed by shells and bombs. Amongst the dead the black soldiers with their long bush knifes particularly stand out. Appalled we turn away from

Right: The mass of French PoWs encountered by *Oberleutnant* Braumann.

Right: *Oberleutnant* Braumann took this picture of a member of his unit in turn photographing the debris on the beach at Dunkirk. His original caption stated: 'Overlooking the destroyed fleet at Dunkirk; in the background is the burning harbour.'

those horrible images in order to go through Dunkirk. However, given that Dunkirk itself is a vast expanse of rubble full of barricades and collapsed, still burning, houses, we are forced to make a detour, past the oil tanks that are still smouldering and harbour full of bombed ships, to reach the beach.

'At the beach we are granted an unprecedented sight: the English have aligned vehicle after vehicle to form a single runway, by driving them into the sea and placing planks over their roofs. On this wobbly bridge they tried to escape the murderous attacks by the Stukas and to maybe reach salvation on a ship. The many wrecks of bombarded transport ships protruding from the sea and the myriad of dead bodies floating in thick oil slick and washed ashore are proof that not many fugitives have been successful. Was the driver whose uniform we found earlier in the car was amongst them?

'We encounter a terrible mess in the hotels where the English have dwelt. Most roofs have been blown away by the German bomb blasts. In the few intact rooms where our enemies had lived we still find the remains of recently half-eaten meals; the walls are decorated with musical instruments like saxophones etc. of the bandsmen; we are greeted by tail wagging dogs left behind by their masters; hockey and tennis rackets as well as champagne and wine bottles left behind testify what kind of "promenade to Berlin" the English officers had planned to lead.

'We are keen to leave this place of terror. We are throwing a last glance back on the beach covered with debris and cadavers ... Only east of La Panne, in the direction of Nieuport, do the traces of the battlefield wear off. But the enduring impression left by the stench of death and by the horrible images we have seen, cannot be erased even by the fresh north wind that we breathe in the famous Spa Ostende.'

Left: Braumann's photograph of the scene on a sector of the beach.

83

Minister of Shipping's Broadcast

Remembering the Role of the Merchant Navy

While much of the glory surrounding the evacuation of the BEF has gone to the civilians who crewed the Little Ships, there were other civilians who played an equally important part, the men of the Merchant Navy. Their contribution was acknowledged in a broadcast by the Right Honourable Ronald Cross, the Minister of Shipping in Churchill's coalition government, on 6 June 1940.

The broadcast painted a realistic, if inspirational, picture of the contribution the Merchant seamen and their ships. 'The men on these ships worked till they dropped,' Cross said. 'Without sleep, often without proper meals, for days on end they passed to and fro across the Channel, under attack by enemy batteries on the coast, by enemy aircraft with bombs and machine-guns, by enemy submarines and motor torpedo boats.'

He made particular reference to deck and engine room officers who responded to the appeal for experienced men: 'Engineers are now almost all engaged on work of national importance,

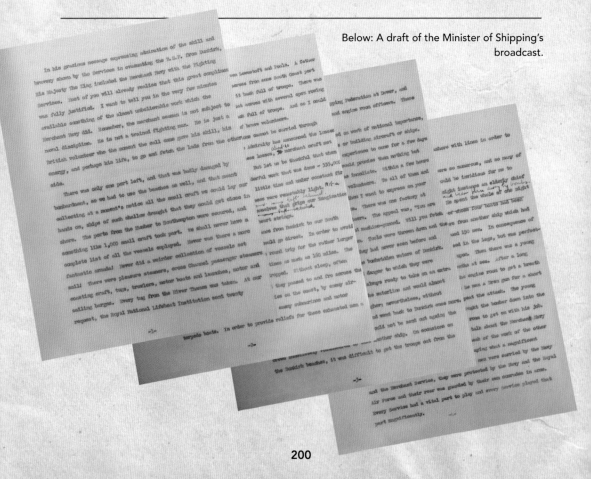

Below: A draft of the Minister of Shipping's broadcast.

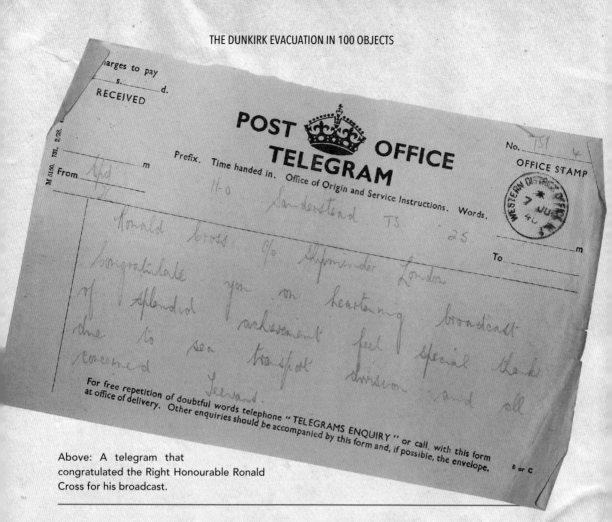

Above: A telegram that
congratulated the Right Honourable Ronald
Cross for his broadcast.

if not at sea they are making munitions or building aircraft or ship. We appealed to engineers with seagoing experience to come for a few days to help in evacuating the troops. We could promise them nothing but fatigue and danger, but the response was immediate. Within a few hours, we had the received the names of about 350 volunteers ... There was one factory at Ramsgate, on which we called for volunteers. The appeal was "You are going to hell. You will be bombed and machine-gunned. Will you fetch back the lads?" There was no hesitation. Tools were thrown down and the engineers went straight down to ships they had never seen before and within twenty minutes had sailed for the bomb ridden waters of Dunkirk.'

Cross then gave one or two general examples: 'In spite of the constant strain and anger to which they were subjected, the officers and crews were always ready to take an extra risk. One ship was badly holed above the waterline and would almost certainly have sunk had the sea got rougher; nevertheless, without hesitation, the crew turned her round and went back to Dunkirk once more. Two others were so badly damaged they could not be sent out again; the crews immediately volunteered to take another ship. On occasions on the Dunkirk beaches it was difficult to get the troops out from the shore to ships; Merchant seamen swam ashore with lines in order to help the troops to embark.'

He concluded by mentioning the fact that Operation *Dynamo* was, as he put it a 'concerted' affair. 'The men were carried by the Navy and the Merchant service, they were protected by the Navy and the Royal Air Force and their rear was guarded by their own comrades in arms. Every service had a vital part to play and every Service played that part magnificently.' Thus the 'spirit of Dunkirk' was born.

84

The Minister of Shipping's Letter

Sent to the Master of the SS *Killarney*

As well as delivering a broadcast on the BBC to the nation, and the wider world, thanking the Merchant Navy and civilian ships and boats for their efforts in Operation *Dynamo*, the Right Honourable Richard Cross, Minister of Shipping, sent letters of gratitude to the individual ships. One such letter was sent to the master of the SS *Killarney*, a 2,050 ton, Liverpool-registered passenger ship that had been requisitioned and employed by the Admiralty as a troopship.

Captain R. Hughes
Master of the "Killarney"

17th June, 1940.

I write on behalf of the Government to convey to you and to the members of your ship's Company the gratitude and admiration felt for the help freely given and the courage and endurance displayed by you all in the evacuation from Dunkirk.

This operation, in which the Merchant Navy joined as partner of the fighting services, was carried to a successful conclusion in the face of difficulties never before experienced in war.

I am proud to pay tribute to your share and that of your Ship's Company in a great and humane adventure destined to occupy a place of honour in the pages of history.

(signed) RONALD CROSS
Minister of Shipping.

SEAL.

Killarney received orders to sail for Dunkirk during the late afternoon, or early evening, of 28 May, arriving off Dunkirk at around 05.00 hours the next morning. Whilst waiting outside the port *Killarney* was not far from *Mona's Queen* when the latter was mined and sunk. Finally, however, *Killarney* tied up against the East Mole and took off some 900 men – who were, according to one account, 'squeezed into every available foot of space below and on the open decks'.

Approximately one hour later *Killarney* cast off and headed back to the UK along Route Z. This took her south past Gravelines where she was spotted by three German-controlled coastal artillery batteries mounting 5.9-inch guns. The first volley of three shells fell short of the port side by

Left: A contemporary copy of the letter sent by the Minister of Shipping to the Master of the SS *Killarney*. A former Irish Sea ferry, *Killarney* was the oldest of the larger personnel vessels to participate in Operation *Dynamo*.

the bridge, and for the next forty minutes she had to endure a persistent bombardment.

As soon as the shelling began, the Master, Captain R. Hughes, immediately made smoke and swung *Killarney* round to face to the north-west presenting the much smaller target of her stern to the enemy. Then, at full-speed *Killarney* sped away, making smoke and zig-zagging. The Germans fired ninety shells, and one struck the after end of the boat-deck. Eight men, one of whom was a member of the ship's crew (Able Seaman Arthur Gott who is buried in Dover (St. James) Cemetery), were killed and thirty injured.

Killarney finally steamed out of range of the German guns, but she was not out of danger, for she was then attacked by a German bomber. But a Spitfire appeared and the German aircraft was sent crashing into the sea 600 yards off *Killarney*'s port. Then three other RAF planes flew overhead, signalling for Captain Hughes to change course.

Hughes obliged and the reason for the change in direction soon became clear – ahead was a flimsy-looking raft with one French officer and two Belgian soldiers perilously trying to escape across the Channel. When they were picked up it was found that the raft had been knocked together with a door and some wood. They had with them two tins of biscuits, six demijohns of wine and a very old-looking bicycle lashed down on the makeshift deck!

The crew of *Killarney* was willing to take on board the biscuits and the wine, but persuaded the newcomers that there really was no room for the ancient bike. All safely on board, *Killarney* made its way back to Dover.[100]

Above: The wording of the Minister of Shipping's letter was used to create this plaque that hung in the saloon entrance of *St Seiriol*, another of the many vessels that participated in the evacuation – and which also features in Object 85. Below: An aerial photograph of evacuation vessels of all shapes and sizes off Dunkirk during Operation *Dynamo*. Note the superstructure of a merchant ship in the foreground.

85

The Major's Mistake

The Story of One Merchant Navy Seaman

When the Minister of Shipping, the Right Honourable Richard Cross, delivered his broadcast on the BBC on 6 June, he singled out a few individuals. This included 'a Deal boatman who took his motor boat across with several open rowing boats in tow and brought them all back full of troops.' Mr Cross then referred to a man he described as an elderly chief officer, well past the prime of life: 'Three of the four boats on his ship had been blown away by bombs. He spent the whole of one night in the remaining boat, picking up survivors from another ship which had been sunk. He and his boat's crew rescued 150 men. He became partially paralysed in the legs, but was perfectly ready to make another trip if called upon.'

From Sir James German

Tribute to a Brave Boatman

Sir,—Those who were privileged to hear the Minister of Shipping broadcast last week were thrilled with the wonderful story of the Deal boatman who, with his motor-boat, towed rowing boats to and from Dunkirk, saving numbers of lives, until his legs became paralysed through exhaustion.

Some friends are anxious to pay a tribute to him and relieve any anxiety during his illness. If any of your readers would like to make a contribution I will see that it reaches him.—Yours, &c., JAS. GERMAN.

This story inspired the nation, people demanding to know who this tough old man was. Major Sir James German, for example, wrote an open letter to the *Western Mail* suggesting that he himself and others would like to make a financial contribution to the unnamed Deal boatmen to help him after suffering the paralysis in his legs. Unfortunately, Major German misheard, or became 'muddled', not realising that these were two separate people.

The Ministry of Shipping wrote to the Major explaining that the sailor who had suffered so severely in helping rescue the soldiers was not from Deal but was in fact Joseph McNamee, the Chief Officer of *St. Seriol* who, an employee of the Liverpool & North Wales Steamship Co., lived in Liverpool. Following his experiences at Dunkirk, McNamee had 'been in bed for several days wrapped in cotton wool and was still under doctor's orders, though making progress, and was at last able to hobble down to the offices of the company for which he worked'. The Deal boatman, meanwhile, was perfectly well and had not suffered at all from his efforts.

In a letter dated 24 June 1940, Captain Norman Moore of the Shipping Federation recalled his encounter with McNamee, on *St. Seiriol* at Dover, on 30 May: 'I became fully aware of the prevailing conditions and the arduous tasks the men concerned with the evacuation were

performing. The *St. Seiriol*, a small, unarmed coasting passenger vessel, had already made several trips to Dunkirk in circumstances, which as you know, would be most trying to crews of warships.

'I found most of the crew in a very fatigued and nervous state … Mr McNamee would have to be relieved immediately as he was suffering from a form of nervous paralysis from the waist downwards, which rendered him incapable of standing for any length of time. The [ship's] Doctor then informed me that in his opinion Mr McNamee's condition was entirely due to the excellent work he had been performing during the night. Apparently, the *St. Seiriol* had made contact with a vessel which was sinking from the result of enemy action and went to the rescue.

'Unfortunately, only one of the *St. Seiriol's* four lifeboats remained at the time. This was quickly launched and Mr McNamee took charge of it. Throughout the period, in which a large number of men were rescued, he worked untiringly, directing the operations and assisting in pulling the survivors from the water into the lifeboat which, apart from anything else would impose a great physical strain on him. To sum up, I quote the actual words used by the Doctor … "That man has guts".'

Opposite top: A cutting from the *Western Mail* showing Major Sir James German's letter. Above: A view of the ship on which Joseph McNamee served during *Dynamo* – the Training Ship *St Seiriol*. Despite working off both the beaches and from the port itself, *St Seiriol* is only listed as having evacuated 672 men. This is almost certainly the total for her first crossing, on the 27th, a latter one on the 28th/29th having been seemingly overlooked. Below: A few of the 'Little Ships' under tow to Dunkirk – note the warship in the background. Close examination of this image suggests that it depicts the skoot *Hilda* that is seen here towing a collection of smaller boats. *Hilda* had been lying at Poole when she was taken over by a crew commanded by Lieutenant A. Gray RN. During her three trips she transported 835 men.

An Improvised Rear Admiral's Flag

Raised on MTB 102, a Dunkirk Survivor

MTB 102 was designed by Commander Peter Du Cane CBE, Managing Director of Vosper Ltd., in 1936. She was completed and launched in 1937, and ran trials on the Solent. When she was purchased by the Admiralty and brought into service she was named MTB 102 (the 100 prefix denoting a prototype vessel, making her the first MTB of the modern era). Her captain during Operation *Dynamo* was Lieutenant C.W.S. Dreyer.

The boat reached Dunkirk for the first time on 30 May, undertaking a variety of tasks, but she earned her place in history when Rear Admiral Wake-Walker, the senior naval officer afloat off Dunkirk, began using her to help organise the huge

numbers of vessels moving in and out of the evacuation areas. Wake-Walker's flag had been raised in the destroyer HMS *Keith*, with MTB 102 being employed by the admiral to move rapidly between the other ships. However, on 1 June, *Keith* was repeatedly bombed, and was abandoned before she sank. So Wake-Walker transferred to MTB 102, but his flag was left behind on the sinking destroyer.

By this stage of the operation, daylight evacuations had been cancelled due to heavy losses from German aircraft and artillery, and so, after seeing all the ships away that day, Wake-Walker returned to Dover in MTB 102. Upon its arrival, Dawkins, the boat's torpedo operator, decided that an admiral's flag should fly on Wake-Walker's tiny flag-ship. Dawkins took a rather smart new dishcloth which had a red stripe down the centre. To this, he added another red stripe to create a St George's Cross. Dawkins then painted two red blobs on the inner quarters, to complete a rear admiral's flag. Another crew member sewed on a length of rope so that it could be hoisted. The new flag was ready to be presented to Wake-Walker. He declared that he was delighted with the flag and agreed that it should be flown from MTB 102's mast.

The motor boat returned to Dunkirk to continue its vital task, speeding in and out of the harbour and along the evacuation beaches, passing messages and offering help and guidance amid the wrecked ships and the mass of boats moving to and from the beaches and the larger warships anchored out at sea.

Its final trip was on the last night of the evacuation, 3-4 June. This was to carry off the remaining senior officers. It meant that as well as a rear admiral, MTB 102 was able to claim the distinction of transporting the Senior Naval Officer ashore at Dunkirk, Captain William Tennant, as well as two generals, one of whom was Major General H.R.L.G Alexander who commanded the rear-guard of the BEF. As soon as 102 was clear of Dunkirk harbour, the officers went below. There they were offered sandwiches and between them drank a bottle of whiskey. The officers, who had been on duty almost continuously for days on end, were soon sound asleep and were not disturbed until the tiny flagship pulled into Dover Harbour.

Opposite page: Rear Admiral Wake-Walker's improvised flag that flew from MTB 102 during Operation *Dynamo*. Both the flag and MTB 102 have survived, being in the care of the MTB 102 Trust. For more information on the Trust's work, how to support 102, or even where she can be seen, please visit: www.mtb102.com. (Courtesy of Richard Basey/MTB 102 Trust) **Main image: MTB 102 underway.** (Courtesy of Lisa Larsson, www.flickr.com)

87

Fortunino Matania's Depiction of Dunkirk

'The Brilliant Rescue of the BEF'

During and immediately after the evacuation from Dunkirk, newspapers and magazines fueled an almost insatiable demand for images and pictures of the events surrounding Operation *Dynamo*. To quench this hunger, a number of artists created their own interpretation of scenes on the opposite side of the Channel – often drawing their inspiration from first-hand accounts. One of these individuals was the artist Fortunino Matania.

Born in Naples, the son of artist Eduardo Matania, Fortunino studied at his father's studio, designing a soap advertisement at the age of 9 and exhibiting his first work at Naples Academy at just 11. By the end of the First World War, his work had ensured that he was a household name. 'Accuracy and authenticity were the key characteristics of his work,' notes one account, 'which had an almost photographic realism. He took particular pains to recreate uniforms, costume and weaponry correctly. During the Great War, he visited the Front on several occasions to gather material first-hand. At other times, he took eyewitness accounts from wounded men in hospital.

'His illustrations for *The Sphere* covered all aspects of the war, from battle charges and entertainment behind the lines to munitions work on the home front. More emotive subjects include his famous *Goodbye, Old Man*, a heart-wrenching picture of a gunner bidding farewell to his wounded horse. Originally painted for the Blue Cross Fund, it was distributed in several versions by *The Sphere*. As busy as ever in his later years, he was still producing illustrations with his customary skill and accuracy during the Second World War.'[101]

Fortunino's depiction of the scene at Dunkirk, seen here, appeared on the front of *The Sphere* on 8 June 1940. Under the illustration, *The Sphere*, which described itself as 'the Empire's illustrated weekly', ran with the following editorial:

'Chronicled in this issue is the great event of the last ten days – the withdrawal of the British Expeditionary Force from the triangle into which it had retreated after the defection of the Belgian Army. Behind a "Corunna" line, held apparently by the aristocracy of the British Army at any cost to itself, the remainder of the Expeditionary Force was enabled to reach the sandy beaches of Dunkerque. Spreading out for some seven miles in each direction, the forces were able to avoid the heavy casualties which at' first seemed inevitable. The shallowness of the waters there made it necessary to employ light draught vessels, 222 naval and no less than 665 civil, including famous river paddle steamers.'

THE BRILLIANT RESCUE OF THE B.E.F. The Scene on the Beaches at Dunkerque

A colourised version of Fortunino Matania's drawing of the Dunkirk evacuation, entitled 'The Brilliant Rescue of the BEF'.

88

'The Curlew At Dunkirk'

A Broadcast on the BBC's *London Calling* Radio Programme

At least four vessels named *Curlew* are believed to have participated in Operation *Dynamo*. One of these was a twin-screw motor yacht built by Vosper & Co. at Portsmouth in 1929 and which was owned by Sir R. Holme. In the days after the evacuation one of *Curlew*'s crew recorded a broadcast of his involvement in the evacuation for the BBC's *London Calling* radio programme:

'So far as I was concerned, the affair started about midnight on Wednesday, May 29, when I received a telephone message asking me to get out the motor yacht *Curlew*. She had been laid up in a shed all winter on the upper Thames at Maidenhead. She's thirty-seven feet long and fitted with two engines of thirty horse-power each.'[102]

It was from Ramsgate that *Curlew* finally set out across the Channel on 1 June. 'My crew consisted of a friend of mine as engineer and two young Naval seamen lent to me as deckhands and to work the Bren gun, but soon after sailing I learned that neither of these two young seamen had had much sea experience, neither had either of them ever fired a Bren gun! My engineer, however, was a magnificent help. We sailed in company with another fine little motor yacht, the *Cairngorm*, which was in the charge of a Lieut.-Commander R.N.R.'

Eventually *Curlew* arrived off Dunkirk, as the unidentified speaker recalled: 'As we made our way up the channel leading to the port we could see the flashes from the artillery holding the coast and a vast pall of smoke hung over the town itself. One of our destroyers, apparently damaged, was tied up to the mole and firing furiously, but our orders were not to stop at the harbour but to push on past it to a beach about two miles to the east. The whole place was littered with wrecks, and the only vessels under way were *Cairngorm* and ourselves. *Cairngorm* sounded her way carefully towards the beach, and we were able to follow in her wake at full speed. So we drew up to her and both of us went alongside a pair of Thames barges, the *Glenway* and the *Lark*, which were aground and apparently deserted. But they made good landing-stages for us, though we could not tie up because of the danger of grounding on the ebbing tide. Had we touched bottom we probably could not have got off again.'

'We were at the beach from 4.40 until 6.25 and this was the most uncomfortable hour and three-quarters that I have ever spent, because until we had got our troops aboard it was a question of putting our engines astern and ahead, astern and ahead, so as to hold the boat just clear of the sand. Meanwhile, we were bombed at intervals, and so were the troops waiting on the beach.

'It had been our plan, had there been any destroyers or other large vessels nearby, to put our troops aboard them and go ashore for more, but the only other vessel was the destroyer that was firing shells from her berth at the mole. A small steamer anchored off-shore was bombed just as we were trying to make up our minds whether there was anybody aboard her. So we had no option but to make off for Ramsgate with our load of troops.' In all, *Curlew* rescued twenty-four men.

Right: German soldiers pose by a Thames barge, similar to that described by the crew member from *Curlew*, after the end of the evacuation. The name on the stern indicates that this is *Barbara Jean*, a sailing barge of 144 tons. She was run ashore on 1 June by her skipper, C. Webb, after her cargo of food, water and ammunition had been unloaded. Some accounts state that she was then set on fire, though this image suggests that this was not the case.

89

The Sinking of Bourrasque

The French Navy at Dunkirk

It was not just in defending Dunkirk and holding the perimeter that French forces played a vital part in Operation *Dynamo* – they were also involved in the evacuation itself. French ships, for example, began to arrive on 30 May, when some fifteen vessels reached Dunkirk, including the destroyers *Foudroyant* and *Branlebas* and the torpedo boats *Bourrasque*, *Bouclier* and *Siroco*.

Those French warships and other vessels wearing the French flag that were employed evacuating troops from Dunkirk harbour, and, on the last three nights, from the beaches, included nine destroyers, four Avisos (a medium-sized warship designed for colonial service), three fast motor boats, three sub chasers, six auxiliary minesweepers, and three or four small cargo vessels that, having transported munitions to Dunkirk, returned with troops. At the same time a total of 167 trawlers, drifters and small craft were brought together from ports and harbours along the French coast between Boulogne and Cherbourg, and employed mainly off the beaches. In addition, the French mail packets *Cote*

d'Argent, Cote d'Azur, Newhaven and
Rouen were transferred to the command of the Vice-
Admiral, Dover, and were employed as required side by side with the
British personnel vessels.

The French vessels were not only used for evacuating troops. The two small cruisers Leopard and Epervier, for example, provided covering patrols offshore, whilst the four avisos, when not employed evacuating men, acted as escorts along 'X' Route. In all, a total of 20,525 French troops were landed in the UK from French vessels, whilst an unknown number was transported direct to other French ports.

The French Navy's participation in Dynamo was a costly one. Three of the destroyers were sunk (Bourrasque and Foudroyant by bomb, Sirocco by torpedo), whilst Cyclone was badly damaged by a torpedo and Mistral by bomb. Two trawlers, one drifter and fifteen other small craft were also lost. The packet Cote d'Azur was sunk by bombs before her first trip.

Like Cote d'Azur, Bourrasque's participation in Operation Dynamo was also brief. She left Dunkirk at 15.30 hours on the 30th from the Quai Félix Faure with more than 600 men (and one woman). Around thirty minutes later, as she was passing Nieuport, she came under fire from a German battery. The French boat moved as far over as she could to the edge of the swept channel but when the torpedo boat was about five miles north of Nieuport she was shook by a violent explosion, followed by a second even-more violent one. The ship came to a halt, badly damaged.

Understandably, there was a degree of panic amongst the passengers, who believed the ship was sinking. Even though the captain had not declared that the warship should be abandoned, the ship's boats were lowered but so many crowded into them that they sank. Others jumped into the water. Bourrasque was indeed sinking, having either struck a mine or been hit by artillery, sources disagree on this point, and broke in two. The destroyer Branlebas, with 300 troops on board, was astern of Bourrasque and picked up 100 survivors. The Admiralty drifter Yorkshire Lass, and the armed trawler HMT Ut Prosim also helped. Remarkably, at 05.30 hours on the 31st, the Pickfords' boat Bat picked up another fifteen survivors from the partially submerged wreck. They were found completely naked and covered in oil.

Opposite: The French destroyer Bourrasque sinking on 30 May 1940. Above: A view of the French Navy's Chasseur 9 stranded on the beach at Malo-les-Bains at the end of Operation Dynamo.

90

'Home From Dunkirk'

J.B. Priestley's Description of an 'Excursion to Hell'

For many organisations, both civil and military, the implementation of Operation *Dynamo* placed a great strain on their personnel and resources. This was no different for the British Red Cross. When war was declared in September 1939 the British Red Cross Society and the Order of St John joined forces. As they had done in the First World War, they formed the Joint War Organisation ensuring activities were carried out efficiently and under the protection of the red cross emblem.

Writing in 1940, Field Marshal Sir Philip Chetwode BT, GCB, OM, explained a little of the impact on the organisation of which he was Chairman: 'As the wounded poured back from Dunkirk, the call for help was sent to the Red Cross and St. John War Organisation.. It was answered at once.

'By day and by night, trained stretcher-bearers, nurses and detachments of the two Bodies, without stopping, worked on piers, on quay-sides, in docksheds, and in schools hastily converted into reception and dressing stations for the wounded. . Skilfully, carefully, they moved the wounded from the ships. They dressed their wounds, easing pain and suffering, they conveyed them to trains and hospitals, and in a hundred helpful ways gave their services to the authorities.

'From the hospitals which received the wounded there came urgent appeals for supplies and comforts to supplement official issues. In the space of a few days the War Organisation dispatched over £30,000 worth of Red Cross stores in answer to these demands. That the calls could be so readily met is due to the wide .response of the public to the War Organisation's appeal for funds, and we are very grateful.'

HOME from DUNKIRK

WITH AN INTRODUCTION BY
J. B. PRIESTLEY

In aid of the
BRITISH RED CROSS and **St. JOHN**

Third Printing

46 memorable photographs

1s. NET

JOHN MURRAY

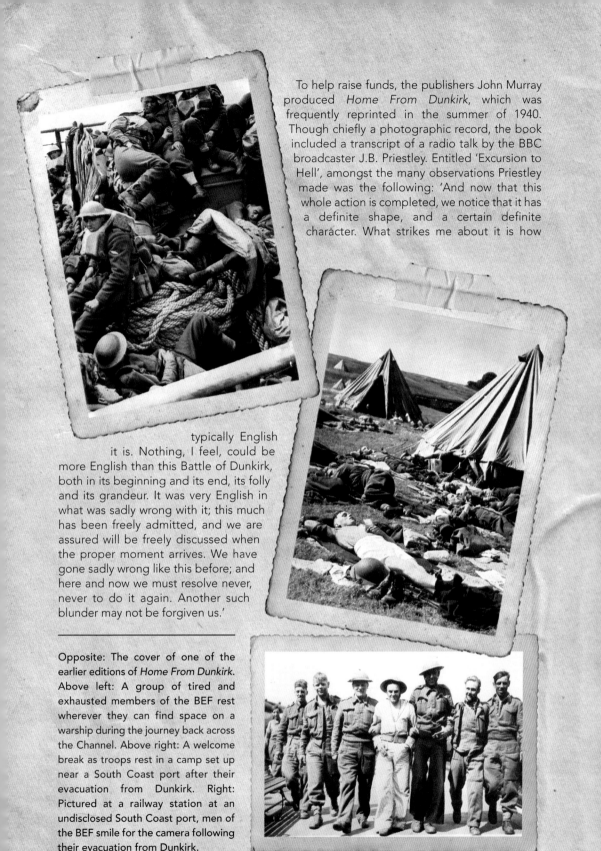

To help raise funds, the publishers John Murray produced *Home From Dunkirk*, which was frequently reprinted in the summer of 1940. Though chiefly a photographic record, the book included a transcript of a radio talk by the BBC broadcaster J.B. Priestley. Entitled 'Excursion to Hell', amongst the many observations Priestley made was the following: 'And now that this whole action is completed, we notice that it has a definite shape, and a certain definite character. What strikes me about it is how typically English it is. Nothing, I feel, could be more English than this Battle of Dunkirk, both in its beginning and its end, its folly and its grandeur. It was very English in what was sadly wrong with it; this much has been freely admitted, and we are assured will be freely discussed when the proper moment arrives. We have gone sadly wrong like this before; and here and now we must resolve never, never to do it again. Another such blunder may not be forgiven us.'

Opposite: The cover of one of the earlier editions of *Home From Dunkirk*. Above left: A group of tired and exhausted members of the BEF rest wherever they can find space on a warship during the journey back across the Channel. Above right: A welcome break as troops rest in a camp set up near a South Coast port after their evacuation from Dunkirk. Right: Pictured at a railway station at an undisclosed South Coast port, men of the BEF smile for the camera following their evacuation from Dunkirk.

THE LORD GOD ALMIGHTY and the LAMB are the light of it

CARITAS

For behold I create new

heavens and a new earth

Wherefore take unto you the whole

armour of GOD

91

Operation Dynamo's First Memorial

Stained-Glass Window in Little Missenden Church, Buckinghamshire

Right in the centre of the Buckinghamshire village of Little Missenden is the parish church of St. John the Baptist. Nestled in the Chiltern Hills, the church has Anglo-Saxon origins. The chancel dates back to the 13th century, whilst the North chapel was added in the 14th century and the porch the following century. It is in the Lady Chapel, however, that part of the church's Dunkirk link can be found for it is there that a stained-glass window remembering the evacuation in 1940 can be seen. Designed by G.E.R. Smith, and crafted by A.K. Nicholson, the window, depicting scenes from both Dunkirk and the Battle of Britain, was unveiled on 22 May 1941.

'The Bishop of Oxford, Dr Kirk, unveiled in the parish church of Little Missenden, Bucks, last evening a stained-glass window to commemorate the completion of 50 years' service in the county of the Bishop of Buckingham, the Right Rev. P.H. Eliot, and dedicated a pair of churchyard gates and tower doors to commemorate the deliverance of the B.E.F. from Dunkirk. This is believed to be the first Dunkirk memorial in this country. Doors, windows, and gates are the gifts of Mr. P.W. Hett, of Chesham Bois. The window has been inserted in the fourteenth-century twin light in the north wall of the Lady Chapel.'[103]

A CALIFORNIAN LINK

Other Dunkirk memorials reported on by *The Times* during the Second World War involved an unusual object once displayed in Pasadena, California. The following description was published in the paper on 26 May 1942:

'There may be a Dunkirk British soldier somewhere today who might be interested to know that he and his greenish oilskin jerkin are held in remembrance in Pasadena, California. During that evacuation a contingent of British troops marched past a French (or Belgian) lady and her husband, who were fleeing to the sea. The husband, all out, lay by the roadside. One of the soldiers spread his jerkin over him. Those fugitives reached America at last: the man succumbed; but months later his widow came to Pasadena, bringing that greenish oil-skin. She gave it to the British War Relief (where it now hangs) as her tribute not to that one soldier alone who, passing by, had cared for her husband, but to him and all his comrades in the British Army.' One can only wonder what became of that leather jerkin?

Opposite: The stained-glass window remembering the Dunkirk evacuation in St. John the Baptist, Little Missenden. (Courtesy of Rob Farrow; www.geograph.org.uk)

Dunkirk Propaganda Tour

Painting of Fire Float Massey Shaw in Action

To Jackson-Lee High School.   " Dunkirk June 1940 ".   Rudolf Haybrook /43.

From the moment Winston Churchill came to power in May 1940 the United States was central to his strategy. His aim was to use all possible means, including propaganda if necessary, to persuade Americans to enter the war. In the summer of 1941, the Ministry of Information was reorganised, following which its American operations were revitalised. One outcome of this was the despatch to the US of a collection of artworks completed by personnel serving in the Auxiliary Fire Service.

The idea of sending an exhibition of artworks by auxiliary firemen had first been suggested by Major F.W. Jackson DSO, Officer Commanding London Fire Services. The tour would both support the UK's propaganda campaign in America and act as a fundraiser, with half of the proceeds of any sales going to the Firemen's Benevolent Fund.

A total of 107 works by twenty-two firemen were selected by Sir Kenneth Clark, director of the National Gallery, London; Sir Walter W. Russell, R.A., keeper of the Royal Academy; and J.B. Mason, former curator of the Tate Gallery, London. The exhibition was sponsored by the British government, under the auspices of the British Library of Information, and by Mayor F.H. LaGuardia of New York.

Before leaving for America, the works were exhibited at the Central School of Arts and Crafts in London in March 1941. It was also decided that three firemen would accompany the works: Rudolph Haybrook, Daniel Ivall and Clarence Palmer. As a result of the bombing in the Blitz, the pictures left the UK much later than the three firemen.

The paintings, noted LaGuardia at the time, 'are not the result of weeks of studio work in the peace and quiet of a pre-war era. Rather are they the result of experiences undergone, horrors and trials bravely faced by sensitive men and women, capable not only of hard, physical labor in defense of their country, but of instant, creative effort, which will record for posterity actual scenes as the artists saw them.'

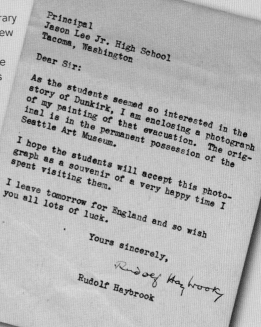

Principal
Jason Lee Jr. High School
Tacoma, Washington

Dear Sir:

As the students seemed so interested in the story of Dunkirk, I am enclosing a photograph of my painting of that evacuation. The original is in the permanent possession of the Seattle Art Museum.

I hope the students will accept this photograph as a souvenir of a very happy time I spent visiting them.

I leave tomorrow for England and so wish you all lots of luck.

Yours sincerely,

Rudolf Haybrook

After the public airing in Washington, the exhibition continued to museums in Canada, then returned to the United States for further viewings. One of Haybrook's paintings that went on the tour was his depiction of the fire float *Massey Shaw* in action during Operation *Dynamo* (see object 44), a scene which he entitled 'Dunkirk in Flames 1940'.

One Portland newspaper noted how Haybrook had been 'a soldier in the last World War at 16. In post war years he won fame as a portrait artist. When war was declared, he joined the Auxiliary Fire Services, and was one of the men who crossed to Dunkirk on the London Fire Boat *Massey Shaw*, and helped to rescue hundreds of men from that hellish beach.'

Haybrook was well placed to inform the American audiences of the events of May and June 1940. One reporter in Oregon wrote that Haybrook 'was the guest speaker at a Clatskanie High School assembly last night. During the 45-minute address everyone was held spellbound as Mr. Haybrook told the thrilling story of the Dunkirk evacuation.'

Rudolf Haybrook's original painting of *Massey Shaw* returning from Dunkirk is believed to reside in a gallery in Seattle.

Opposite: A photograph of Rudolf Haybrook's painting of *Massey Shaw* off Dunkirk during the evacuation. This signed photograph was presented by Haybrook to the Jason Lee Jr High School in Tacoma. Note the smoke from the burning oil tanks in the background. Above: The covering letter Haybrook sent with the photograph of his painting to the Principal of the Jason Lee Jr High School. Right: Auxiliary Fireman Rudolph Haybrook at work in a bomb-damaged street in London in the months after his return from Dunkirk.

Dunkirk Movie Poster

Film Released in 1958

Premiered in London on 20 March 1958, the film *Dunkirk* had an all-star cast that included Richard Attenborough, John Mills and Bernard Lee. The script was based on two novels relating to Operation *Dynamo* – Elleston Trevor's *The Big Pick-Up* and Lieutenant Colonel Ewan Hunter's and Major J.S. Bradford's *Dunkirk*.

The film approaches the events of the evacuation through the eyes of three individuals. Bernard Lee (who later played M in the Bond films) stars as a cynical journalist, John Mills plays a resourceful army corporal, whilst Richard Attenborough is an English factory owner making a handsome living off the Army by manufacturing belt buckles. A review of the film in *The Times* the day after its release gave a brief summary of the story:

'In war the difference between an Army in retreat and a rabble lies in the discipline that is maintained within the smallest units. If disintegration is to be avoided, the weakest link must hold. So long as it adheres to this theme, the British film *Dunkirk* … achieves continuity and purpose. Corporal Binns (Mr. John Mills) is cut off from his company in the early days of the Allied retreat and finds himself, by virtue of his two stripes, in charge of a handful of men who look to him for guidance. Thus leadership is thrust upon him. Bewildered, without any clear purpose, and with but little faith in his own abilities, he sets out indomitably on the long road that is to lead him to Dunkirk, and finally to England. Here, at least, are the seeds of a moving, and even a heroic, narrative.

'The problems which confronted the producer, Sir Michael Balcon, when he set out to make this story must have been formidable … He had to make a film with a factual climax involving a scattered retreat of hundreds of thousands of men while harassed by a remorseless enemy – their deployment along 20 miles of open beach under merciless attack from the air; and their final rescue and return to England with the aid of the Royal Navy and innumerable small boats. His technical assets for telling such a story were limited, and the only possible solution to his many problems lay in a closely-knit screenplay of the highest quality: expert direction, particularly in the specialized field of handling large crowd scenes; and, in its final composition, a finished film which could be assembled with unflagging tempo.'

The beach scenes were filmed at Camber Sands in East Sussex, where as many as 2,000 extras were employed to play the part of the BEF, whilst the streets and harbour of nearby Rye were adapted to represent the port of Dunkirk. Many of the buildings that appear in the film, including Rye's church and some of the warehouses, still exist.

The film's director, Leslie Norman, later recalled: '*Dunkirk* was bloody difficult to make from a logistics point of view. Yet it was made for £400,000 and came in under budget … I was the council school boy who became a major in the war, and that had a lot to do with the way I felt about Dunkirk. I didn't think that Dunkirk was a defeat; I always thought it was a very gallant effort but not a victory.'

The film, which was made with the cooperation of the Royal Navy, the French Navy and the Admiralty, was the second most popular production at the British box office in 1958.

Opposite: A promotional poster for the film *Dunkirk*. (Courtesy of Tony Matthews) Below: British soldiers wade out into the surf at Camber Sands during the filming of *Dunkirk* in May 1957.

94

The Dunkirk Medal

For Service during Operation *Dynamo*

Just seven days after Winston Churchill's speech in the House of Commons, in which he described Operation *Dynamo* as 'a miracle of deliverance, achieved by valour, by perseverance, by perfect discipline, by faultless service, by resource, by skill, by unconquerable fidelity', the subject of recognising the actions of those involved was first discussed in the same building.

During a debate in 11 June 1940, Mr Ellis Smith, the MP for Stoke-on-Trent, 'asked the Prime Minister whether he will consider awarding a special British medal to all men and women who went to the assistance of Belgium by land, air and sea and who also took part in the Dunkirk evacuation; and, if so, whether the medal will be presented to British, French and Belgian allied men?' In reply, the Lord Privy Seal, Mr Attlee, stated that 'the question of instituting a British medal for war service will be considered in due course. Awards of decorations and medals for gallantry and for good service are already made from time to time and special services rendered since the invasion of Belgium will be dealt with in accordance with the usual practice.'

There was little discussion on the subject during the remainder of the war. It was on 22 July 1946, that questions were again asked about a specific Dunkirk medal. On this occasion it was the MP for Gravesend, Mr Garry Allingham, who raised the topic. He 'asked the Prime Minister whether he will arrange for a special medal to be struck, similar to the Mons Medal of the 1914–18 war, to commemorate the action of men who fought through the Dunkirk campaign'.

The then Prime Minster, Clement Attlee, replied thus: 'The 1939–45 Star is granted to men who took part in the operations in France and Belgium between 10th May and 19th June, 1940, and there is no time qualification. These men will also qualify for the War Medal. It is not proposed to recommend the institution of any further general award for service in these operations.'

Allingham was not prepared to leave the matter at that: 'Does not the Prime Minister realise that these men did make a distinct and distinctive contribution to the war effort, and that, just as the Mons effort was recognised, it would give great satisfaction to these particular men if their effort was recognised?'

I do recognise that a great many men in various theatres gave distinctive service,' continued Attlee. 'The whole matter is one of great difficulty, and I do not think we should carry it any further by trying to draw parallels between other wars.'

Though a separate medal for involvement at Dunkirk was not issued by the Committee on the Grant of Honours, Decorations and Medals in 1946, a concession was made in that service in Operation *Dynamo* was recognised by waiving, for those involved, the eligibility criteria for the 1939-1945 Star.

It was in 1948 that the Dunkirk Commemorative Medal, which is also referred to as the Dunkirk Star, was established by the French Government, under the patronage of the town of Dunkirk. In 1970 authority was given by Her Majesty the Queen for the medal to be awarded to British personnel who served in operations at Dunkirk in 1940.

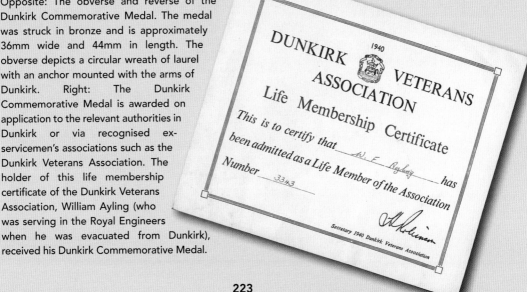

Opposite: The obverse and reverse of the Dunkirk Commemorative Medal. The medal was struck in bronze and is approximately 36mm wide and 44mm in length. The obverse depicts a circular wreath of laurel with an anchor mounted with the arms of Dunkirk. Right: The Dunkirk Commemorative Medal is awarded on application to the relevant authorities in Dunkirk or via recognised ex-servicemen's associations such as the Dunkirk Veterans Association. The holder of this life membership certificate of the Dunkirk Veterans Association, William Ayling (who was serving in the Royal Engineers when he was evacuated from Dunkirk), received his Dunkirk Commemorative Medal.

DUNKIRK VETERANS ASSOCIATION
1940
Life Membership Certificate
This is to certify that W. E. Ayling has been admitted as a Life Member of the Association
Number 3343
Secretary 1940 Dunkirk Veterans Association

95

The Dunkirk Veterans' Memorial

Unveiled by Major-General John Carpenter CB, MBE

Located on Dover's seafront, by Waterloo Crescent, the Dunkirk Veterans' Memorial commemorates all those involved in Operation *Dynamo*.

The memorial takes the form of a cairn with a bronze figure on one side disembarking from a boat. On the opposite side of the cairn is a plaque which bears the following inscription: 'During the period May 10th to 1st June 1940, 202,306 British, Commonwealth and Allied troops were evacuated to Dover. This memorial not only pays tribute to the bravery and discipline of the servicemen, but to the courage of the crews of the armada of Little Ships which assisted, and the people of the Port of Dover who received them.'[104]

The memorial was unveiled by Major-General John Carpenter, the then national president of the Dunkirk Veterans' Association, on Saturday, 16 August 1975 – the 35th anniversary of the evacuation. On behalf of the town, Dover's Mayor, George Ruck, laid a wreath and a flypast salute was made by an Air Sea Rescue helicopter from RAF Manston.

Born in Exeter on 21 June 1921, Victor Harry John Carpenter had been educated mainly at Army and local schools. After Sandhurst, he was commissioned into the Royal Army Service Corps and, when the Second World War broke out, was sent to France with 522 Company RASC, part of 50th (Northumbrian) Infantry Division.

Carpenter's platoon had been tasked with supplying 'the infantry and divisional artillery with ammunition, but when the Germans, who had air superiority, cut the rail lines of communication, Carpenter and his men were reduced to scavenging for ammunition; sometimes this involved unloading one end of a train while the other end was on fire and exploding.'[105]

At dawn on 31 May, still three weeks short of his 19th birthday and by his own admission a very green subaltern second-lieutenant, Carpenter found himself, along with other members of his platoon, on the beach at Bray Dunes, six miles east of Dunkirk. Speaking on the occasion of the 60th anniversary of the evacuation, he gave the following account of his escape:

'I can remember the evacuation vividly. We were in the dunes; all our heavy equipment was destroyed and as it got light I looked out to sea. There was not a ship to be seen.

'When eventually we saw ships on the horizon, I knew I had to get out to them because they couldn't get too close to the shore. Then I spotted a lifeboat drifting. I waded out to it with some of my men and we dragged it ashore. We managed to cram 60 people into it.

'We rowed around two miles to a Dutch coaster which was under machine-gun fire from bombers. Eventually we made it to Ramsgate and I think if so many soldiers had not been pulled off the beaches, Hitler might have invaded us that summer.'

In recognition of his services to the Dunkirk veterans and liaison with the Belgian authorities, he was appointed Commander of the Order of Leopold II by the King of the Belgians in 1992.

Opposite page: The Dunkirk Veterans' Memorial near Dover's Waterloo Crescent. Right: Men of the BEF at Dover after their evacuation from Dunkirk. One soldier assists a wounded comrade who walks with the aid of a stick. The soldier second from the left has been identified as Alec J. Harrison, a member of the Royal Army Medical Corps who 'was among the last soldiers to be evacuated'.

96

Vice-Admiral Sir Bertram Ramsay's Despatch

Published in *The London Gazette* in 1947

Dating back to the seventeenth century *The London Gazette* has been the official publication of the English and in the eighteenth century the British Government. Included in its pages throughout the decades have been the official reports of British admirals and generals from the seat of war. Before the advent of radio and television, these reports were the only official medium through which the British public could learn about the battles and campaigns as they were being fought. Commanding officers, therefore, had to word their despatches with care because they knew that every word would be scrutinized by thousands, and later as literacy levels increased, millions of people.

Above: The supplement to The London Gazette that contained Vice-Admiral Ramsay's Dunkirk despatch. Opposite: Troops under fire on the beach during Dynamo.

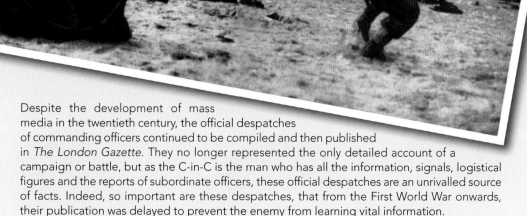

Despite the development of mass media in the twentieth century, the official despatches of commanding officers continued to be compiled and then published in *The London Gazette*. They no longer represented the only detailed account of a campaign or battle, but as the C-in-C is the man who has all the information, signals, logistical figures and the reports of subordinate officers, these official despatches are an unrivalled source of facts. Indeed, so important are these despatches, that from the First World War onwards, their publication was delayed to prevent the enemy from learning vital information.

Such a policy, however, was not universally accepted. During a debate in the House of Lords on 1 February 1945, for example, Viscount Trenchard posed the following question: 'Are we giving up the time-honoured custom of publishing the communiqués as we have given up publishing the Despatches of the Commander-in-Chief? We have not even got Despatches about Dunkirk and Crete and other places. Are we giving up the publication of Despatches without protest from anybody?'

Consequently, though Vice-Admiral Sir Bertram H. Ramsay, KCB, MVO submitted his despatch on Operation *Dynamo* to the Lords Commissioners of the Admiralty on 18 June 1940, it was not published in *The London Gazette* until after the war – more specifically on 17 July 1947.

Ramsay's despatch, however, contains a wealth of precise detail not given in other publications. Though Ramsay's despatch does not contain the dramatic eye-witness accounts usually associated with the Dunkirk evacuation, it does contain a wealth of precise detail not always given in other publications – such as the signals sent to and from Ramsay which provide a mounting drama of their own as events unfold on the beaches and in the Channel. As well as providing the official figures of the numbers of troops taken off the beaches and from Dunkirk, it listed all the losses suffered by the Royal Navy and the larger civilian vessels.

Ramsay, however, never lived to see the official publication of his despatch, for he was killed in a plane crash at Toussus-le-Noble, to the south-west of Paris, on 2 January 1945. The aircraft he was a passenger in had been taking-off to transport him to a meeting with General Montgomery in Brussels when it crashed.

97

Relics of Operation Dynamo

Data Plates From British Army Vehicles

Such was the scale of Operation *Dynamo* that it is not surprising that evidence of the evacuation is still being uncovered to this day – as a visit to the Dunkerque 1940 museum in Bastion 32 will testify. From badges and insignia, through to razors and rifles, just a few of the objects recovered from the beaches, big and small, can be seen.

For those with the correct permits and permissions (metal detecting and archaeological excavations in France are tightly controlled by the authorities) such finds can still be made. The selection of manufacturer's data plates seen here are just a few examples – and they are almost certainly some of the only tangible evidence of the improvised piers or jetties constructed on the beaches – such as that recalled by Lieutenant J.G. Wells in Object 25.

Another veteran who recalled these piers was Sapper Thomas John Garrett, 225 Field Company Royal Engineers, who found himself awaiting evacuation from the beach at La Panne: 'Along the beach being lapped and rolled about by the tide were hundreds of bodies, some of them still with their packs on. One could not see how they died. I presume a lot had tried to

wade or swim out to the crafts that had been lying off shore, and had been drowned in the attempt.[106]

'We then realised that because of the shallow water the boats could not come in very close. Once the problem was created, a solution was soon forthcoming. I do not

Both pages: A selection of vehicle data plates recovered from the beaches east of Dunkirk. (Courtesy of Johann Tytgat). Below: German personnel inspecting the battered remains of one of the improvised piers east of Dunkirk.

know whose idea it was to construct a rough temporary pier with the vehicles that were available. All trucks, lorries with superstructure were to be used; another Field Company was to construct another pier farther up the beach.

'Starting above the tidemark the lorries were packed nose to tail as close as possible out towards the sea. When the water was reached as the tide went out so more vehicles were added. While this was being carried out others collected tailboards, planks or anything else that could be used for a catwalk. This was then lashed down to the top of the superstructure of the vehicles thus completing with the other one 2 temporary piers out into the deeper water. These 2 piers cut down the distance between the shore and the boats, which we expected to appear soon. It was surprising how firm and solid they were, a job well done!'

Below: The effects of time and tide are clear to see on the vehicles used in of the piers.

Together Again

The Association of Dunkirk Little Ships

Above: The Dunkirk Jack is the House Flag of the Association of Dunkirk Little Ships, under permission of the Admiralty, the College of Heralds and the City of Dunkirk. The jack consists of the Cross of St. George (the flag of Admiralty) defaced with the Arms of Dunkirk. This jack can be worn by Member Ships at any time when the owner is aboard. Member Ships are limited to civilian vessels that took part in the Dunkirk rescue operation between 27 May and 4 June 1940.

To mark the 25th anniversary of Operation *Dynamo*, in May 1965 the radio and TV presenter Raymond Baxter organised and assembled a flotilla of forty-three of the original 'Little Ships' to return to Dunkirk. It was decided that such a unique assembly should not be allowed to disperse into obscurity and the Association of Dunkirk Little Ships was subsequently formed in 1966.

The object of the Association is to keep alive the spirit of Dunkirk by perpetuating for posterity the identity of those Little Ships that went to the aid of the BEF in 1940 by forming a registered association of their present-day owners and of those closely associated. The Association organises several meetings 'on the water' each year where the Little Ships may be seen and appreciated by the public. Every five years, the Little Ships, over 100 of which are represented by the Association, return under their own power to Dunkirk.

It was during the 70th anniversary celebrations in 2010 that the image overleaf was taken. After their journey across the Channel, some of the Little Ships berthed together in Dunkirk Harbour, presenting us with this remarkable scene of forty-four Dunkirk veterans – one more than the inaugural sailing in 1965.

1. *Greta*. Built in 1892 and the oldest boat in the anniversary flotilla. **2**. *Silver Queen* (now *Fermain V*). Considered expendable, no-one expected her to come back from Dunkirk and she actually sank but was refloated. **3**. *Papillon*. Went to Dunkirk on 2 June and returned with soldiers the following day. **4**. *Skylark* (now *Tahilla*). Abandoned during the rescue operation but towed back to England. **5**. *Seymour Castle* (now *Devon Belle*). Sailed from Dartmouth to Ramsgate – no other Little Ship came from further west. **6**. *Betty* (now *Nyula*). After Dunkirk she was refitted and went on to serve as a Royal Navy patrol boat. **7**. *Hulfranor*. She was abandoned by her crew but French soldiers sailed her back to Ramsgate. **8**. *Jonga* (now *Gentle Layde*). Evacuated troops from Bray-Dunes and Malo-les-Bains under heavy artillery fire. **9**. *Wairakei* (now *Brown Owl*). Despite her considerable draft of five feet, she returned from Dunkirk with her hull undamaged. **10**. *Elvin*. Set off for Dunkirk with no passage charts and simply sailed towards the fires and the shell-bursts. **11**. *Endeavour*. Her rudder was smashed collecting soldiers from the Mole and the inner harbour. She was towed back to Britain. **12**. *Princess Freda*. Still operates as a ferry on the Thames. **13**. *Minnehaha* (now *Thamesa*). Found in Ramsgate harbour after Dunkirk with her wheelhouse badly burnt. **14**. *Surrey* (now *L'Orange*). Previously owned by Raymond Baxter. **15**. *Tom Tit*. Two brothers took her to Dunkirk without the owner's permission. **16**. *Southern Queen*. Towed across to Dunkirk and back by one of the tug boats. **17**. *White Heather* (now *RIISI*). Went to Dunkirk on 1 June and then abandoned. Subsequently taken over by the Royal Navy. **18**. *Susan K* (now *MB 278*). Until recently, still had evidence of a row of bullet holes along her hull. **19**. *Wanda*. All that is known of *Wanda* is that she ferried troops off the beaches on 1 June. **20**. *Chalmondesleigh* (*Chumley*). Was owned by comedian Tommy Trinder when she sailed to Dunkirk. **21**. *Ryegate II*. Capsized several times when too many soldiers tried to climb aboard. **22**. *Lazy Days*. Badly damaged at Dunkirk and had to be rebuilt. **23**. *Gay Venture*. Survived a serious fire on the return from Dunkirk. **24**. *Lijns*. Steel-hulled, built in Holland just before the war. **25**. *MTB 102*. Made eight trips during the evacuation, and a one point served as Rear Admiral Wake-Walker's flagship. As

she carried no Rear Admirals' flag, one was created with an Admiralty dishcloth and some red paint. Was the third to last vessel to leave Dunkirk. **26**. *Ferry Nymph*. A harbour ferry boat which carried up to ninety soldiers at a time. **27**. *Fleury II* (now *Mada*). Had to travel all the way from Christchurch in Hampshire to join the flotilla at Ramsgate. **28**. *Lady Gay*. In 1939 her owner, Lord Dunhill, handed her to the Royal Navy as a patrol boat. **29**. *Kitty* (now *Aureol*). Was used to lift troops from the beaches to the transport ships off-shore. **30**. *Blue Bird* (now *Bluebird of Chelsea*). Her twin propellers were fouled by debris and her engines stopped so she had to be towed back across the Channel. **31**. *Mermaiden* (now *Amazone*). In her four trips between Dunkirk harbour and the transport ships offshore, the deck and wheelhouse were riddled with machine-gun bullets. **32**. *Maid Marion*. Diverted to Le Havre and collected soldiers from there. **33**. *Margo II*. Once owned by Walter Young who installed in her the compass from the Wellington bomber he flew during the war. **34**. *Iorana*. For Operation *Dynamo* she was collected by the Admiralty from Littlehampton. **35**. *Reda* (now *Janthea*). Towed whalers full of troops from La Panne beach to the off-lying ships. **36**. *Wairakei II*. Requisitioned by the Navy early in the war she was armed with a machine-gun on her foredeck and rifle racks around her decks. **37**. *Bounty*. Fouled her propeller while carrying 150 troops from the beaches out to destroyers off-shore. **38**. *Bluebird II* (now *Blue Bird of 1938*). Requisitioned by the Navy, she was operating with the Customs Examination Service when called to Dunkirk. **39**. *Atanua* (now *Mary Scott*). Beached and abandoned at La Panne after helping rescue over 200 men. **40**. *Rosa Woodd and Phyllis Lunn* (now *Dowager*). Former Shoreham By Sea lifeboat. At Dunkirk her naval officer protected his crew by constructing a makeshift wheelhouse from steel plates. **41**. *Cecil and Lillian Philpott*. Another former lifeboat. Saved fifty-one soldiers but was stranded by the tide and did not return until 3 June. **42**. *Sylvia* (now *Wendy Ken*). Holed by machine-gun fire, she reached England so low in the sea that water was almost up to her engines. **43**. *Anne*. Her shallow 3 feet 3 inches draft made her ideal for collecting troops from the Dunkirk beaches. **44**. *Mimosa*. Made three round trips during Operation *Dynamo*.

99

The 1940 Dunkirk Veterans' Association Memorial

A Symbolic Battlefield Grave

Located within the 150-acre site of the National Memorial Arboretum near Alrewas in Staffordshire, the 1940 Dunkirk Veterans' Association Memorial was unveiled in 2014, even though the association had ceased to exist for a number of years.

Formed in Leeds in 1953, the 1940 Dunkirk Veterans' Association was established for those British service veterans 'who served at Dunkirk and other ports of evacuation between 10 May and June 1940', including those who were taken prisoner. Associate membership was available to those 'otherwise not qualified, but who had assisted at the ports of evacuation'. At its peak, the association supported a membership of over 20,000.

With numbers dwindling, the association was disbanded on 30 June 2000, following the last official reunion on the 60th anniversary of the evacuation. During this event, over fifty of the remaining members gathered at the Imperial War Museum in London. This group included the oldest and youngest members, William Stone, 99, and Joe Barnes, 74.

A Chief Petty Officer during Operation *Dynamo*, Stone served on the minesweeper HMS *Salamander* at the time. He later recalled that 'Dunkirk was the worst experience of my life': 'We did five trips to Dunkirk in all, rescuing 200 to 300 men each time. Things got worse each trip we made … I was often stationed on the quarterdeck helping men get aboard *Salamander* as they swam out from the beach. Other groups of men had managed to find boats and row out to the ship. On one occasion I had a rope around a badly injured soldier who had bones sticking out of his trousers. Just as I tried to pull him in, the ship went ahead and I lost him. I don't know what happened to him.'

Joe Barnes has been described as the youngest person to participate in the evacuation. Aged just 14, he stowed away on the Thames tug *Sun XII* when it sailed for Dunkirk.

The 1940 Dunkirk Veterans' Association Memorial was built by a team of National Lottery winners from around the UK. The memorial takes the form of a symbolic temporary battlefield grave for a British soldier, this being created by a Short Magazine Lee-Enfield rifle being placed muzzle-down into sand with a steel helmet balanced upon it. The sand spread around the rifle and its accompanying plaque was brought from the beaches around Dunkirk.

Opposite: The 1940 Dunkirk Veterans' Association Memorial at the National Memorial Arboretum. (Courtesy of Robert Mitchell) Below: Almost certainly photographed in the dunes to the east of Dunkirk, such as at Bray, these wooden crosses mark the spot where British casualties, and possibly one French soldier, were buried during Operation *Dynamo*.

100

The Dunkirk Memorial

Unveiled by Her Majesty Queen Elizabeth The Queen Mother in 1957

Standing within the grounds of the British War Graves Section of Dunkirk Town Cemetery is the Dunkirk Memorial. Designed by Philip Hepworth, the memorial stands at the end of a broad avenue flanked by large columns, on which are engraved the names of the dead. These panels commemorate more than 4,500 casualties of the BEF who died in the campaign of 1939-40 or who died in captivity having been captured during this campaign and who have no known grave.

As the following account by a *Times* special correspondent reveals, the memorial's unveiling on 29 June 1957 was a remarkable event:

'Along the dusty, sun-baked streets of the new Dunkirk, which is rising from the shattered remnants of the war, veterans of the evacuation of 17 years ago yesterday tried to plot the path which brought them down to the beaches and eventually to safety. These veterans were part of a pilgrimage more than 2,000 strong. For most of the pilgrims, however, the journey was in memory of those who did not come back, the 4,700 men of the British Expeditionary Force who have no known grave and are commemorated on the Dunkirk memorial, which was unveiled by Queen Elizabeth the Queen Mother.

'Mothers, widows, and orphans joined with the Field-Marshals, the Admirals, and the Air Marshals in a simple service of dedication. … The pilgrimage, organized by the British Legion,

included people from all parts of the British Isles; women – mothers and widows – outnumbered the men. To make the journey they had to forgo two nights' sleep, for there was no sleeping accommodation in the cross-channel ships that were chartered.'[107]

As the Queen Mother unveiled each panel with its list of names a roll of drums accompanied the falling of the Union flag to the ground. The Queen Mother then addressed 'the great congregation' from the silver-topped pavilion that had been erected in the centre of the cemetery. 'That fighting retreat, side by side with many brave French comrades, will remain one of the treasured memories of the British Army and one of the great moments of our age,' she solemnly declared. 'Whilst this memorial is to soldiers, it is fitting that we should recall too the sailors and airmen without whom deliverance would have been an impossibility. The countless little ships have their honoured place in history, but it was ever the Royal Navy which bore the brunt of the task.

'Today we pay our tribute to the undying memory of all those brave men, soldiers, sailors, and airmen, who died in the hour of seeming defeat in order that in the fullness of time it could be turned to victory. Many of them rest in honoured graves, tendered by skilled and reverent hands, others in the swaying fortunes of swift battle lay where they fell, and have no known resting place. They are commemorated in this beautiful setting amid the scent of English flowers in a comradeship of 4,700 gallant soldiers.'

Main image: The Dunkirk Memorial in Dunkirk Town Cemetery. During the unveiling ceremony on 29 June 1957, more than 625 wreaths were laid. The memorial is in the care of the Commonwealth War Graves Commission. (Paul Daniels/ Shutterstock) Right: The Cross of Sacrifice and some of the graves in Dunkirk Town Cemetery. (Paul Daniels/ Shutterstock)

Notes and References

1. Grehan, J., and Mace, M., *The BEF in France 1939-1940: Manning the Front Through to the Dunkirk Evacuation* (Pen & Sword, Barnsley, 2013), pp.45-6.
2. The National Archives (TNA), WO 197/134.
3. Imperial War Museum (IWM), Department of Document, reference Documents.56; duplicated transcript message from the Admiralty.
4. TNA, ADM 199/788B.
5. Article A2310715, BBC WW2 People's War website.
6. ibid.
7. TNA, AIR 27/252.
8. *The Sunday Times*, 5 October 2014.
9. TNA, ADM 199/788A.
10. TNA, ADM 199/789.
11. TNA, ADM 199/786.
12. Jackson, Robert, *Dunkirk: The British Evacuation, 1940* (Cassell, London, 2001).
13. TNA, ADM 199/789.
14. Quoted on the Association of Dunkirk Little Ships' (ADLS) website, .
15. TNA, ADM 199/789.
16. Devine, David, *The Nine Days of Dunkirk* (Ballantine, New York, 1959), p.96.
17. TNA, ADM 199/789.
18. Anon, *Dunkirk-Margate, 1940-1950*, a commemorative booklet published by the Borough of Margate in 1950.
19. Craig, Olga, 'Wormhoudt: 'Every day I thank God we did our duty', The *Telegraph*, 23 May 2010.
20. Quoted in Sebag-Montefiore, Hugh, *Dunkirk: Fight to the Last Man* (Penguin, London, 2007).
21. The evening of Saturday, 25 May 1940, found HMS *Pangbourne* berthed alongside the quay at North Shields. A Hunt-class minesweeper launched in 1918, *Pangbourne* was a half-leader of the 5th Flotilla – the Fighting Fifth. It was shortly before midnight when her captain, Commander (Acting) Francis Douglas-Watson, received orders to sail for Harwich. Those officers and men ashore were immediately recalled. The duty officer remembered that it was 'a pretty tall order to recover sixty men in a town the size of North Shields', though within hours the task had been completed and the minesweeper underway. By 11.00 hours the next morning *Pangbourne* had docked at Harwich and work began immediately to prepare the small warship for whatever lay ahead.

22. The first part of the un-named sub-lieutenant's account was published in *The West Australian* on 9 June 1945; part two followed a week later.

23. Quoted on the BBC's *People's War* website, Article No.A3542339.

24. Anon, *Dunkirk-Margate, 1940-1950*.

25. ibid.

26. Anon, *Dunkirk-Margate, 1940-1950*.

27. TNA, ADM 199/788A.

28. Ellis, Major L.F., *The War in France and Flanders 1939-1940* (HMSO, London, 1954), p.249.

29. BBC People's War website, Article No.A2493876.

30. The Scout Association's Weekly News Bulletin, No.519, 25 June 1940.

31. The full story of *Minotaur* can be found on the following excellent website: scoutguidehistoricalsociety.com/minotaur.htm.

32. Quoted in Brann, Christopher, *The Little Ships of Dunkirk* (Collectors' Books Limited, Kemble, 1989), p.104.

33. Richards, John, *Dunkirk Revisited* (Privately Published, 2008), p.49.

34. Quoted in Mace, Martin, *The Royal Navy at Dunkirk* (Frontline Books, Barnsley, 2017), pp.241-4.

35. TNA, WO 361/19.

36. ibid.

37. Plumber, Russell, *Paddle Steamers at War, 1939-1945* (GMS, Peterborough, 1995), p.34.

38. TNA, ADM 199/788B.

39. Mace, Martin, *They Also Served: The Story of the Sussex Lifeboats at War 1939-1945* (Historic Military Press, Storrington, 2001).

40. Mace, Martin, *The Royal Navy at Dunkirk*, p.68.

41. TNA, WO 361/12.

42. ibid.

43. The husband of Grace Pridham of Ashton-under-Lyne, Lancashire, 28-year-old Sergeant Edward Pridham's body was never recovered or identified, and he is commemorated, along with many other casualties from the loss of *Gracie Fields*, on the Dunkirk Memorial.

44. Plummer, Russell, *The Ships that Saved an Army, A Comprehensive Record of the 1,300 'Little Ships' of Dunkirk* (Patrick Stephens, Wellingborough, 1990), pp.224-5.

45. See Plummer, Russell, *The Ships that Saved an Army*, pp.85-6.

46. Robins, Nick, *The Coming of the Comet: The Rise and Fall of the Paddle Steamer* (Seaforth Publishing, Barnsley, 2012).

47. Kay, Wing Commander Cyril Eyton, *The Restless Sky: The Autobiography of an Airman* (London, Harrap, 1964).

48. TNA, AIR 81/694.

49. For more information see, Franks, Norman, *Air Battle Dunkirk 26 May – 3 June 1940* (Grub Street, London, 2000).

50. IWM, Department of Sound, 12209. Interview recorded 27 August 1991.

51. *The London Gazette*, Supplement 34909, 26 July 1940, p.4659.

52. TNA ADM 199/786.

53. Tucker, Lionel, *Memories of The Maid of Orleans*, quoted on the BBC WW2 People's War website.
54. Quoted on the Association of Dunkirk Little Ships' website: www.adls.org.uk.
55. See *Tom Tit*'s entry, Certificate No.1618, on the National Historic Ships UK website: www.nationalhistoricships.org.uk.
56. Quoted on the ADLS website.
57. See *Tom Tit*'s entry on the National Historic Ships UK website.
58. Quoted on the ADLS website.
59. TNA, ADM 199/787.
60. TNA, AIR 27/411.
61. TNA, AIR 50/19-91.
62. Riley, Gordon, *Hawker Hurricane Survivors* (Grub Street, London, 2015), p.16.
63. TNA, ADM 199/786.
64. TNA, WO 361/16.
65. Quoted in Mace, Martin, *The Royal Navy at Dunkirk*, p.68.
66. For Crosby's full account, please see Russell Plummer's excellent book, *The Ships that Saved an Army*, p.209.
67. ibid, p.212.
68. TNA AIR 27/1941.
69. Franks, Norman, *Air Battle Dunkirk 26 May – 3 June 1940*, p.125.
70. *The London Gazette*, Issue 34873, 14 June 1940, p.3623.
71. IWM Department of Sound, Catalogue No.7196.
72. Quoted in Joshua Levine, *Forgotten Voices of Dunkirk* (Ebury Press, London, 2010), p.377.
73. TNA, AIR 27/1371/1.
74. C. Vince, *Storm on the Waters: The Story of the Life-Boat Service in the War of 1939-1945* (Hodder & Stoughton, London 1946), p.25.
75. ibid, p.33.
76. TNA, WO 334/83.
77. Quoted from the Thames Sailing Barge Trust website: www.bargetrust.org/dunkirk.
78. Gardner, W.J.R., *The Evacuation from Dunkirk: Operation Dynamo, 26 May-4 June 1940* (Routledge, 2000), p.71.
79. Murland, Jerry, *Retreat and Rearguard - Dunkirk 1940: The Evacuation of the BEF to the Channel Ports* (Pen & Sword, Barnsley, 2016).
80. *Life* Magazine, 24 June 1940, p.89.
81. Murland, Jerry, ibid.
82. IWM Department of Documents, reference 9144.
83. *Life* Magazine, 24 June 1940, p.89.
84. TNA, WO 197/134.
85. BBC People's War website, article No.A6985740.
86. Quoted in Joshua Levine's *Forgotten Voices of Dunkirk* (BBC Audiobooks Ltd, London, 2010), p.254.
87. Martin Summers, *Bluebird* (Collectors Books Ltd, 1990).

88. Quoted on the BBC People's War website, article No. A2304677.

89. TNA, ADM 199/788B.

90. Quoted from .

91. Costobadie's full account can be seen in the author's book, *The Royal Navy at Dunkirk: Commanding Officers' Reports of British Warships In Action During Operation Dynamo* (Frontline, Barnsley, 2017), p.142.

92. The original drawing is held at The National Archives, file reference INF 3/1578.

93. Franks, Norman L.R., *Royal Air Force Fighter Command Losses of the Second World War*, Volume 1, 1939-1941 (Midland Publishing, Hersham, 2008), p.30.

94. Major-General M.G. Holmes CBE, MC, speaking in a BBC broadcast on 16 April 1943.

95. Quoted on the following website: www.dunkirk1940.org.

96. Longden, Sean, *Dunkirk, The Men They Left Behind* (Constable, London, 2008) pp.46-7.

97. Cited in Sebag-Montefiore, Hugh, *Dunkirk: Fight to the Last Man* (Penguin, London, 2006) pp.434-5.

98. Patrick Wilson, *Dunkirk, From Disaster to Deliverance* (Leo Cooper, Barnsley,1999), p.153.

99. IWM Sound Archive, reference 6552.

100. E. Keeble Chatterton, *The Epic of Dunkirk* (Kindle version), location 2215-3322.

101. For more information, see: www.illustratedfirstworldwar.com.

102. Quoted on the BBC Archive website: www.bbc.co.uk/archive/dunkirk.

103. 'Dunkirk Memorial', reported in *The Times*, 23 May 1941.

104. Quoted from the Imperial War Museum's UK War Memorials register: www.iwm.org.uk/memorials/search.

105. *Daily Telegraph*, 12 August 2009.

106. Contributed to the BBC People's War website by Lee Richard; Article No.A2330812; www.bbc.co.uk/history/ww2peopleswar.

107. 'The Queen Mother Unveils Dunkirk Memorial', in *The Times*, 1 July 1957.